The Dutch in America

The Dutch in America

Immigration, Settlement, and Cultural Change

Edited by Robert P. Swierenga

RUTGERS UNIVERSITY PRESS
New Brunswick, New Jersey

To Willard C. Wichers
for his indefatigable efforts
to promote Dutch-American
history and culture

Publication of this book has been aided by a grant from the National Endowment for the Humanities.

Library of Congress Cataloging in Publication Data
Main entry under title:

The Dutch in America.

Includes index.
1. Dutch Americans—History—Addresses, essays, lectures.
I. Swierenga, Robert P.
E184.D9D87 1985   305.8'3931'073   84—6785
ISBN 0—8135—1063—5

Frontispiece photograph: Courtesy of Heritage Hall Archives, Calvin College.

Contents

Figures

Tables

Preface

Research in immigration and acculturation of the many ethnic groups in American society has flourished in the last decade after forty years or more of neglect. There has been renewed interest in the meaning of ethnic identity, in the process of community formation, and in the effects of migration on the sending and host societies. The computer revolution of the 1950s in academia also helped prepare scholars for a new focus in migration studies, by making possible individual-level research on the vast scale required to understand the complexities of the immigration process. The major characteristic of the "new" immigration studies is that it is "human-centered"; its goal is to describe how people acted as well as what they said about themselves. Migration is viewed as a social process that involved the transplanting of individuals and kin groups from specific local communities abroad to specific communities in North America. Themes such as these are the focal point of this book on Dutch immigration and settlement in the nineteenth and twentieth centuries.

There has been a resurgence of scholarly interest in the past decade on the subject of Dutch immigration and the processes of acculturation and assimilation in America. In recent years, scholars in North America and in the Netherlands have published a number of scholarly monographs on the first-wave migration of the 1840s, the significance of Dutch immigrant letters, the formation of Dutch-American rural and urban communities, and institutional and cultural developments. Primary documents have also been published, including three vast computer-readable files of Dutch emigrants and immigrants. At least eight doctoral dissertations and as many masters theses have been written on aspects of Dutch immigration and community development. The first periodical devoted to Dutch-American history and culture, *Origins*, appeared in 1982, and in 1979 a comprehensive annotated bibliography of printed secondary sources was published.

This intellectual ferment shaped the scholarly commemorations of the Netherlands-American bicentennial in 1982, of which this book is a product. The essays in this collection were first presented at the conference on "Dutch Immigration to America, 1782–1982," held at the Balch Institute for Ethnic Studies in Philadelphia on September 22–24, 1982. The purpose of the conference, and of this book, is to provide a synopsis of the latest research findings and to offer guidance and direction for the next generation. New sources, concepts, and research methods are introduced including computer-aided techniques and family linkage. The contributors are specialists in history, geography, language, literature, religion, economics, and library science. They have sought to summarize the current knowledge about Dutch-American immigration and socialization patterns and to specify the major questions and topics that deserve further attention. In short, this is a progress report that reveals not only how far we have come, but how far we have to go in comprehending the history of the Dutch in America.

The Dutch are not a large immigrant group. Only half a million Dutch nationals emigrated to the United States since the founding of New Amsterdam. Dutch nationals and Americans of Dutch ancestry number approximately six million according to the 1980 Census Bureau records. They rank eleventh among American ethnic groups; yet, the continuing cultural influence of the Old Yorkers and the dogged resistance to assimilation of the nineteenth century Dutch in the Midwest have given Dutch-Americans a far greater presence than their numbers might warrant. They remain a self-conscious ethnic group after many generations in America.

Without the active support and interest of many persons, this volume and the conference that gave it birth would not have been possible. The National Endowment for the Humanities (grant BD-20267-82), the United States International Communications Agency, and the Netherlands Ministry of Foreign Affairs provided substantial funding support for the conference. Mr. Gene Wise of NEH and Mr. Peter Antico of USICA offered advice and support in the critical early stages of planning. Several Netherlands government officials provided unusual encouragement and generous assistance. They are The Honorable Dr. John H. Lubbers, Netherlands Ambassador to the United States; The Honorable Mr. Theo. J. M. van den Muijsenberg, Ambassador for Press and Cultural Affairs; Mr. H. A. Barvoet, First Secretary for Press and Cultural Affairs; The Honorable Mr. Simon Van Nijspen, Consul General of the Netherlands, Chicago. Mr. Charles R. Tanguy, Executive Director of the Netherlands-American Bicentennial Commission, gave unfailing encouragement and advice, as also did Mr. Willard C. Wichers, Executive Director of the Netherlands Museum (Holland, Michigan), whose credits are noted elsewhere. Dr. James R. Tanis, Director of Libraries and Professor of History, Bryn Mawr College, and Dr. Mark Stolarik, Executive Director of the Balch Institute for Ethnic Studies, Philadelphia, helped in planning the conference from its inception and freely contributed their considerable administrative and scholarly talents. Joan Boomker Swierenga typed a number of the manuscripts in her usual efficient manner. Finally, I wish to acknowledge with deep appreciation the cooperative spirit of each of the contributors to this volume. Without their willingness to share their expertise and knowledge and to accept graciously the weight of my editorial pen on their writings, this enterprise could not have succeeded.

Robert P. Swierenga
Kent, Ohio

Introduction

Robert P. Swierenga

The Dutch presence in America is as historic as that of the Puritans. For more than 350 years, since the founding of New Netherland in the 1620s, Dutch immigrants have settled these shores and trekked westward along with the pioneers. Dutch blood and culture are deeply embedded in American life. In the seventeenth century Dutch expansion at the mouth of the Hudson River was primarily an adjunct of the fur-trading ventures of the Dutch West India Company. But commerce eventually led to colonization, and by 1664, when the English seized control of the colony, seven thousand Dutch settlers lived there. From this small base, Dutch influence dominated the New York City region for centuries. In 1790, 80 percent of the one hundred thousand persons of Dutch birth or ancestry resided within a fifty-mile radius of the city.

The major phase of Dutch immigration coincided with the epic northern-European migration of the nineteenth century, when more than 250,000 Netherlanders came to America. This so-called free migration led mainly to the Midwest, where the Dutch again clustered in homogeneous colonies, many of which survive to the present. Because this migration was the most influential and significant in shaping Dutch-American culture and history, the contributors to this book focus largely on this era.

Following the horrendous Second World War, the Dutch again became emigration minded and nearly a million people left, many assisted by their government. But less than one hundred thousand reached their preferred destination in the United States

1

because of the restrictive immigration quotas. Canada and Australia welcomed many of the remainder with open arms. Thus, after a hiatus in immigration of two generations, these post-war newcomers revived the waning ethnic identity among the Dutch-Americans, just as the young-Dutch in the nineteenth century had renewed the old-Dutch of the seventeenth century.

The Dutch in North America faithfully have reflected the characteristics of their small but diverse nation. Following the Eighty Years War (1568–1648), when the Protestant Dutch led by the house of Orange successfully revolted against Catholic Spain, the modern Dutch nation was officially established as a Protestant state linked with the privileged Dutch Reformed Church, whose Calvinist confessional standards were formulated in the Heidelberg Catechism (1563), the Belgic Confession (1561), and the Canons of Dort (1619).

During the next century the Netherlands enjoyed its Golden Age, when Holland merchant princes founded a worldwide commercial empire, with colonies in Asia, Africa, and the Americas. Subsequently, beginning in the eighteenth century, Dutch glory became tarnished by military defeats at the hands of more powerful neighbors—England, France, and much later, Germany. Napoleon controlled the nation from 1806 to 1813 but the Congress of Vienna (1814–1815) re-established Dutch independence and attached the ten Belgian provinces to the nation. The Belgians successfully rebelled in 1830, however, and won their independence, taking all but two of the Catholic provinces in the south of the Netherlands (Limburg and Noord-Brabant). These provinces remain to this day the overwhelmingly Catholic part of the Netherlands.

The Dutch in America are composed of four major linguistic and cultural subgroups that historically have intermingled with Netherlanders. The vast majority are Hollanders who speak the Dutch language. Next in importance are Frisians, who constitute a national minority in the Netherlands and Germany and who speak the Frisian tongue, which is a related but distinct language from Dutch. Friesland was for centuries an independent maritime country along the coast of the North Sea. After becoming absorbed into the Netherlands in the late Middle Ages, the states of Friesland enjoyed a semi-autonomous status within the former

Dutch Republic until 1795. Two smaller subgroups in America are Flemish-speaking Belgians from the south of the Netherlands, whose language is virtually identical to Dutch, and Dutch-speaking Germans from Hanover (Graafschap Bentheim) and Ost Friesland, which are eastern border areas with historic cultural ties to the Dutch.

Although the Dutch language is a Low German linguistic form, and the word *Dutch* is philologically the same as Deutsch, the Dutch in America have always carefully maintained their separate identity, even to the point of calling Germans "Duitschers" and themselves "Hollanders" or "Netherlanders." The U.S. government, in its census reports and statistical compilations, has always followed a simple nationality rule, including Hollanders and Frisians but excluding Belgian and German-born peoples who are Dutch-speaking, even though the latter associate and intermarry with Hollanders.

In addition to religious and language divisions, the Netherlands comprises numerous subregions, based on variations in dialect, soil type, economic activity, and cultural traditions. One's village or province often took pride of place over the nation. Emigrants carried this localism to America as part of their cultural baggage and often created segregated neighborhoods within the larger Dutch settlements. This extreme type of local differentiation often withered away during the pioneer period because of the common struggle to adjust to the larger American community, but local pride created tensions and rivalries in the early years.

Conflict in the Protestant settlements also stemmed from the Old Country religious disputes and schisms that immigrants invariably carried into the American daughter denominations. In 1834, the first of several major secessions from the National or Reformed Church created a group known simply as the Seceders. These separatists claimed that the Reformed Church was succumbing to the theological liberalism of the Enlightenment and to the Erastianism of the house of Orange under Willem I. The Seceders objected to the doctrinal heterodoxy and government-imposed reorganization of the Reformed Church. Their opposition struck a responsive chord in rural parts of the Netherlands, and the Seceders grew rapidly. Dutch ecclesiastical and political authorities viewed the *Afscheiding* (Secession) as a civil threat that could not be tolerated. Seceder leaders were arrested and heavily fined, and followers sometimes lost their jobs. The persecution, coupled with the potato blight and economic depression of 1845 and 1846, caused five thousand Seceders to emigrate to the United States before 1850. These Seceders formed the nucleus of the Holland and Zeeland, Michigan and Pella, Iowa colonies. Their orthodoxy, individualistic faith-life, and cultural conservatism and clannishness gave form and substance to their community life for generations.

The American Reformed churches were further influenced by a second secession (known as the *Doleantie*) from the Dutch Reformed Church, which occurred in 1886 under the leadership of Abraham Kuyper, head of the Christian Anti-Revolutionary party and founder of the Free University of Amsterdam (1880). This ardently Calvinist party won control of the Dutch government in 1892, and Prime Minister Kuyper reshaped social institutions along religious lines, notably by providing for public tax support of sectarian schools and eventually universities. Emigrants to America from the *Doleantie* group (often identified as Kuyperians) were imbued with a Calvinist "world and life view," and they sought to organize their social, economic, and educational life around Reformed principles. Although the followers of Kuyper were a small minority among American Hollanders, it was their impetus in the pre–World War I decades that led to the establishment of Reformed institutions such as schools and social agencies.

Religious life among the Calvinist Hollanders in America since the mid-nineteenth century has been largely influenced by the *Afscheiding* and *Doleantie* heritages, with their differing individualist and totalistic emphases. Organizationally, the Dutch Calvinists are divided into two major and several minor denominations. The major duo are the Reformed Church in America, founded in 1628 in the New Netherland colony (and thus one of the oldest denominations in the United States) and its daughter church, the Christian Reformed Church, which originated in an 1857 schism in western Michigan. People of the *Afscheiding* tradition joined both American denominations, but *Doleantie* immigrants almost exclusively affiliated with the Christian Reformed Church, where they comprised the leadership elite and dominated the denominational seminary faculty. In the Canadian branch of the Christian Reformed Church, which grew rapidly after World War II, the Kuyperian followers have been even more influential. This has strengthened the radical cultural triumphalism of the *Doleantie* wing in the Christian Reformed Church, but it has also acerbated tensions with the majority group, the individualistic children of the *Afscheiding*.

Despite their internal religious struggles, Calvinist immigrants preserved their Dutch language and culture far more successfully than did the Dutch Catholics, who were quickly absorbed into multi-ethnic parishes. This indicates that religious structures were the key factor in differing Protestant and Catholic rates of assimilation, in-group marriage practices, language retention, literature and periodicals, and the survival of an ethnic identity in America.

The contributors to this book address these issues of immigration behavior and adjustment in America. Part One describes the general patterns of nineteenth century Dutch migration both within Europe and to North America. Part Two provides three examples of the process of settlement in the Midwest and the economic successes enjoyed by one rural community. Part Three focuses on religious and cultural aspects of the Americanization process and stresses the salience of ecclesiastical structures and personalities for acculturation. In Part Four, Dutch-American literature and periodicals are described, and the authors show that immigrant writings display similar religious distinctions.

The opening chapter evaluates the primary record sources for the study of Dutch immigration from 1820 to 1920, which I have largely converted into computer files for detailed analysis. Official statistics underreport Dutch immigration to the United States by at least one-third; nevertheless, the bias in surviving records is measurable, and the records series can be used for the structural analysis of Dutch transatlantic migration. The picture that emerges is one of a regularized and rational transplanting of families and communities from a relatively few Old Country villages that were most adversely affected by agricultural modernization, to a relatively few New World farm colonies and urban neighborhoods near the Lake Michigan shoreline. The pace of industrialization of the Dutch economy and availability of land on the American frontier were underlying secular factors; business cycles in the Atlantic economy determined the short-term ebb and flow of migration.

Dutch emigration to the United States, while the most publicized and analyzed, is only one aspect of population mobility, according to Pieter Stokvis. Cross-border transfers with Germany, Belgium, France, and England are also important, Stokvis argues persuasively. In fact, in the first half of the nineteenth century, more foreigners immigrated into the Netherlands than Dutchmen departed from it. After midcentury, for several decades the number of Dutch settling in the United States exceeded those in neighboring European countries, but by 1900 the situation was reversed and Dutch emigrants preferred Europe to America. Dutchmen in Germany alone in 1905 outnumbered those in the United States. Stokvis thus confirms the famous law of E. W. Ravenstein that short-distance migration exceeds long-distance migration, barring such unusual circumstances as the attractive free-land policies in the United States and the desire of the Seceders for religious freedom. Finally, Stokvis offers an alternative census-based method of estimating the underreporting of Dutch immigration to the United States, which is surprisingly close to my estimates derived from nominal record linkage. Stokvis's point is clear: migration was a complex phenomenon involving both short- and long-distance moves, and for every out-migration there is a counterbalancing in-migration. Students of European emigration to North America must consider all aspects of international migration if they hope to understand the transatlantic aspect.

Henry van Stekelenburg, a specialist in Dutch Roman Catholic emigration to North America, demonstrates the important influence of religious structures on immigration patterns. Dutch Catholics were a suppressed minority like the Seceders, and they also immigrated in community and family groups led by their priests, as did the Seceders under their dominies. But the international character of the American Catholic church undermined the attempt of the Dutch Catholics to maintain their ethnic identity, whereas the separatist Calvinists successfully sustained their Dutchness. Van Stekelenburg has enriched Dutch historiography by comparing Catholic and Calvinist immigration patterns and by demonstrating the behavioral similarities in the removal process, despite strikingly different outcomes.

Hille de Vries addresses another historiographical shibboleth, that the severe Dutch agricultural depression in the 1880s was causally linked to the spurt in Dutch emigration to the United States that occurred in that decade. De Vries argues that fewer Dutch departed in the 1880s than in the pre–World War I decade. The agrarian depression was a normal cyclical phenomenon that may incidentally have stimulated emigration to the United States, but the overwhelming cause was the long-term structural effects of agricultural modernization with its larger farms and reduced labor demands. The "excess" farm laborers comprised the bulk of the emigrant population, for whom the liberal American land policy provided the irresistible lure.

Yda Saueressig-Schreuder's study of Catholic immigration to frontier Wisconsin exemplifies the newest technique of family history in migration research, that of tracing individual families from origin to destination. In this meticulous manner, she demonstrates the importance of family ties in creating a chain-migration pattern. Saueressig-Schreuder explores the economic and social context in three villages in Noord-Brabant and then follows the migrants to the Fox River Valley in Wisconsin. Her diagrams portray the intricate social links among the emigrant households and prove the interactive nature of the overseas resettlement process.

David Vanderstel uncovered similar localistic patterns in his study of Dutch immigrant neighborhood development in Grand Rapids, Michigan in the second half of the nineteenth century. Instead of the standard "concentration zone" model, he discovered that immigrants from different cultural and geographic regions of the Netherlands tended to settle in their own homogeneous neighborhoods in this growing urban center. Even subsequent migration within the city followed localistic lines. At the center of each neighborhood stood the church, which Vanderstel views as the most important institution in the community. Eventually, the churches and schools as communitywide institutions broke down the isolation and promoted a "commonality" among the Dutch in the city; but in so doing, these institutions perpetuated the continuation of a common Dutch culture.

That the Dutch in America are clannish and hard working is a truism. Richard Doyle demonstrates that in the Iowa farming colony of Pella the truism was also the reality. The Dutch immigrants in Pella in the seventy-five years after the founding of the colony maintained a church-centered, homogeneous, and stable village. The decadal persistence rates of the Pella Dutch surpassed the normal frontier rates by 50 percent or more. More than half of the workers improved their relative wealth status in each decade from 1850 to 1925. Whether economic success encouraged persistence or vice versa is problematic, but Doyle suggests that persistence was a cultural trait stemming from the Dutch desire to remain within a supportive homogeneous community. Even after the available farm land was gone and before industrial employment opened up around 1900, Dutch workers chose to remain in Pella even at the expense of a declining rate of increase in their property holdings. In the long run, this persistence resulted in economic success and the accumulation of property far in excess of that of their American neighbors.

The essays in the second half of the book direct attention from family and farming to faith and culture. But the essential question remains: What was the process of religious and cultural institutional transference and how successful were the Dutch in transplanting their social and intellectual institutions and life styles?

Elton Bruins offers the broadest picture of the process of Americanization in the predominant Dutch Reformed denominations from the 1620s until the twentieth century. Bruins notes that the Canons of Dort, written by the Netherlands Synod of Dort (1618–1619), provided the quintessential definition of Reformed orthodoxy among the Dutch Calvinists both in Europe and North America. Despite their commitment to this standard, the Dutch immigrants reluctantly had to adapt gradually to American religious practices in order to survive. The English take-over of New Netherland made English the official language in New York. Then the Great Awakening brought English free-will doctrines and revivalist practices into the Reformed Church. Finally, the growing American nationalism in the mid-eighteenth century forced the Dutch Reformed to sever their ecclesiastical ties to the mother church in Amsterdam and to organize independently. In the early nineteenth century, the Dutch Reformed began to Americanize rapidly. Their prominent clerics and lay leaders joined Masonic Lodges, and most congregations slowly introduced English-language services. At this very time, thousands of orthodox Seceders emigrated to America, and many joined the Reformed Church. This hastened Americanization, but it also created tensions in both groups, and ultimately a minority withdrew and formed the more isolationist Christian Reformed Church, Thereafter, newcomers had the choice of affiliating with the "Dutch Church" or the "American Church." Bruin's survey proves again that immigrants may forestall Americanization temporarily, but eventually the process is inevitable.

The crucial decade of forced Americanization for Continental European emigrants such as the Germans and Dutch was the period during and following World War I. James Bratt explores the process by which the various Dutch Reformed groups responded to these heightened pressures. He likens the picture to that of a kaleidoscope, which highlights the many layers of the mosaic. Bratt's first principle is that "the Dutch Reformed guided their entry into American life by mentalities established in their European past." These mind sets he uncovered in the multitudinous pamphlets, periodicals, sermons, and writings of the Dutch Reformed community, most of which expressed religious themes, since religion served as the prime cultural medium. Bratt identifies four groups and shows how their differing mentalities explain the heresy trials, conflicts over "social issues," and political clashes of the 1920s. This behavioral analysis of ideology suggests that acculturation is a very complex phenomenon; it is a two-way rather than a one-way street. But assimilation is the ultimate outcome, nonetheless.

Herbert Brinks, like Bratt, discovered intellectual continuities when he studied the theological background of the Dutch-American clerics involved in the schism of 1857 in Michigan that gave birth to the Christian Reformed Church. This secession, Brinks shows, had direct roots in the earlier *Afscheiding* of 1834 in the Netherlands. That schism fractured into at least three subgroups, and the immigrant pastors who trained under the personal tutelage of the various leading Dutch clerics carried the theological controversies to America as part of their cultural baggage. Who trained with whom in the Old Country is the decisive question in understanding the theological conflicts in newly transplanted religious communities in America.

If religious conservatism delayed assimilation, did any other institutions serve that purpose as well? Herman Ganzevoort investigates this question in his study of contemporary Dutch-Canadian culture, which is largely a post-1945 community of four hundred thousand strong. Ganzevoort finds that the Canadian Dutch have little interest in language retention, they ignore the ethnic press, they resent their churches being regarded as the "Dutch church," their credit unions serve non-Dutch clients, and their ethnic social clubs espouse open membership policies. While these are typical characteristics of first- and second-generation immigrants, Ganzevoort offers an alternative explanation. The Canadian Dutch yield their birthright willingly because, as lower class peasant folk, they never valued it in the first place. Such immigrants, claims Ganzevoort, "were hardly the most ideal carriers or transmitters of high native culture." Nor did the Dutch-Canadians settle in homogeneous clustered communities to the same degree as the Dutch-Americans. Thus, Ganzevoort concludes that the Dutch-Canadian "is a 'vanishing species'" and "willingly so."

Dutch literary culture in America provides another window on the immigration story. Walter Lagerwey opens that window by carefully selecting a sampling of the literture and translating and interpreting it for English-language readers. The sampling includes not only the writings of the orthodox Protestants but also the generally ignored Catholic Dutch and Flemish immigrant writings. The early literature of the founding period in the nineteenth century displays an overwhelming sense of uncertainty, of pathos and suffering; but the semi-centennial celebrations at the turn of the century convey a different spirit, one of satisfaction, pride in accomplishment, and gratitude for prosperity. The Dutch-American patriotic literature seems quaint and archaic to modern ears, but it faithfully reflects a filiopietistic idealism and is a sure sign of Americanizing forces at work. The literary outpourings remained typically Dutch in their didactic and sentimental religious motifs, their ridicule of pride and place, and their deep emotions. Lagerwey concludes, with a note of sadness, that the "sun has set on the poets of Dutch and Flemish America." The loss of the native language has taken its toll.

Conrad Bult's comprehensive survey of the Dutch-American periodical press portrays the same language declension as in literary culture generally. At the turn of the century, Dutch journalism displayed a "vigorous vitality," and newspapers and magazines served every taste and purpose. News of the various Dutch-American settlements and of the homeland dominated the newspapers, and the journals and magazines focused on religion and politics. But in the post–World War II decades, the periodicals succumbed, one by one, until only one religious periodical remains, and that is now scheduled to cease publication at the end of 1985. Bult provides an extensive historiographical review of the literature on the subject of Dutch-American journalism and concludes with a current inventory of surviving files and suggestions for their use. Bult notes that, while the journalistic efforts themselves deserve study, their outpourings are crucial to an understanding of Dutch-American settlements, their religious life, and their attitudes toward American society. The periodicals, Bult argues persuasively, are an "unrivaled" embodiment of the Dutch-American heritage.

Although the contributors to this book approach their subjects from differing viewpoints and use a wide variety of sources and research techniques, their efforts add to a common corpus of knowledge about immigration and its effects on ethnic identity and survival. Despite all that has been written on this subject in the past decade, many questions about the process of removal and resettlement continue to challenge scholars. If this book has sharpened and refined these issues, and if it points the way for future students to study these questions, the efforts of the contributors will have been richly rewarded.

PART ONE

Dutch Immigration and Settlement in America

1. Dutch Immigration Patterns in the Nineteenth and Twentieth Centuries

Robert P. Swierenga

From the outset of heavy European overseas emigration in the early nineteenth century, government officials and scholars have displayed a keen interest in the facts and figures of the movement.[1] The American government in 1820 responded to the massive outpouring of Europe's peasants after the Napoleonic War by implementing a record-gathering system that required ship captains to submit sworn passenger manifests to customs agents at all major east coast ports.[2] These manifests, over 100,000 in number, provided the basis for the official United States immigration statistics published annually by Congress.

With similar national interests in mind, Dutch officialdom likewise responded to the first large emigration of the mid-1840s by creating an administrative system to identify the citizens who were leaving the fatherland for distant shores. Each January, municipal clerks were instructed to compile lists of all overseas emigrants of the previous year for provincial and national officials.[3] Emigration lists such as these have provided the raw material for economic and social theorists to interpret the significance of emigration, or as was often the case, to offer prescriptions for

15

stemming or encouraging the outflow. Thus, we lack neither raw information on emigration nor interpretations of its meaning.

Computers and Migration Records

Record-keeping in the nineteenth century was at best an inexact science. The amount of information collected was so huge that few could gain control over it, assess its validity, or find the meaning within the mass of data. Only with the recent advent of computers for information storage, retrieval, and analysis has it become possible to reconstruct the behavioral patterns of thousands of persons who participated in the great nineteenth century emigration from Europe. Few countries provide a better data base than the Netherlands for such a study, because of its rich archival resources and the manageable size of its emigrant population, which totaled only 380,000 from 1820 to 1920.

The secret weapon of contemporary scholarship in social and economic history is exploitation of the computer's capacity to process large bodies of information on individual persons. For example, instead of using only published information on the volume and types of emigration from one country to another, it is now possible to reconstruct that emigration flow from the bottom up, by considering both the individuals and families involved and the larger economic, social, religious, and geographical groups of which they were a part. An emigrant movement is more than the sum of its parts; it is a collection of families and communities that must be studied small scale.

With computers we can also link biographical information on individual immigrants in various record series, including those from the various countries involved. In the case of Dutch emigration to the United States, there are three key primary sources. The first is the Netherlands emigration records that list each family or single adult, and state the person's age, occupation, religion, social status, tax class, family size, presumed reason for leaving, intended destination, date of leaving, and place of last residence (Figure 1.1). From 1835 through 1880, the records of officially registered emigrants are more than 95 percent complete.[4] Thereafter, the emigration lists are missing and presumed

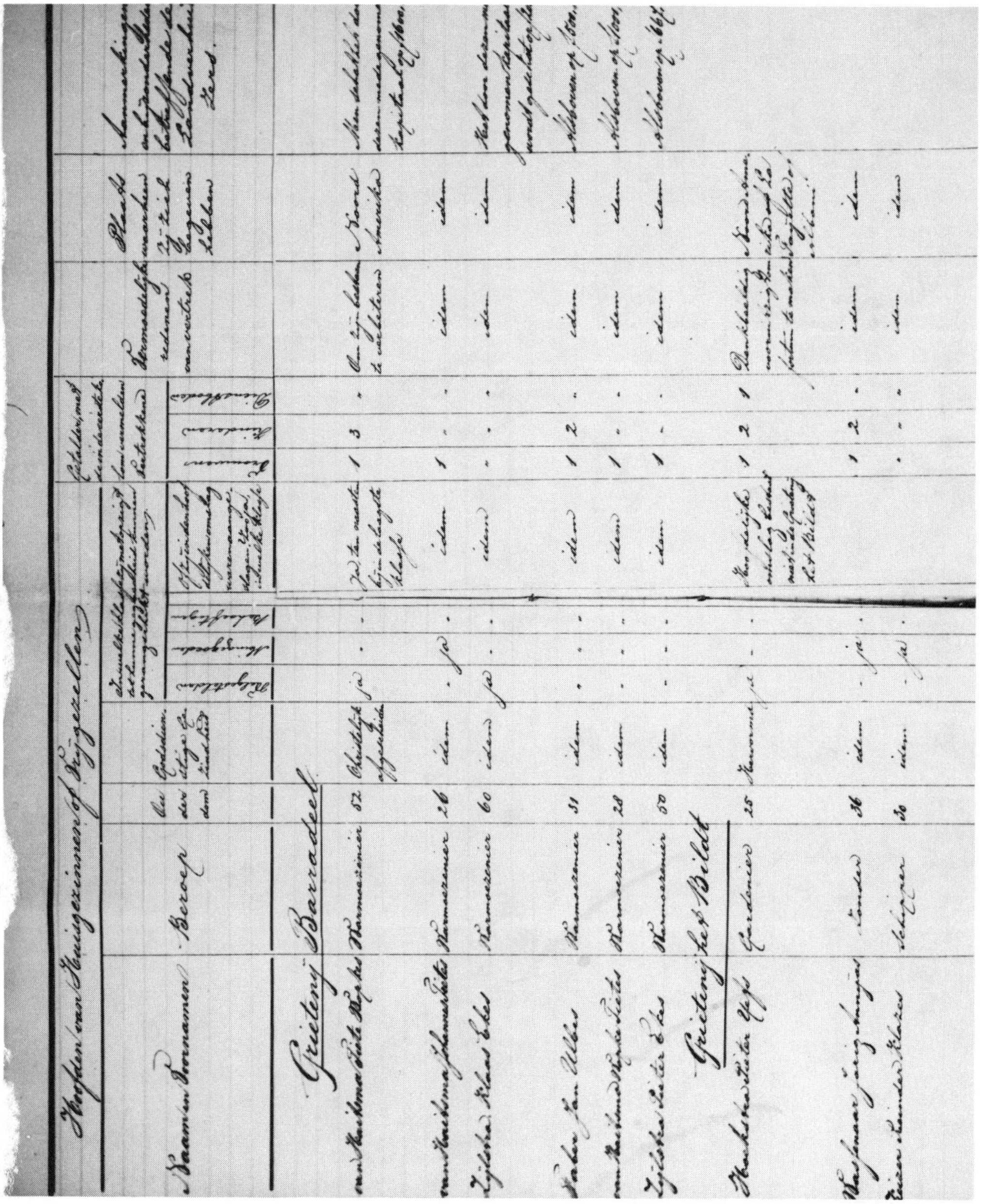

Figure 1.1. Page from Netherlands Emigration Lists, Province of Friesland, 1848

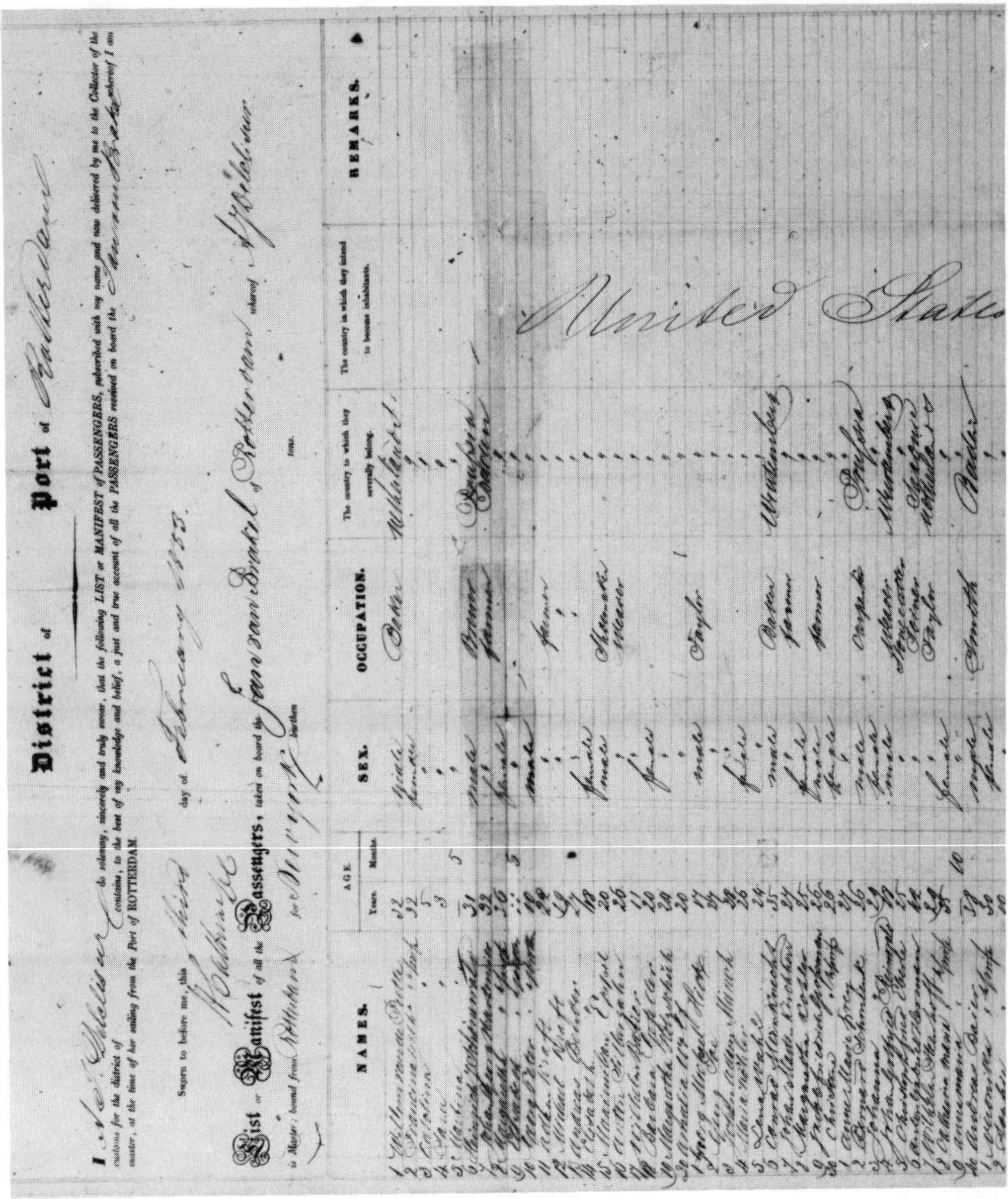

Figure 1.2. Page from U.S. Ship Passenger List of *Jan van Brakel* of Rotterdam, Arrived at New York, February 3, 1853

lost in six of the eleven provinces, and one would have to reconstruct them from the municipal *bevolkingsregisters* (population
registers) from which they were prepared in the first place.[5] For
the years 1835–1880, I have transcribed to computer files all
available lists, which include 21,800 families and single adults
(57,000 persons).[6]

The second record series is the U.S. ship passenger lists,
which beginning on January 1, 1820, name every arriving passenger at the five major ports: New York, Philadelphia, Baltimore,
Boston, and New Orleans. These manifests provide proof of arrival on American shores and state for every person, including
wives and children, the name, age, sex, occupation, country of origin and destination, type of ticket (first or second class or steerage), ports of embarking and disembarking, day of arrival, the vessel's name, type and tonnage, captain, and owner (Figure 1.2). For
the period 1820 through 1880 these manifests include 23,000
Dutch immigrant families or single adults (54,000 persons),
which again have been transcribed into computer files.[7] The U.S.
ship lists have also been linked name by name with the
Netherlands emigration records. The combined file includes 25
categories of personal information including the background and
removal process.

The Problem of Underreporting

More importantly, the linked file provides a way to test the
reliability and accuracy of the official emigration statistics of Holland and the United States. Dutch officials and scholars such as
Jacob van Hinte acknowledged that many people emigrated without being officially registered. Van Hinte estimated that clandes-
tine emigration before 1880 was equal to the official figure.[8]
American immigration statistics likewise suffered from underreporting because of administrative flaws and carelessness.[9]

The linked file of Dutch emigrants and Dutch arrivals at
U.S. ports provides the ideal mechanism for determining the actual or "true" rate of emigration. The linkage procedure results in
three "classes" of emigrants: (1) those listed in Dutch records as
U.S.-bound and who are found in the U.S. ship manifests (25,000);

(2) those listed in Dutch municipal records but not in the ship manifests (32,100); and (3) those Dutch immigrant arrivals listed in the U.S. ship manifests but not in the Dutch emigration records (29,700). The combined total of the three classes is the best estimate of actual Dutch immigration in the years 1835–1880. This "true" total is 86,800, or 28,200 (48 percent) more emigrants to North America than the official Netherlands government figures, and 41,200 (90 percent) more than the official U.S. government figures on Dutch immigration. Thus, although the Dutch figures are twice as complete as the U.S. statistics, they still underreport North American emigration by one-third.

Analysis of the missing third indicates that single emigrants were three times more likely than families to be unregistered.[10] Given the voluntary registration system in the Netherland, in contrast to the mandatory passport regulations enforced by the police in Sweden and Norway, single persons could easily leave Holland unnoticed. The departure of families, on the other hand, would most likely come to the attention of local officials except in the largest and most densely populated cities. Apart from the problem of unregistered singles, the linked and nonlinked ship passenger files do not differ significantly in other respects. Thus, the surviving serial records, incomplete as they are, provide relatively unbiased sources for the structural analysis of Dutch transatlantic migration. The remainder of this essay will report on some of these findings.

The Journey Across— Ships and Ports

Dutch immigrants in the period 1820–1880 crossed the ocean on more than 2,000 different ships, but in the 1860s, as the packet steamers came to replace sailing vessels whose departures were often irregular, the Dutch, like other European travellers, increasingly took passage on relatively few, specially designed immigrant ships that shuttled the Atlantic on regular schedules. As the large number of ships carrying Dutch immigrants would suggest, most travelled singly or in single families. Of 500 ships crossings with Dutch aboard in the years 1820–1844, only a third

(38 percent) had 10 or more Dutch passengers, and only one carried more than 100.[11] After 1845, with the beginning of the Great Migration, more than half the Dutch crossings had 10 or more, and 102 ships had more than 100 Dutch, the largest group numbering 486 on a crossing in 1873.[12] But the transatlantic passage was a trickle rather than a flood, except for the group migration of 1846–1847.

The ports of embarkation for the Dutch were largely determined by the fact that English, Dutch, French, and German shipping companies dominated the northern European passanger trade. Prior to the 1840s, the ports of Amsterdam and Le Havre vied for dominance in the Dutch immigrant traffic, with Bremen gaining ground in the 1830s. But after 1840, Rotterdam became the dominant port, except for the decade of the 1860s when Liverpool and London far surpassed the premier Dutch harbor by capturing half of all Dutch traffic. over the 60-year period 1820–1880, 46.7 percent of the Dutch emigrants sailed to the United States directly from Rotterdam, and another 18.5 percent transshipped via Liverpool; 11.4 percent left Antwerp, and 6 percent each departed from Amsterdam, London, and Le Havre. Bremen, Hamburg, and Glasgow shared the remaining 4.5 percent (Table 1.1).

Convenience, price, scheduling, comfort and familiarity, and the activity of shipping company agents were all factors in the selection of the port of sail and the particular vessel of passage. The Dutch transportation network of canal boats and later railroads made the port cities of Rotterdam and Amsterdam easily accessible to immigrants. Southern Netherlanders, by the same token, sometimes travelled to nearby Antwerp or more distant Le Havre. Liverpool, though inconvenient, gained its share of the Dutch traffic only because of its low prices. To reach Liverpool, however, Dutch immigrants first had to cross the North Sea from Rotterdam to Hull, and then cross England by train to Liverpool. This added a week or more to the total voyage. Ninety percent of the Dutch travelled in steerage class, while 10 percent enjoyed the comforts of the first- and second-class cabins (Table 1.2).

The preferred immigrant port of entry in the United States was New York (Table 1.3). In the 60 years from 1820 through 1880, 89 percent of the Dutch disembarked at New York. Most

Table 1.1. Port of Embarkation by Decade, Dutch Immigrants, 1820–1880

Port	1820–1829		1830–1839		1840–1849		1850–1859		1860–1869		1870–1880		All years	
	N	%	N	%	N	%	N	%	N	%	N	%	N	%
Netherlands														
Amsterdam	179	42	328	33	1,897	15	842	6	57	1	1	0	3,304	6.1
Rotterdam	13	3	85	9	7,964	62	7,138	48	1,585	19	8,475	52	25,260	46.7
Nieuwdiep	0	0	0	0	119	1	1	0	0	0	0	0	120	0.2
England														
Liverpool	34	8	36	4	165	1	2,200	15	2,217	26	5,380	33	10,032	18.5
London	7	2	33	3	348	3	337	2	2,038	24	244	2	3,007	5.6
Glasgow	0	0	0	0	0	0	3	0	539	6	457	3	999	1.9
Other Atlantic														
Antwerp	39	9	21	2	951	7	2,526	17	1,286	15	1,361	8	6,184	11.4
Le Harve	94	22	286	29	872	7	1,651	11	175	2	63	0	3,141	5.8
Other	2	0	1	0	294	2	0	0	4	0	18	1	319	0.6
North Sea/Baltic														
Bremen	1	0	130	13	286	2	211	2	484	6	163	1	1,275	2.4
Hamburg	5	1	9	1	4	0	51	0	90	1	47	0	206	0.4
Other	0	0	0	0	1	0	0	0	13	0	0	0	14	0.0
Mediteranean	2	0	1	0	3	0	2	0	0	0	0	0	8	0.0
Latin America	40	9	47	5	23	0	47	0	37	0	46	0	240	0.4
E. Indies/Africa	2	0	1	0	0	0	1	0	5	0	2	0	11	0.0
United States	2	0	3	0	2	0	0	0	0	0	0	0	7	0.0
British No. Amer.	2	0	0	0	2	0	0	0	3	0	9	0	16	0.0

Source: U.S. ship lists study data.

Table 1.2. Ship Accommodations by Decade,
Dutch Immigrants, 1820–1880

Decade	Cabin[a]		Steerage		N.A.[b]
	N	%	N	%	
1820–1829	0	N.A.	19	N.A.	404
1830–1839	0	N.A.	13	N.A.	968
1840–1849	13	N.A.	4,032	N.A.	8,880
1850–1859	1,418	16.3	7,289	83.7	6,345
1860–1869	853	10.3	7,408	89.7	273
1870–1880	1,470	9.1	14,761	90.9	35
All years	3,754	10.1	33,522	89.9	

Source: U.S. ship lists study data.
[a] Includes all non-steerage passengers.
[b] Data not regularly reported until 1855.

arrived healthy. Chroniclers and popular historians have made much of burials at sea due to shipboard epidemics and accidents, but very few Dutch died at sea. In all 60 years, with more than 55,000 crossings, mostly in steerage, only 507, or 1.1 per 1,000 passengers, died en route (Table 1.4). Two thirds of them were children, usually infants; nineteen infants were born on board and survived the voyage. A quarter of those who died at sea were husbands and wives; their deaths dealt a far more serious blow to the family. The low death rate was a result of the relatively good health of the Dutch emigrants and the proverbial Dutch cleanliness. Few Dutch emigrants were in dire poverty or various advanced stages of starvation, as were German emigrants in the 1830s and the "famine Irish" in the 1840s.

The Dutch emigrants also were careful to take passage during the spring in the healthiest time of the year (Table 1.5). Almost half arrived in April, May, and June, before the summer epidemics broke out but after the most dangerous winter storms on the north Atlantic. The Dutch emigrants had not always planned so carefully. In the early decades they travelled later in the year, under the July and August sun, or in the late fall, arriving in October, November, and December after the Great Lakes shipping season had ended. Few laboring jobs were available during the winter, however.

The leaders of the first Seceder groups, which arrived in the

Table 1.3. Port of Arrival by Decade, Dutch Immigrants, 1820–1880

Port of arrival	1820–1829 N	1820–1829 %	1830–1839 N	1830–1839 %	1840–1849 N	1840–1849 %	1850–1859 N	1850–1859 %	1860–1869 N	1860–1869 %	1870–1880 N	1870–1880 %	All years N	All years %
New York	273	65	618	63	10,122	78	14,042	93	8,066	95	15,237	94	48,358	89
Baltimore	0	0	45	5	1,538	12	226	2	173	2	301	2	2,283	4
New Orleans	29	7	94	10	879	14	574	4	36	0	55	0	1,667	3
Boston	18	4	51	5	229	7	162	1	213	2	257	2	930	2
Philadelphia	85	20	170	17	163	1	48	0	8	0	416	3	890	2
Other Atlantic and Gulf ports	18	4	3	0	2	0	0	0	38	0	0	0	61	0

Source: U.S. ship lists study data.

Table 1.4. Deaths at Sea, by Family Status, Age,
and Decade, Dutch Immigrants, 1820–1880

	N	%
Status and age group		
Husband	76	15.0
Wife	47	9.3
Infants (below age 1)	91	17.9
Children (age 1–13)	251	49.5
Other adults (age 14 +)	42	8.3
Total	507	100.0
Deaths by decade		
1820–1829	0	0.0
1830–1839	1	0.2
1840–1849	147	29.0
1850–1859	206	40.6
1860–1869	103	20.3
1870–1880	50	9.9
All years	507	100.0
Death rate 1.1 per 1,000		

Source: U.S. ship lists study data.

winter of 1846, changed the pattern by writing strong letters of advice to the 1847 contingent, urging a spring departure if possible. In the next decades, over 40 percent of the Dutch arrived in May and June, when the weather was good and jobs plentiful. Only in the 1870s, when the more reliable steam packets had largely replaced sailing vessels, did the prime arrival time move ahead slightly to April and May, rather than May and June. The Dutch emigrants, it is clear, planned their transoceanic voyage as carefully as they made the decision to migrate in the first place and chose their ultimate destinations.

Origins and Destinations

The Netherlands emigration records, as I have noted, state the village or city in which the immigrants last resided and their intended country of destination, but it is not possible to follow them to their actual place of settlement without linking the

Table 1.5. Month of Arrival by Decade, Dutch Immigrants, 1820–1880

Month of arrival	1820–1829		1830–1839		1840–1849		1850–1859		1860–1869		1870–1880		All years	
	N	%	N	%	N	%	N	%	N	%	N	%	N	%
January	17	4.0	41	4.2	583	4.5	456	3.0	343	4.0	281	1.7	1,721	3.2
February	7	1.7	20	2.0	40	.3	357	2.4	155	1.8	372	2.3	951	1.8
March	20	4.7	19	1.9	152	.1	165	1.1	330	3.9	1,643	10.1	2,329	4.3
1st quarter	44	10.4	80	8.1	775	5.9	978	6.5	828	9.7	2,296	14.1	5,001	9.3
April	33	7.8	15	1.5	842	6.5	952	6.3	693	8.1	3,253	20.0	5,788	10.7
May	26	6.2	63	6.4	2,017	15.6	2,864	19.0	1,677	19.7	3,377	20.8	10,024	18.5
June	42	9.9	260	26.5	3,135	24.2	2,936	19.5	1,908	22.4	1,452	8.9	9,733	18.0
2d quarter	101	23.9	338	34.4	5,994	46.3	6,752	44.9	4,278	50.1	8,082	49.7	25,545	47.1
July	82	19.4	92	9.4	1,884	14.6	1,494	9.9	690	8.1	1,117	6.9	5,359	9.9
August	21	5.0	244	24.9	1,085	8.4	1,128	7.5	389	4.6	1,229	7.6	4,096	7.6
September	34	8.1	43	4.4	1,063	8.2	1,673	11.1	722	8.5	1,231	7.6	4,766	8.8
3d quarter	137	32.5	379	38.6	4,032	31.2	4,295	28.5	1,801	21.1	3,577	22.0	14,221	26.2
October	74	17.5	35	3.6	871	6.7	1,652	11.0	602	7.1	854	5.3	4,088	7.5
November	43	10.2	48	4.9	595	4.6	740	4.9	690	8.1	887	5.4	3,003	5.5
December	24	5.7	101	10.3	666	5.2	635	4.2	335	3.9	570	3.5	2,331	4.3
4th quarter	141	33.2	184	18.8	2,132	16.5	3,021	20.1	1,627	19.1	2,311	14.2	9,422	17.4
Decade	423	0.8	981	1.8	12,933	23.9	15,052	27.8	8,534	15.8	16,266	30.0	54,189	100.0

Source: U.S. ship lists study data.

Dutch records to American population censuses. Therefore, I searched the federal population census manuscripts of 1850, 1860, and 1870 for all counties in which groups of Hollanders were known to have lived, and the census questionaires of all first- and second-generation Dutch-Americans were abstracted and again converted to a computer file. This census file, which includes 105,000 individuals and is arranged alphabetically by families or single adults (24,000 in all), was then linked, name by name, with the Netherlands emigration records.

The resulting combined file provides biographical information both before and after migration that permits a point-to-point study of Dutch emigration from Old World to New World homes. Moves within the United States can also be traced at 10-year intervals. Likewise, a search of the municipal population registers would reveal if the emigrant families had moved within the Netherlands prior to their overseas move. We know that the Dutch, like other northern Europeans, were a mobile people and that overseas emigration was merely a redirection or rechanneling, prompted by disturbances at home and new opportunities in North America, of a small part of the traditional internal migration. Despite the internal mobility, my investigation of the population registers in Haarlem and Amsterdam indicate that almost all the overseas emigrants from these cities had been born there and lived there until leaving for America. There was little so-called stage migration from the Netherlands, that is, removal first from rural regions to the urban centers and then overseas emigration.

The "distant magnet" of North America also exerted a limited force on Hollanders. Only 380,000 Dutch nationals emigrated overseas in the century from 1820 to 1920. This was a moderate rate of 72 per 100,000 population (Table 1.6), which places the Netherlands tenth among European nations; only France, Belgium, and Luxemburg had a lower percentage of emigrants. The Dutch were simply not as emigration-minded as most of the rest of Europe. Those who did depart, however, followed the general northern European emigration cycle of four periods (Figure 1.3): (1) 1847–1857, when the Calvinist Seceders and Roman Catholic groups led the way; (2) 1865–1873, when the pent up desire to emigrate was released by the ending of the American Civil War; (3) 1880–1893 during the severe agricultural crisis in the northern Netherlands; and

Table 1.6. Annual Overseas Emigration per 100,000
Dutch Population, 1820–1920

Year	Population on Dec. 31 (1,000s)	Overseas emigration	Rate per 100,000
1820–1829 ave.	2,424	39[a]	2
1830–1839 ave.	2,737	96[a]	4
1840	2,894	107	4
1841	2,931	103	4
1842	2,957	127	4
1843	2,989	296	10
1844	3,020	321	11
1845	3,053	874	29
1846	3,061	2,831	92
1847	3,050	8,090	265
1848	3,055	3,103	102
1849	3,057	3,143	103
1850	3,031	1,299	43
1851	3,080	1,771	57
1852	3,128	1,951	62
1853	3,163	2,653	84
1854	3,195	5,074	159
1855	3,216	3,087	96
1856	3,252	3,050	94
1857	3,282	2,844	87
1858	3,303	1,363	41
1859	3,309	713	22
1860	3,336	1,163	35
1861	3,373	863	26
1862	3,410	931	27
1863	3,453	1,333	39
1864	3,492	1,036	30
1865	3,529	1,814	51
1866	3,553	3,727	105
1867	3,592	4,923	137
1868	3,628	3,520	97
1869	3,580	4,018	112
1870	3,618	2,288	63
1871	3,637	2,520	69
1872	3,675	4,447	121
1873	3,716	5,576	150

Table 1.6., continued.

Year	Population on Dec. 31 (1,000s)	Overseas emigration	Rate per 100,000
1874	3,767	1,719	46
1875	3,810	1,245	33
1876	3,865	875	23
1877	3,925	603	15
1878	3,982	832	21
1879	4,013	1,553	39
1880	4,061	4,670	116
1881	4,114	7,462	181
1882	4,173	5,975	143
1883	4,225	3,433	81
1884	4,278	2,611	61
1885	4,336	1,782	41
1886	4,391	1,758	40
1887	4,451	4,214	95
1888	4,506	4,461	99
1889	4,511	7,495	166
1890	4,565	3,143	69
1891	4,622	3,825	83
1892	4,670	5,934	127
1893	4,733	5,724	121
1894	4,796	1,357	28
1895	4,859	1,457	30
1896	4,929	2,299	47
1897	5,004	1,543	31
1898	5,075	1,175	23
1899	5,104	1,472	29
1900	5,179	1,548	30
1901	5,263	2,886	55
1902	5,347	3,603	67
1903	5,431	5,296	98
1904	5,510	4,030	73
1905	5,591	3,927	70
1906	5,672	4,958	87
1907	5,747	7,221	126
1908	5,825	4,680	80
1909	5,858	6,769	116

Table 1.6., continued.

Year	Population on Dec. 31 (1,000s)	Overseas emigration	Rate per 100,000
1910	5,945	7,136	120
1911	6,022	7,752	129
1912	6,114	7,774	127
1913	6,213	8,503	137
1914	6,340	6,275	99
1915	6,450	4,131	64
1916	6,583	3,905	59
1917	6,725	1,983	29
1918	6,779	2,182	32
1919	6,831	5,574	82
1920	6,926	11,924	172
Totals: 1820–1920	380,104	272,882	72

Sources: Emigration figures, 1830–1880 are derived from the author's analysis of the *Landverhuizers* records and U.S. ship lists (see notes 6 and 7). Emigration data, 1881–1920, are in *Bijdragen tot de Statistiek van Nederland*, and in *Bijdragen* . . . (Nieuwe Volgreeks), Central Bureau for Statistics, The Hague. Population data are from the *Jaarboekje over* . . . , 1841–1864. and the *Bijdragen tot de Statistiek* . . . , 1865–1920.
    [a] U.S. immigrants only: 1820–1829 = 387, 1830–1839 = 958.

(4) 1903–1913, the pre-war decade of intense emigration, when 66,000 Dutch left for overseas places under the adverse impact of the industrial revolution in the Netherlands.

This migration of the early twentieth century differed markedly from previous patterns. Instead of the agricultural provinces, particularly the sea clay regions, leading the way as they had for a half century, the primary emigration field shifted to the so-called Randstad region, the concentration of cities from Dordrecht to Amsterdam. Between the 1880s and World War I, the share of emigrants from the three sea clay provinces—Zeeland, Groningen, and Friesland—dropped sharply from 20 percent to under 5 percent, whereas the share from Noord-Holland and Zuid-Holland rose threefold, from 10 percent to over 30 percent. These shifts signify a fundamental change in the social structure of Dutch emigration, a change from a rural to an urban movement that coincided with the belated but rapid industrialization of the Dutch economy after 1900[13]

The dramatic reversal in the type of Dutch emigration coincided with a shift in overseas destinations. The United States had

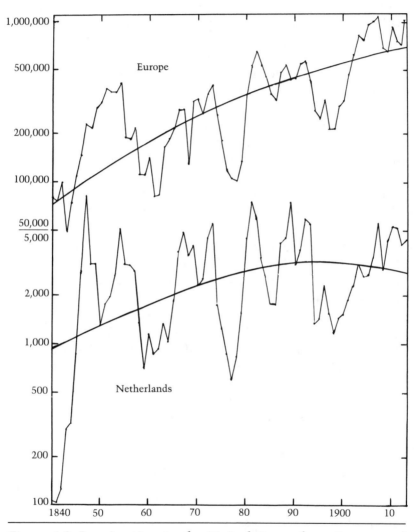

Figure 1.3. Immigration to the United States from Europe and the Netherlands, 1840–1913

Source: Brinley Thomas, *Migration and Economic Growth* (1954), 286; Swierenga study data derived from the Netherlands Emigration Records and U.S. Ship Passenger Lists.

always been the region of choice for Hollanders. Java or the Cape of Good Hope might offer advantages to aspiring civil servants, young professionals, military men, and large planters, but these areas did not attract rural farm folk and village craftsmen. Until the 1890s, nearly 90 percent of all Dutch emigrants went to the United States (Table 1.7). Begnning in 1894, following the census bureau's announcement that the agricultural frontier had closed, and in the midst of a severe economic depression that lasted until 1897, the Dutch preference for America dropped rapidly, reaching a low point of 44 percent in 1897. Between 1901 and 1920, only 56 percent of all Dutch overseas emigrants chose the United States; the remainder preferred Indonesia and South Africa.

The key variable in determining the America-centeredness of Dutch emigration was always rurality of origin. Rural peasants and craftsmen sought the free land offered in the American West, whereas ambitious sons of urban middle class families looked to the Dutch colonies for opportunities to advance into white-collar positions and higher income and prestige. The few urban immigrants who did come to the United States settled in New York City, Cincinnati, St. Louis, Chicago, and other large cities. Most rural immigrants, by contrast, went directly to rural Dutch colonies and farms.

How did the resettlement process occur? What factors determined who went where? If we could interview all the emigrants, we would find as many different factors involved as there were people. The overall pattern of the removal process, however, provides some clues, which seem to be confirmed by immigrant letters and other writings. Dutch emigration, it appears, can best be understood as a series of local movements, a sort of migration chain, tying together specific Dutch villages and specific American communities. It is a remarkable fact that only a relatively few communities in Holland and America participated in the Dutch migration. Of the 1,156 municipalities (*gemeenten*) in the Netherlands in 1869—the equivalent of American counties—only 134 municipalities (12 percent) provided nearly three-quarters of all overseas emigrants in the period 1820–1880. One-half of all emigrants came from only 55 municipalities (5 percent), and one-third hailed from a mere 22 municipalities (2.0

Table 1.7. Dutch Overseas Emigration by Continent, 1835–1920 (Official Statistics Only)

Decade	All	U.S.A. N	U.S.A. %	S.E. Asia N	S.E. Asia %	Africa N	Africa %	S. America N	S. America %	Other[a] N	Other[a] %
1835–1840	35	31	88.6	4	11.4	0	0.0	0	0.0	0	0.0
1841–1850	10,310	9,631	93.6	64	0.1	14	0.0	48	0.0	553	5.4
1851–1860	15,850	13,175	83.2	328	2.1	767	4.8	920	5.8	660	4.2
1861–1870	20,904	18,717	90.0	951	4.6	471	2.3	400	1.9	365	1.8
1871–1880	15,314	14,149	93.0	447	2.9	288	1.9	92	0.0	338	2.2
1881–1890	42,330	40,760	96.3	14	0.0	1,066	2.5	N.A.		490	1.2
1891–1900	26,416	22,524	85.3	36	0.0	3,745	14.2	N.A.		111	0.0
1901–1910	50,588	34,369	68.1	10,016	19.8	3,141	6.2	2,964	5.9	98	0.0
1911–1920	60,503	27,396	45.7	26,021	43.4	1,626	2.7	4,960	8.3	500	0.1
1835–1920	242,250[b]	180,752	74.9	37,881	15.7	11,118	4.6	9,384	3.9	3,115	1.3

Sources: R. P. Swierenga, comp., Dutch Emigrants to the United States, South Africa, and Southeast Asia, 1835–1880: An Alphabetical Listing by Household Heads and Independent Persons (Wilmington, Del.: Scholarly Resources, 1982); Bijdragen tot de Statistiek van Nederland, 1881–1900; Bijdragen tot de Statistiek van Nederland, Nieuwe Volgreeks, 1901–1920.
[a] Includes Australia, 618; Middle East, 15; British North America, 50; Continental Europe, 143; and "unknown," 584.
[b] 2,933 missing records.

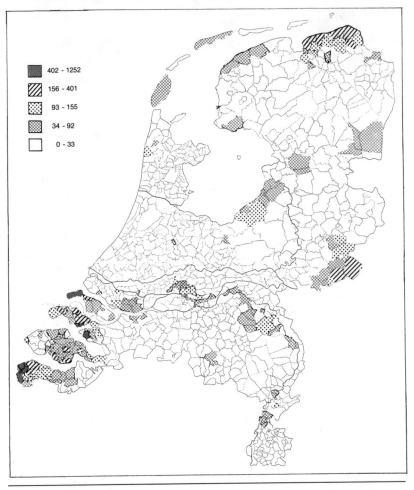

Figure 1.4. Emigration Rate per Municipality, 1835–1880, per 1,000 Average Population, 1830–1878

Source: Robert P. Swierenga, comp., *Dutch Emigrants to the United States, . . .* (Wilmington, Del., 1982); *Volkstelling*, 1 Jan. 1830; *Bijdragen tot de Algemene Statistiek van Nederland*, 1878, *Bevolking, Oppervlakte* I, 1–73.

percent). Figure 1.4 depicts the major emigration areas in terms of their population density.

The primary emigration fields in the Netherlands were: in the east, the Gelderland Achterhoek region on the German border; in the north, the sea clay farming region along the North Sea coast; in the southwest, the Zuid-Holland island of Goeree-Over-flakkee and the Zeeland islands of West Vlaanderen, Walcheren, Schouwen-Duiveland, and Zuid Beveland; in the south, the area of the Brabantse peel in Noord-Brabant.

In the United States there was an even greater concentration of settlement. Of the 1,626 counties nationwide in 1850, spread among 35 states, 72 percent of the Dutch immigrants lived in only 16 counties (less than 1 percent). At the township or city ward level—called "minor civil divisions" in census jargon—half (51.2 percent) of the Dutch were squeezed into only 15 townships or wards within these counties. At the time, there were more than 30,000 minor civil divisions in the United States. By 1870, after 25 years of continuous immigration, the Dutch had begun to spread out, but even then, 56 percent resided in only 18 counties (out of 2,295 nationwide), and 40 percent lived in a mere 55 townships or city wards (out of over 30,000 nationwide).

The primary Dutch settlements ranged within a 50-mile radius of the southern Lake Michigan shoreline from Muskegon, Grand Rapids, and Holland on the east shore to Chicago, Milwaukee, and Green Bay on the west shore. Secondary areas were in central Iowa, western New York, and metropolitan New York City, including Paterson and Passaic in northern New Jersey. Subsequently, the Dutch dispersed themselves over a much greater area of the northern plains and west coast in search of cheap farmland. But few immigrant groups of comparable size clustered together more than did the clannish Dutch. Living in such close proximity has doubtless nurtured and sustained the strong sense of "Dutchness" that is evident today, five and six generations later.

The primary mechanism of the Dutch migration was the removal over a period of time of related families and friends from particular Dutch communities to their particular American counterparts. First, a few families would emigrate, and they in turn would induce relatives and friends to follow in a type of migration chain.[14] Additional evidence of a community-type migration is the strong familial character of the Dutch emigration. More than three-fourths of all emigrants sailed with family members, according to the ship manifests.[15] Two-thirds of these were young couples with still growing families, and the other third were single-parent families or childless couples. The family pattern of Dutch emigration increased the likelihood of concentrated settlement near relatives and friends in America.

Because of this local linkage, an emigration movement that might appear to be random was actually a regularized transplanting, governed by community and family ties.[16] Dutch overseas migration was channeled rather than scattered; there was a consistency in the direction and goal of migration. Dutch localities in which the migration tradition began in the early days of the 1840s continued to send out more emigrants in a self-generating process. Neighboring villages might also be affected later, as the word spread about opportunities and successes in America, but large areas of the Netherlands, particularly in the central and western region, remained entirely untouched by emigration fever.

Socio-economic and Religious Aspects

The individual and local factors in migration were always influenced by larger socioeconomic and religious forces. Wars and depressions in America halted immigration at times and at other times agrarian crises and religious controversies in the Netherlands stimulated it. The earliest emigration in the mid-1840s began in communities that were severely depressed economically or suffering from religious turmoil. Winterswijk in Gelderland and Oudorp and Goedereede in Zuid-Holland are prime examples of economic migration. Religiously driven emigration in the 1840s occurred among strict Calvinist Seceders in Ommen and Staphorst in Overijssel, Dwingeloo and Sleen in Drenthe, and Ulrum and Lopersum in Groningen. Roman Catholics, also a minority still facing handicaps, emigrated from the villages of Boekel, Zeeland, and Uden in Noord-Brabant. As among the Seceders a few clerical leaders also instigated this movement.

But ultimately economic conditions in the countryside were decisive. The Netherlands consists of three major soil regions: marshy areas with active dairying in the west, higher eleva-

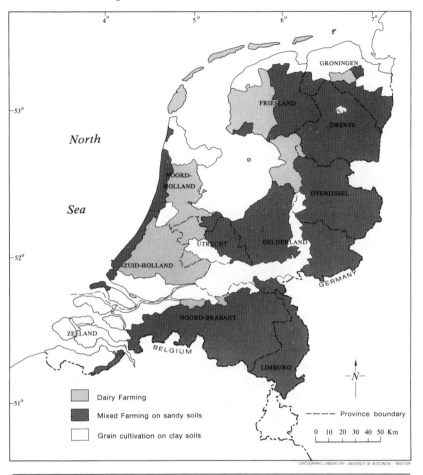

Figure 1.5. Major Agricultural Regions of the Netherlands

Source: Derived from *Verslag van den Landboum in Nederland: Grootte der Gronden tijdens de invoering van het kadaster* [Report of Agriculture in the Netherlands: Size of the Land at the Introduction of the Land Registry] ('sGraven-hage: Van Weelden en Mingelen, 1875).

tion sandy soils in the east, and fertile sea clay regions along the North Sea coast in the north and southwest (Figure 1.5). Over half (55 percent) of all emigrants originated in the clay areas, a third (31 percent) came from the thin sandy regions, and only a seventh (14 percent) hailed from dairy areas.[17]

The clay soil emigrants were mainly excess farm laborers

who were vulnerable in the periodic agricultural depressions and were unable to find nonfarm employment at home because of the slow pace of Dutch industrialization.[18] The prolonged agrarian crises beginning in the late 1870s drove tens of thousands of these so-called "free" farm workers to migrate to America, where they could hope to become farm owners themselves under the homestead law. In the sandy soil regions, farm owners themselves emigrated in greater numbers in the 1840s and 1850s in order to escape their small, low-yield farms and provide land for their sons. Village craftsmen also emigrated in large numbers, having been squeezed out by license fees, onerous taxes, and lack of work in a sluggish economy.[19] Dairy farmers, on the other hand, had little propensity to emigrate because their small, single-family operations enjoyed stable prices and underwent little technological change.

Religious forces interacted with economic developments and to a large extent gave shape to the group migrations of the 1840s and the planting of colonies in the American Midwest.[20] The triumph of religious tolerance in the Netherlands had since the seventeenth century led to a pluralistic society of Protestants, Roman Catholics, and Jews. According to the census of 1849, the Hervormde Kerk (Reformed Church) held its premier place as the church of the Orange monarchy, with 55 percent of the populace. Other Protestant groups, all small in number, were the Evangelical Lutherans with 2 percent, the Seceders of 1834 (who separated from the Hervormde Kerk) with 1.3 percent, and Mennonites with 1.2 percent. Catholics in 1849 numbered 38.5 percent and Jews 1.9 percent.

The overseas emigration of the period 1835–1880 generally follows this ranking: 65 percent were Hervormden, 20 percent Catholics, 13 percent Seceders, and Jews 2 percent. The predominant Hervormden and minority Seceders were thus *over*represented among emigrants; Catholics were *under*represented, because they had a greater personal resistance to emigration and their clerical leaders generally discouraged it. Nevertheless, Catholic emigrants far outnumbered the much more publicized Seceder emigration.

Together Seceders and Catholic emigrants contributed only

one-third of the total before 1880. Yet, because they emigrated in large groups in the early years and founded rural colonies, they perpetuated their ideals and group identity. Their colonies of Holland, Pella, Sheboygan, and Little Chute, among others, in turn mothered myriad other colonies to create places for their sons and daughters and for later arrivals from the homeland. Even though up to half of the Dutch immigrants did not settle in religiously oriented colonies, these communities retained a dominant influence for generations because of their strong clerical leaders, educational and cultural institutions, and ethnic newspapers that circulated far and wide.

Conclusion

The salient characteristic of Dutch immigration to the United States that is revealed by this analysis of the primary sources is the rationality of the movement. The notable "planned migration" after World War Two, when the Dutch government took an active part, had its counterpart in the nineteenth century, when religious congregations and families managed and directed the Dutch diaspora. These organs channeled the resettlement from point of origin to ultimate destination in a regular manner. The Dutch usually selected their destination before departing. Less than one in five Dutch emigrant families were classified as needy; very few were desperately poor and on the verge of starvation. Most were not in an extremity but had time to assess family goals and to weigh alternatives, such as moving within the Netherlands, crossing the border to neighboring countries, or emigrating to one of the Dutch colonies.

Other indicators of rational decision making are the moderate level of Dutch transatlantic migration, its America-centeredness and its cyclical flow in response to American socioeconomic and political conditions, the strong links between particular sending and receiving communities, and the mediating role of family and friends. There was a strategy behind the Dutch immigration. The goal was to preserve family ties, faith commitments, and cultural values and institutions in a strange and sometimes unfriendly environment. Dutch-American society to-day testifies to the strength of that vision and the fruition of many of these goals.

Notes

1. Excellent surveys of the literature are J. D. Gould, "European Inter-Continental Emigration 1815–1914: Patterns and Causes," *Journal of European Economic History* 8 (1979): 593–679; and R. Paul Shaw, *Migration Theory and Fact: A Review and Bibliography of Current Literature, Bibliography Series, Number Five* (Philadelphia, Regional Science Research Institute, 1975).

2. "Act of Congress of March 2, 1819, An Act Regulating Passenger-Ships and Vessels." Copies of this act and all others pertaining to immigrant passengers are conveniently published in William J. Bromwell, *History of Immigration to the United States . . .* (New York, 1856; reprinted New York: Arno Press, 1969), 206–225. The 1819 Act is on pp. 208–209.

3. By order of the Minister of the Interior (Binnenlandse Zaken) of 21 December 1847, Number 100, municipal governments were required each year to send to provincial governors a list of all known overseas emigrants: *Staat der Landverhuizingen naar Noord Amerika of andere overzeesche gewesten [List of Emigrants to North America or Other Overseas Places]*. These lists through the year 1877 are in the Algemeen Rijksarchief in The Hague. A photocopied set for the period 1847–1877 is in the Heritage Hall Archives of Calvin College, Grand Rapids, Michigan.

4. For a detailed analysis of the official Netherlands emigration lists, see Robert P. Swierenga, "Dutch International Migration Statistics, 1820–1880: An Analysis of Linked Multinational Nominal Files," *International Migration Review* 15 (Fall 1981): 445–470.

5. The provinces with extant emigration lists after 1880 are: Groningen until 1901 (except the year 1889), Overijssel until 1918, Utrecht until 1905, Zeeland until 1901, and Zuid-Holland until 1899.

6. Robert P. Swierenga, *Dutch Emigrants to the United States, South America, South Africa, and Southeast Asia, 1835–1880: An Alphabetical Listing by Household Heads and Independent Persons* (Wilmington, Del.: Scholarly Resources, 1982).

7. Robert P. Swierenga, *Dutch Immigrants in United States Ship Passenger Manifests, 1820–1880: An Alphabetical Listing by Household Heads and Independent Persons* (Wilmington, Del.: Scholarly Resources, 1982).

8. J. Van Hinte, *Nederlanders in Amerika: Een Studie over Landverhuizers en Volkplanters in de 19e en 20st eeuw in de Vereenigde*

Staten van Amerika (2 vols., Groningen: Noordhoff, 1928), I, 197. William S. Petersen, *Planned Migration: The Social Determinants of the Dutch-Canadian Movement* (Berkeley: University of California Press, 1955) estimates underreporting of 20–40 percent in the period 1880–1924 (45–46).

9. E. P. Hutchinson, "Notes on Immigration Statistics of the United States," *Journal of the American Statistical Association* 53 (Dec. 1958): 963–1025; Swierenga, "Dutch International Migration," 446–447.

10. Swierenga, "Dutch International Migration," 462–465.

11. The exception was the ship *XYZ* from Bremen to New York, arriving on August 2, 1832, with 116 Dutch nationals aboard.

12. This was the ship *Maas* from Rotterdam to New York, arriving April 17, 1873.

13. The best studies of Dutch economic conditions in the nineteenth century are J. A. De Jonge, "Industrial Growth in the Netherlands, 1850–1914," *Acta Historiae Neerlandica*, 5 (1971): 159–212, which is a synopsis of *Industrialisatie in Nederland tussen 1850 en 1914 [Industrialization in the Netherlands Between 1850 and 1914]* (Amsterdam: Scheltema and Holkema, 1968, reprinted Nijmegen: Sun 1976); Joel Mokyr, *Industrialization in the Low Countries, 1795–1850* (New Haven and London: Yale University Press, 1976).

14. Robert C. Ostergren, "Kinship Networks and Migration: A Nineteenth Century Swedish Example;" *Social Science History* 6 (Summer 1982): 293–320; Robert E. Bieder, "Kinship as a Factor in Migration," *Journal of Marriage and the Family* 35 (Winter 1973): 429–439; John S. McDonald and Leatrice D. McDonald, "Chain Migration, Ethnic Neighborhood Formation, and Social Networks," *Millbank Memorial Fund Quarterly* 42 (Jan. 1964): 82–97; and Sune Åkerman, Bo Kronborg, and Thomas Nilson, "Emigration, Family and Kinship," *American Studies in Scandinavia* 9 (1977): 105–122.

15. For specifics, see Robert P. Swierenga, "Dutch Immigrant Demography, 1820–1880," *Journal of Family History* 5 (Winter 1980): 390–405.

16. An elaboration of this point is in Robert P. Swierenga, "Exodus Netherlands, Promised Land America: Dutch Immigration and Settlement in the United States," in J. W. Schulte Nordholt and Robert P. Swierenga, eds., *A Bilateral Bicentennial: A History of Dutch-American Relations, 1782–1982* (Amsterdam: Meulenhoff, and New York: Octagon Books, 1982), 127–147. Additional evidence is provided in two recent case studies: Yda Saueressig-Schreuder, "Emigration, Settlement, and Assimilation of Dutch Catholic Immigrants in Wisconsin, 1850–1905," (Ph.D. dissertation, University of Wisconsin, 1982); David G. Vanderstel, "The

Dutch of Grand Rapids, Michigan, 1848–1900: Immigrant Neighborhood and Community Development in a Nineteenth Century City" (Ph.D. dissertation, Kent State University, 1983).

17. Details are in Robert P. Swierenga, "Dutch International Labour Migration to North America in the Nineteenth Century," in Herman Ganzevoort and Mark Boekelman, eds., *Dutch Immigration to North America* (Toronto: Multicultural History Society of Ontario, 1982), 1–34.

18. E. W. Hofstee, "Population Increase in the Netherlands," *Acta Historiae Neerlandica* 3 (1968): 43–125; Hofstee, "De Landbouw en de migratie" [Agriculture and Migration], *Economische Statistiek Berichten* 35 (1950): 1024–1026; J. Haveman, "Social Tensions Between Farmer and Farm Laborer in Northern Holland," *American Journal of Sociology* 60 (Nov. 1954): 246–254.

19. A primary source on this point is B. W. A. E. Sloet tot Oldhuis, "Over de oorzaken van landverhuizing der Nederlanders naar de Vereenigde Staten," [About the Causes of Emigration from the Netherlands to the United States], *Tijdschrift voor Staathuishoudkundige en Statistiek* 25 (3rd ser., 2nd pt., 1866): 87–102. This important pamphlet is published in English translation, edited by Robert P. Swierenga, under the title "The Cause of Dutch Emigration to America: An 1866 Account" in *Michigana* 24 (Spring 1979): 56–61; (Summer 1979): 92–97.

20. A recent careful analysis of the 1840s is Pieter R. D. Stokvis, *De Nederlandse Trek naar Amerika, 1846–1847* [The Dutch Emigration to America, 1846–1847] (Leiden: Universitaire Pers, 1977), 36–57 and passim. For a broader statistical analysis see Robert P. Swierenga and Yda Saueressig-Schreuder, "Catholic and Protestant Emigration from the Netherlands in the Nineteenth Century: A Comparative Social Structure Analysis," *Tijdschrift voor Economische en Sociale Geografie* 74 (1983): 25–40. An expanded version of this article is Yda Saueressig-Schreuder and Robert P. Swierenga, "Catholic Emigration from the Southern Provinces of the Netherlands in the Nineteenth Century," Working Paper no. 27, Netherlands Interuniversity Demographic Institute.

2. Dutch International Migration 1815–1910

Pieter R. D. Stokvis

The postwar experience of massive emigration overseas and equally massive immigration from the former colonies and the Mediterranean world makes one wonder to what extent the Netherlanads had known these phenomena in the past. In order to decide whether the Netherlands was an emigration or immigration country during the nineteenth century we have to know how many Dutchmen went abroad permanently, where they preferred to settle, and how migration patterns changed over time. This seems easy, but migration statistics have too many deficiencies to answer these questions by themselves. The combination of migration data and census data, however, may provide us with fairly accurate answers and enable us to take a closer look at the stereotype of Dutch home attachment. Dutch international migration always had two components. One was migration to and from neighboring countries, and the other was migration overseas primarily to North America. Overseas migration was largely one way and resulted in a sustained population loss, but European migration was reciprocal, and it brought at times more people into the Netherlands than the number leaving. In all census years from 1849 to 1909, about three-fifths of those Netherlanders residing abroad lived in Europe. Thus, the picture of Dutch immigration to the United States, which has almost exclusively captivated historians, must be modified to incorporate the even greater population movements across adjacent borders. In this chapter, it is shown that Dutch net migration was dominated by German and Belgian immigration in the 1820s and 1830s, by overseas migration to the United States from the 1840s onward, and around 1900 by a still larger emigration to Germany. As a result, in the wake of the First World War more Netherlanders, proportionately, lived abroad than ever before or after.

The facts of Dutch migration are derived from arrivals and departures for municipalities, provinces, and the country as a whole. According to E. W. Hofstee's recent résumé, the migration records were not sufficiently complete to portray geographical mobility before 1850 in any detail.[1] By deducting the birth surplus from the population growth, Hofstee arrives at an immigration surplus of 143,000 for the period 1815–1849. As a contrast, the period 1865–1910 showed an emigration surplus that equaled almost the total emigration overseas, which was mainly to the United States. Arrivals and departures, rising from 5,000 to 10,000 in 1865 and to 30,000 in 1910 kept each other more or less in balance. The early nineteenth century immigration surplus, which had its origins in the surrounding countries, had apparently disappeared in the second half of the nineteenth century. Again according to Hofstee, after 1865, the emigration surplus caused by the transatlantic migration was comparatively small.

In 1949 Hofstee had already recorded this image of migration to and from the Netherlands.[2] In 1958 an English version appeared which invoked reflections from others on the causes of the minimal Dutch overseas emigration.[3] Taking up Hofstee's findings, the American sociologist William S. Petersen suggested possible explanations for the apparently slight Dutch inclination to move. Petersen noted that the Dutch had an underdeveloped class consciousness, the working class lacked enterprise, Dutch living standards rose after 1870, and emigration itself shifted from a group to an individual character.[4] In his well-known report of 1960, Frank Thistlethwaite also espoused Hofstee's picture and suggested that push circumstances did not result in actual emigration because of the strong Dutch home attachment. Thistlethwaite conjectured that the general unwillingness of Dutch society to change, and particularly to move, reflected a high degree of cohesion, homogeneity, and stability of community patterns.[5] Thus the idea of an immobile Dutch population took root.

In his model explaining that late industrialization in the Netherlands stemmed from the high level of wages, Joel Mokyr likewise assumed labor to be immobile. Immigration from Belgium before 1850 was supposed to be insignificant, and on the authority of Thomas Malthus, Mokyr believed that immigration from Germany found a premature end in the graveyard.[6] In their recent summaries of demographic development in the Netherlands, H. Knippenberg, J. Hofker, and A. C. de Vooys also maintained in the wake of Hofstee that external migration hardly influenced population structures and trends.[7]

One of the few writers to consider emigration to European countries and other destinations overseas other than to the United States has been J. A. A. Hartland. He noted that the annual departure of several thousands to the United States appealed more to the imagination, whereas the yearly Dutch crossing of the German border involved tens of thousands.[8] An indication that the arrival and departure figures may not be the best or sole means to measure migration is a calculation by F. W. A. van Poppel. If one compares the expected population outcome for the period 1830 to 1980, calculated on the basis of births, deaths, departures, and arrivals in the Netherlands since 1830 with the actual population present in 1980, then 241,000 persons have disappeared without a trace.[9] My suggestion is that their trace leads abroad. I hope to prove my case by concentrating on census figures concerning foreigners in the Netherlands and Netherlanders abroad. From census and migration figures, one can determine to what extent the Netherlands was an immigration or emigration country and when structural changes took place.

Both sets of figures point out that by the middle of the nineteenth century the Netherlands changed from an immigration country into an emigration country. Table 2.1 shows large migration surpluses for the 1820s and 1830s. The deficit of 1815–1819 is probably due to adjustments after the French occupation: remigrants and Dutch officials and military personnel sent to the newly acquired Belgian provinces and the restituted colonies.

Table 2.1. Netherlands Population Increase, Birth Surplus, and Migration Surplus, 1815–1909 (in thousands)

Years	Population increase	Birth surplus	Calculated migration surplus	CBS migration surplus	Registered overseas migration surplus
1815–1819	79	92	− 13	—	—
1820–1829	301	211	+ 90	—	—
1830–1839	237	215	+ 22	—	—
1840–1849	196	202	− 6	− 9.3	− 12.4
1850–1859	252	261	− 9	− 10.3	− 15.8
1860–1869	271	346	− 75	− 66.8	− 23.8
1870–1879	433	449	− 16	− 13.0	− 2.8
1880–1889	498	566	− 68	− 67.0	− 34.9
1890–1899	593	675	− 82	− 82.0	− 56.0
1900–1909	754	841	− 87	− 85.0	− 84.1
1840–1909	2,997	3,340	−343	−333.4	−333.4

Note: The 1815–1839 figures, which exclude Limburg, are calculated from E. W. Hofstee, *De demografische ontwikkeling van Nederland in de eerste helft van de negentiende eeuw* [The Demographic Development of the Netherlands during the First Half of the Nineteenth Century] (Deventer: Van Loghum Slaterus, 1978), 190–198. The 1840–1909 figures are taken from Brian R. Mitchell, *European Historical Statistics 1750–1970* (New York: Columbia University Press, 1975), 32, 92, 96, 103, 146, 148, 152. In 1843–1865 only intercontinental emigration via Dutch ports was recorded, from 1865 onwards departures and arrivals to and from overseas were recorded in local registers of resident population. The Central Bureau of Statistics (CBS) figures concern all migration abroad and are taken from CBS, *Bevolking van Nederland naar geslacht, leeftijd en burgerlijke staat 1830–1969* [Population of the Netherlands by Sex, Age, and Civic Status] (s'-Gravenhage: Staatsuitgeverij, 1970), 25. The migration surplus which Hofstee in the above mentioned study (p. 207) computed from the provincial balances for 1840–1850 and 1880–1890 respectively, + 43,737 and − 22,038, seem to be erroneous.

The migration scales tipped in the 1840s. Until 1860 immigration from neighboring countries still compensated partly for the upsurge of overseas emigration. After 1860, overseas migration took a growing share of the migration deficit except in the 1870s. According to these calculations the migration balance for the period 1840–1909 points to a loss of 230,000 people overseas and 113,000 within Europe. Because departures to neighboring countries were matched by a steady influx, the actual loss of Netherlanders within Europe was far greater than 113,000. The foregoing picture of Dutch international migration is confirmed by census figures.[10] If one compares the number of Netherlanders in Germany, Belgium, France, Great Britain, and the United States with the number of foreign residents in the Netherlands, it is clear that the number of Netherlands emigrants per 100 inhabitants had increased from 2.2 in 1849 to 5.8 in 1909, while the number of foreign immigrants per 100 Netherlanders had decreased from 2.3 to 1.6 (Tables 2.2 and 2.3). This percentage of Dutch emigrants is a minimum estimate, because only the important destinations were recorded.

European Immigration

Next to Switzerland the Netherlands was until 1850 the most important immigration country of the continent.[11] However, after 1850 the percentage of foreigners decreased until stabilization was reached in 1869 around 1.6 percent (Table 2.3). Besides, until the mid-nineteenth century, seasonal labor migration of German migrant workers may have been as high as 100,000.[12] In absolute numbers the foreign presence decreased from 1849 to 1869, when it started to increase again, with a retardation in 1889–1899. The Belgian share declined after 1869 and the German shaare after 1899. The German share of the foreign presence in Holland averaged 60 percent from 1849 until 1899, and the number of men per 100 women decreased steadily from 155 in 1849 to 106 by 1879. Initially the Netherlands attracted male Germans qualified to perform heavy labor, skilled crafts, and trades. After Germany spurted into industialization, females looking for domestic employment and spouses equaled males among immigrants. The Germans, mainly from Prussia, preferred to settle in the border provinces of Groningen, Drenthe, Overijssel, and Gelderland, and in the cities of Noord-Holland and Zuid-Holland.[13] The Belgians ranked below the Germans, with a 30 percent share. The balanced sex ratio reflected serving and mating across the borders of Limburg, Noord-Brabant, and Zeeland. The British share was insignificant, and notable only for the predominance of women, who may have been sailors' brides or domestic servants.

Table 2.2. Dutch Nationals in Germany and France and Dutch-born Residents of the United States, Belgium, and Great Britain

Country	1849	1859	1869	1879	1889	1899	1909
Germany	18,000[a]	18,000[a]	19,978[a]	17,598	37,055	88,053	144,175
United States	9,848	28,281	46,811	58,100	81,851	94,992	120,053
Belgium	31,207	33,013	33,854	41,391	47,459	54,491	64,660
Great Britain	6,000[a]	6,000[a]	6,258	5,357	6,064	6,851	7,272
France	3,500[a]	3,800[a]	4,804[a]	5,702[a]	9,925[a]	6,852[a]	6,418
Total	68,555	89,094	111,705	128,148	182,354	251,239	342,578
Per 100 of the Neth. population	2.2	2.7	3.1	3.2	4.0	4.9	5.8

[a] Estimated or averaged.

Emigration within Europe

The number of Netherlanders abroad increased steadily after 1879 at an absolute rate of 1 percent per decade (Table 2.2). The agrarian depression of 1875–1895, the beginning of industrialization, and the improved transportation and communication systems all tended to uproot people and make them move internally and across the border. The number of Netherlanders in neighboring countries by far surpassed the number overseas. After 1905, more Netherlanders were counted in Germany alone than in the United States (Table 2.4).

Next to the Hapsburg Empire, the Netherlands provided Germany with the largest quota of immigrants.[14] After the financial crash of 1873 had ended by 1880, the number of Netherlanders in Germany rose steeply until the eve of the First World War. After 1880, both the Dutch and the Italian share of the foreign presence in Germany had risen the most. In 1900, 11.3 percent of all foreign nationals were Dutch, having increased to 1.56 per 1,000 population in 1900 and 2.22 in 1910.[15] Using 1880 as the base year (1880 = 100), the number accelerated most between 1895 and 1900, and between 1905 and 1910 (Table 2.4).

Initially the Dutch settled mainly in rural municipalities and small towns. In 1867, for instance, 64 out of 100 Netherlanders in Prussia were residing in rural municipalities of whom more than half were in municipalities with less than 2,000 inhabitants. The remainder lived in cities, but only 14 percent were in cities over 20,000 inhabitants. The male/female ratio of 611 in the smaller rural municipalities deviated remarkably from the mean of 141. This may be attributed to the employment structure, in which field labor far surpassed industrial, domestic, and other labor.[16] After 1870 the concentration of Netherlanders within Prussia, who represented 95 percent of all Netherlanders in Germany, shifted from the Rhine provinces to Westphalia, which coincided with the industrial upsurge of the Ruhr area.

Apart from farming and industry, other economic sectors in Germany also attracted Dutch "guest"-workers. On the eve of the First World War, the share of Dutch crews in the herring- and trawl-fleet of the lower Weser River amounted to 15 percent.

Table 2.3. Foreign Born and Foreign Nationals
in the Netherlands, 1849–1909

Year	Total foreign born	Foreign born per 1,000	M/F ratio	Total foreign nationals	M/F ratio
1849	70,855	2.3	139		
1859	61,936	1.9	125		
1869	59,076	1.6	116		
1879	67,776	1.7	105		
1889	75,980	1.7	98	47,884	101
1899	79,673	1.5	94	52,989	112
1909	95,282	1.6	91	69,975	101

Year	Total German born	German born per 1,000 foreigners	M/F ratio	Total German nationals	M/F ratio	German nationals per 1,000 foreigners
1849	41,209	5.8	155			
1859	36,561	5.9	139			
1969	33,766	5.7	124			
1879	42,026	6.2	106			
1889				28,767	101	6.0
1899				31,865	109	6.0
1909				37,531	98	5.4

These Dutch fishermen originated around the Zuider Zee and
were attracted by high wages and modern equipment.[17] Many
Netherlanders in Germany were migrant workers who remained
officially registered in their home municipalities in Holland. In
the Dutch census they remained legal citizens, whereas in Germany they were counted as foreign residents. In the years 1900
and 1901, when the Netherlands required identity cards to be renewed yearly, 44,617 and 34,547 cards were issued to citizens
working abroad. From 1902 to 1906, 15,000 to 30,000 permanent
cards were issued yearly. In 1907, when the Netherlands and
Germany agreed to have the papers renewed every five years,
49,018 cards were issued; in the following years the figures

Table 2.3., continued.

Year	Total Belgium born	Belgium born per 1,000 foreigners	M/F ratio	Total Belgium nationals	M/F ratio	Belgium nationals per 1,000 foreigners
1849	21,556	3.0	101			
1859	19,429	3.1	99			
1869	19,147	3.2	102			
1879	18,816	2.8	100			
1889				13,697	104	2.9
1899				14,903	118	2.8
1909				18,338	104	2.6

Year	Total British born	British born per 1,000 foreigners	M/F ratio	Other foreign born and nationals (after 1889)	M/F ratio	Other foreign born per 1,000 foreigners
1849	1,434	0.2	130	6,656	210	0.9
1859	1,011	0.2	71	5,290	171	0.9
1869	1,007	0.2	67	5,358	136	0.9
1879	1,614	0.2	63	6,515	136	1.0
1889	1,339	0.3	64	5,081	160	1.1
1899	1,307	0.2	58	4,654	133	0.9
1909	2,102	0.3	73	12,005	115	1.7

Source: Derived or computed from the Netherlands census figures.

averaged 30,000 annually.[18] The number of men per 100 women until 1890 was higher for Dutch nationals than for residents born in the Netherlands. Naturalization by marriage seems a feasible explanation. After 1890, migration to enter wedlock, however, became secondary to labor migration. Male nationals then numbered 140 per 100 females, and by 1910 the number decreased to 128. The women were catching up.

The 1900 age distribution of Netherlands-born German residents allows some inferences.[19] Under 16 years of age, the percentage of girls outstripped the percentage of boys by 18 to 13 percent, indicating that young maids were possibly more in demand than young farmhands. In the core of the active ages, from 16 to

Table 2.4. Netherlanders in Germany

Year	Germany				Dutch Nationals		Prussia			
	Total Dutch nationals	M/F ratio	Total Dutch born	M/F ratio	Per 1,000 inh.	Index 1880 = 100	Total Dutch nationals	M/F ratio	Total Neth. born	M/F ratio
1867	18,311	—					16,955	141	—	—
1871	21,646	—					20,043	165	—	—
1880	17,598	—			0.39	100	—	—	—	—
1885	27,191	—	45,270	111	0.85	154	25,146	132	43,004	111
1890	37,055	—	56,437	119	0.75	211	—	—	53,715	118
1895	50,743	141			0.97	288	47,715	140	—	—
1900	88,053	151	94,477	143	1.56	500	83,944	151	90,208	—
1905	100,997	140			1.67	574	95,969	139	—	—
1910	144,175	128			2.22	819	137,440	128	—	—

49 years, males surpassed females by 10 points, probably because of employment opportunities. In a fifty-year period the relationship was reversed as a result of marriage or family migration, and females outnumbered males by 4 points.

The occupational distribution of Netherlands-born German residents in 1907 shows how important labor migration to Germany was and what sectors attracted the most workers. Of the 100,709 Netherlands-born, 62 percent were economically active, compared to only 39 percent of the Dutch population in 1909. Of these 23 percent were employed in agriculture, compared to 28 percent in the Netherlands, but 56 percent were employed in German industry (construction, mining, and textiles), compared to only 33 percent in the Netherlands. Dutch laborers thus provided much manpower for German economic growth in the pre–World War One years.

The number of Netherlands-born Belgian residents averaged 52,000 between 1849 and 1909 and surpassed the number of Dutch nationals in Germany until 1895 (Table 2.2 and Table 2.5). The Dutch share of the foreign presence in Belgium decreased slightly in these years but averaged 30 percent. The greatest number of Dutch lived in the provinces of Antwerp (36 percent), Liege (20 percent), and Brabant (18 percent), particularly in the industrial cities of Antwerp, Liege, and Brussels. Fewer Hollanders resided in the provinces of Limburg (12 percent) and East Flanders (10 percent). By 1910, six out of ten Dutch nationals lived in the four largest Belgian cities; half were in the thriving seaport of Antwerp.

Migration because of marriage remained an important factor, as appears from the male/female ratio, which was 88 for Dutch nationals. This female predominance may also have been due to servant migration to the Belgium towns. In 1846 the towns numbered 87 men per 100 women, the rural municipalities 112, in 1856 the rates were 82 and 100. Other indications of migration motives may be derived from a comparison between the occupational distribution of Dutch nationals in Belgium in 1910 and in the Netherlands in 1909.[20] The percentage of persons economically active was somewhat higher in Belgium than in the Netherlands; this was particularly true for women. Agriculture

Table 2.5. Netherlanders in Belgium

Year	Belgium		Limburg	Liege	Antwerp	East Flanders	Brabant
	Total Dutch born	Dutch of all foreigners	Percentage of all Netherlanders	Percentage of all Netherlanders	Percentage of all Netherlanders	Percentage of all Netherlanders	Percentage of all Netherlanders
1846	31,207	33	18	15	32	13	15
1856	33,013	35	24	18	30	10	17
1866	33,854	35	14	23	30	10	17
1880	41,391	29	10	22	34	10	20
1890	47,459	28	8	23	36	10	18
1900	54,491	26	8	20	38	10	19
1910 [a]	70,950	28	7	18	45	8	19
64-year Average	51,766	30	12	20	36	10	18

Source: Derived or computed from Belgian census data.
[a] Dutch-Nationals.

attracted little Dutch labor compared to industry, communication, and domestic services. Diamond cutting seems to have attracted many a Dutch specialist to Antwerp.

The number of Dutch nationals in France and Netherlands-born residents in Britain was both negligible, ranging around 5,000 to 7,000 (Table 2.2). In 1871, 77 percent of the Dutch in England lived in London. Here 118 men were counted for every 100 women, in contrast to 141 men per 100 women for all Dutch in Britain.[21] Most men in 1871 earned their living as a merchant, tailor, craftsman, sailor, and especially as a tobacco worker or cigarmaker; most women worked in the textile or garment industry and in domestic service. Out of 2,592 women, 1,557 (60 percent) were classified as housewives. The majority accompanied their Dutch husbands to England or had married a British subject.

Overseas Migration

Dutch emigration overseas until 1914 was mainly directed towards the United States. Data on settlement elsewhere are rare or not available. According to the immigration statistics of the receiving countries, 4,895 Netherlanders were admitted to Canada between 1900 and 1910, from 1911 until 1914 another 4,712 arrived, and from 1915 to 1920 only 1,219 came. Argentina registered 8,751 Dutch immigrants between 1857 and 1929, among whom 4,255 returned. In Brazilian harbors, 2,270 Netherlanders disembarked between 1908 and 1910, 869 from 1911 to 1914, 346 from 1915 to 1920. Australian statistics report 811 Netherlanders for 1902–1910, 1,317 for 1911–1914, and 1,920 for 1911–1920. In South Africa, only 999 Netherlanders arrived in 1913–1920.[22]

Available census data also show a very minimal Dutch presence outside Europe.[23] About 1914 roughly 20,000 Netherlanders lived or worked overseas apart from those in the colonies and in the United Sates; there were approximately 4,000 in Canada, 10,000 in Latin America, 1,000 in Australia, and at least 5,000 in the Union of South Africa. In 1891 the Cape Colony counted only 870 Netherlanders, in 1904 1,663, plus 276 in Natal. South Africa numbered 5,391 Netherlanders in 1911, of which 68 percent were in the Transvaal, 20 percent lived in the Cape, 8 percent in the

Orange Free State, and 4 percent in Natal. In 1891, 75 percent were settled in urban areas; in 1904, 84 percent; and in 1911, 80 percent. Women showed a 10 percent stronger urban preference than men. The male/female ratio was also lower in urban areas and declined steadily to 141 in 1911. The overall sex ratio declined to 159 for the Union of South Africa in 1911. The settlement pattern indicates that those Dutch that went to South Africa were probably mainly of urban backgrounds seeking employment in commerce, services, and industry.

On the average, the number of people coming from the colonies to the Netherlands in the early twentieth century (4,300) surpassed the number going to the colonies (4,050). In 1914, 12,000 Netherlanders resided in the colonies. Between 1895 and 1905, an average of 10,584 Dutch-born persons lived in the East Indies, 229 men for every 100 women. In Surinam for the same decade, an average of 929 Europeans were counted between 1908 and 1904, 201 men for every 100 women. The Netherlands Antilles only averaged 422 Netherlands-born persons.[24] The Dutch colonies were not preferred settlement areas, as compared with North America and to a lesser degree Latin America. In toto, including the colonies but excluding the United States, 32,000 Dutch-born persons resided overseas in 1914. This was a mere trifle compared to the 120,053 in the United States in 1910.

Between 1865 and 1905 the number of Dutch-American residents was higher than comparable numbers in Belgium and Germany. Dutch overseas migration, especially to the United States, was more conspicuous in this half century than migration to neighboring countries, where they met few linguistic or cultural barriers and could remain in touch or return home easily. Settlement in America was more complicated and irrevocable.

The number of Netherlanders in the United States increased steadily from 1850, but was overtaken around 1905 by the number in Germany (Table 2.2). The Dutch share of the foreign-born in the United States rose from 0.4 percent in 1850 to over 0.9 percent from 1880. Together with the general zenith of foreign-born in America, the share of those born in the Netherlands and those having at least one Dutch parent culminated in 1930 at 133,133 and 280,833, respectively.[25]

From the census data concerning Netherlands-born residents, I have computed the immigration during the preceding decades (Table 2.6) using the formula: immigration equals the sum of the decade increase in Dutch-born, plus the sum of the death rate per 1,000 average decadal population in the Netherlands, plus the estimated 5 percent remigration before 1870 and 15 percent after 1870. Based on the formula, from 1820 to 1880, 94,000 Netherlanders emigrated to the United States, almost twice the officially registered number (Table 2.7). From linking nominal Dutch and American records, Swierenga also inferred that the actual Dutch emigration in 1835–1880 was 48 percent higher than the official Dutch figures and 89 percent higher than the American ones.[26] For 1841–1850 my estimate corresponds to the number counted in the original passenger lists. Swierenga's higher estimate rests on comparisons made for the whole period 1820–1880. For 1841–1880 my estimates are higher, but if the younger age structure of an immigrant population is taken into account, the two estimates are nearly identical. Thus a census-based estimate confirms Swierenga's nominal linkage-based conclusions about the enormous discrepancies between official figures and actual numbers. The correspondence of official figures and my estimates for 1881–1910 points to stricter registration in American harbors. Almost 130,000 Netherlanders disembarked in these thirty years, making a total of 220,000 prior to 1914.

Conclusion

During the first half of the nineteenth century the Netherlands still experienced large-scale immigration. The emigration surplus from 1840 onwards did not equal the comparatively small emigration to the United States, as Hofstee suggests. Neither did any exceptional attachment to their homes keep the Dutch from migrating as Petersen, Thistlethwaite, and Mokyr assume. Systematic scrutiny of census data, however, provides ample opportunity to revise and amend the image of international migration based on arrivals and departures.

Until the 1840s the Netherlands ranked as a top immigration country. Of the nineteenth century settlers, 60 percent came from Germany and 30 percent from Belgium. After 1850 the

Table 2.6. Dutch Immigration to the United States Estimated from Census Figures, 1841–1910

Census	$C_2 - C_1$	$\dfrac{C_1 + C_2}{2}$	Mortality[a]	Estimated deaths	Estimated net migration	Estimated remigration	Estimated immigration per decade
1850	9,848	9,848	0.263	2,590	12,438	622	13,060
1860	18,433	19,064	0.255	4,861	23,294	1,165	24,459
1870	18,530	37,546	0.249	9,348	27,878	1,394	29,272
1880	11,289	52,455	0.245	12,851	24,140	3,621	27,761
1890	23,751	69,975	0.213	14,904	38,655	5,798	44,453
1900	13,141	88,421	0.187	16,534	29,675	4,451	34,126
1910	25,061	107,522	0.156	16,773	41,834	6,275	48,109
1850–1910				77,861	197,914	23,326	221,240

Source: Census data in H. S. Lucas, Netherlanders in America (Ann Arbor: University of Michigan Press, 1955), 642–643.
[a] Ten times the average death rate in the Netherlands during the preceding decade. H. C. Bos, "Long-term Demographic Development in the Netherlands (mimeo, Netherlands Economic Inst., Rotterdam, 1956), 3, Table 6.
[b] Estimated remigration of 5 percent before 1870 and 15 percent thereafter.

Table 2.7. Dutch Immigration to the United States, 1820–1910

Period	U.S. emigrants Netherlands records	Dutch U.S. emigrants recorded in Dutch harbors	Officially recorded Dutch arrivals in U.S. harbors	Dutch nationals on ship lists	Nominal linkage-based estimate	Census-based estimate
1830–1840	31		2,539	1,678	1,452	
1841–1850	9,631		8,251	13,758	19,635	13,060
1851–1860	13,175		10,789	14,551	21,010	24,459
1861–1870	18,717		9,102	8,814	22,381	29,272
1871–1880	14,149		16,541	15,877	23,318	27,761
1820–1880	55,703		47,222	54,558	87,796	94,552
1881–1890	40,736	41,022	53,701			44,453
1891–1900	22,454	23,261	26,758			31,126
1901–1910	34,464	25,212	48,262			48,109
1820–1910	153,357		175,943			221,240

Source: Computed from R. P. Swierenga, "Dutch International Migration" note 26 in this chapter and *Jaarlijkse Statistiek van den Loop der Bevolking van Nederland* [Yearly Statistics of the Population Development of the Netherlands], 1881–1910.

Netherlands lost increasingly more people than it gained from abroad. Indeed, judging from Swierenga's calculations and mine, the loss to the United States alone up to 1880 was twice as great as official statistics had indicated. Germany also attracted hosts of Netherlanders after 1880, first in agriculture and later mainly in industry and construction. After 1900 more Netherlanders lived and worked there than in the United States. Emigration to Belgium was mainly motivated by employment in industry and domestic services. Out of ten Netherlanders, two belonged to a religious order and two lived on rental income. Before 1914 roughly 20,000 Netherlanders lived overseas, and 12,000 resided in the colonies, but all these overseas Dutch comprised at most one-third of the number in the United States alone.

Although the comparatively small overseas emigration was compensated for by a significant emigration to neighboring countries, the total Dutch emigration lagged behind emigration from other northern European countries, as for example, Norway and Sweden. Of the 17.6 percent of Norwegians who resided abroad, 16.9 percent resided in the United States and only 0.7 percent were in neighboring Sweden and Denmark. Of the 13.3 percent of Swedes who lived elsewhere, 12 percent were in the United States.[27] While the Norwegians and Swedes abroad had predominantly crossed the ocean, the majority of Netherlanders abroad only crossed the border. Intracontinental migration prevailed over intercontinental migration in the Netherlands and should therefore not be overlooked nor underestimated.

Notes

1. E. W. Hofstee, *Korte demografische geschiedenis van Nederland van 1800 tot heden* [Short Demographic History of the Netherlands from 1800 to the Present] (Bussum: Fibula-Van Dishoek, 1981), 86–100.
2. E. W. Hofstee, "De functie van de internationale migratie" [The Function of International Migration], *Tijdschrift voor Economische en Sociale Geografie* 40 [1949]: 10–22.
3. E. W. Hofstee, "Netherlands," in Brinley Thomas, ed., *The Economics of International Migration* (London: Macmillan, 1958), 96–107.

4.   William S. Petersen, *Planned Migration: The Social Determinants of the Dutch-Canadian Movement* (Berkeley: University of California Press, 1955), 42–48, 58–60.

5.   Frank Thistlethwaite, "Migration from Europe Overseas in the Nineteenth and Twentieth Centuries," in *XIe Congrès International des Sciences Historiques. Stockholm 1960, Rapports V, Histoire Contemporaine* (Göteburg-Stockholm-Uppsala: Almquist & Wiksel, 1960), 54.

6.   Joel Mokyr, "Industrialization and Poverty in Ireland and the Netherlands," *Journal of Interdisciplinary History* 10 (Winter 1980): 449.

7.   H. Knippenberg, "De demografische ontwikkeling van Nederland sedert 1800: En overzicht" [The Demographic Development of the Netherlands Since 1800: An Overview], *Geografisch Tijdschrift* 14 (1980): 63–65; J. Hofker, *De demografische ontwikkeling van Nederland sedert 1800* [The Demographic Development of the Netherlands Since 1800] (Amsterdam: Meulenhoff Educatief, 1980), 10, 15; A. C. De Vooy, *De demografische ontwikkeling in Nederland in de 19e en in de eerste helft van de 20e eeuw* [The Demographic Development in the Netherlands During the 19th and the First Half of the 20th Century] (Amsterdam: Meulenhoff Educatief, 1979), 137–138, 141.

8.   J. A. A. Hartland, *De geschiedenis van de Nederlandse emigratie tot de Tweede Wereldoorlog* [The History of Dutch Emigration Until the Second World War] (The Hague: Nederlandse Emigratiedienst, 1959), 130–131.

9.   F. W. A. Van Poppel, *Demografische ontwikkelingen in Nederland, 1850–1950* [Demographic Developments in the Netherlands, 1850–1950] (Voorburg: Netherlands Interuniversity Demographic Institute, 1981), 1–2.

10.   Centraal Bureau voor Statistiek, *Bevolking van Nederland naar geslacht, leeftijd en burgerlijke staat, 1830–1969* [Population of the Netherlands by Sex, Age and Civil Status, 1830–1969] (s'–Gravenhage Staatsuitgeverij, 1970), 25. Hofstee's diverging calculations seem unwarranted. Hofstee, *Korte demografische geschiedenis*, 140.

11.   Alfred Legoyt, *L'émigration européenne, son importance, ses causes, ses effets* [European Emigration, Its Importance, Its Causes, Its Effects] (Paris: Guillaumin & Co., 1861), xlvi.

12.   G. F. Van Asselt, "De Hollandgängerei" [(German) Emigration to the Netherlands], *Spiegel Historiael* 12 (1977): 4, 233.

13.   *Volkszahlung Preussen 1871* [Prussian Census 1871] (Berlin: 1875), 111, 74.

14.   Wolfgang Kollman, *Bevolkerung und Raum in Neuer and Neuester Zeit* [Population and Territory in Recent Times and Today] (Würzburg: 1965), 96.

15. *Die Volkszahlung im Deutschen Reich 1900* [The Census in the German Empire 1900] (Berlin: 1903), Vol. 1, 134.

16. *Preussiche Statistik V. Die Ergebnisse der Volkszahlung und Volksbeschreibung 1867* [Prussian Statistics V. The Results of the Census and Population Classification, 1867] (Berlin: 1869), 178–219.

17. G. Rohdenburg, "Saisonarbeit im Unterweserraum. Binnenländer als Seeleute in der Hochseefischerei 1895–1914" [Seasonal Labor in the Upper Weser Area. Landlubbers as Sailors in Ocean Fishing 1895–1914], *Breunsches Jahrbuch* 55 (1977): 221–241.

18. Henri Willem Methorst, *Résumé rétrospectif de l'Annuaire statistique des Pays-Bas* [Retrospective Résumé of the Statistical Yearbook of the Netherlands] (The Hague: [Soc. aan "Drukkerij trio"], 1911), 23.

19. *Die Volkszahlung im Deutschen Reich 1900* [The Census in the German Empire 1900] (Berlin: 1902), Vol. 2, 120ff.

20. *Recensement général 1910* [General Census 1910] (Brussels 1916), Vol. 5, 674ff; and Centraal Bureau voor Statistiek, *Algemene volkstelling 1960* [General Census, 1960], Vol. 10C.

21. *Census of Great Britain 1871*, LI, Table XXIII–XXVII.

22. W. I. Willcox and I. Ferenczi, comps., *International Migrations, Volume I, Statistics* (New York: National Bureau of Economic Research, 1929), 364–367, 545, 551–556, 952, 1057.

23. See *Fifth Census of Canada 1911* (Ottawa: 1913), Vol. II; *Census of the Commonwealth of Australia 1911* (Melbourne: 1914), Vol. II; *Censo de la Republica de Chile 1907* [Census of the Republic of Chile 1907] (Santiago: 1908); *Census of the Colony of the Cape of Good Hope 1891* (Cape Town: 1892); *Census of the Colony of the Cape of Good Hope 1904* (Cape Town: 1905); *Census of the Colony of Natal 1904* (Marienburg: 1905); *Census of the Union of South Africa 1911* (Pretoria: 1913), Vol. VII.

24. Centraal Bureau voor Statistiek, *Tachtig jaren statistiek in tijdreeksen 1899–1979* [Eighty Years of Statistics in Serials 1899–1979] (The Hague: Staatsuitgeverij, 1979), 28; and *Jaarcijfers voor het Koninkrijk der Nederlanden, Kolonien 1917* [Statistical Data for the Kingdom of the Netherlands, Colonies 1917] (The Hague: Staatsuitgeverig, 1919), 5, 164, 184.

25. E. P. Hutchinson, *Immigrants and their Children* (New York: Wiley, 1956), 5, 10.

26. R. P. Swierenga, "Dutch International Migration Statistics 1820–1880: An Analysis of Linked Multinational Nominal Files," *International Migration Review* 15 (Fall 1981): 445–470.

27. Computed from the figures in U.S. Bureau of the Census, *Historical Statistics of the United States* (Washington, D.C.: Government Printing Office, 1960), 66; *Folktaellingen in kongeriget Danmark*

1911 [Census of Denmark 1911] (Kopenhagen: 1913), Vol. 1, 13, 43; *Folketaeling in Norge 1910* [Census of Norway 1910] (Kristiania: 1914), Vol. 5, 34, 135; *Folkrakningen 1910* [Census of Sweden 1910] (Stockholm: 1918), Vol. 4, 13, 23.

3. Dutch Roman Catholics in the United States

Henry A. V.M. van Stekelenburg

There is a dearth of historical research concerning the Roman Catholic Dutch in the United States, although their numbers are quite substantial.[1] That Dutch Catholic and Protestant emigrants during the ninteteenth century differed in occupation and socioeconomic status in the Old World has recently been demonstrated by a quantitative analysis of emigrant records.[2] Catholic emigrants were less agricultural in background and ranked higher socioeconomically than Protestants. For this reason, and because of the international character of the Catholic church, Dutch Catholic immigrants assimilated much easier than did the Protestant Dutch in the United States.

Manuscript sources, particularly local community and church records, can supplement the quantitative emigration data that have formed the basis of current research. These traditional materials are the primary sources for this essay, which attempts to complete the picture of the emigration and adaptation of Dutch Catholics in the United States in the nineteenth century.

Regional Diversity

Eminent scholars have pointed out the importance of a regional approach to the history of emigration.[3] In the mid-nineteenth century, when education, communication, and transportation were very limited and the rural economy was locally based, personal contacts often did not reach beyond a few hours walking distance. To talk about the Dutch, Frisians, Brabantines, and the like reflects an administrative point of view and overlooks much differentiation that is important to understand human beings. The regional division into agricultural areas—clay soil, sand soil, and dairy areas—forms a beginning for understanding regional differentiation, but this division is also too broad and requires refinement.

Likewise, it is incorrect to portray the Netherlands as a Protestant nation. The Catholic population never fell below 33 percent and in fact approached 40 percent during the nineteenth and twentieth centuries.[4] Thus, the customary partition into the Prostestant North and the Catholic South is not correct. In the provinces of Noord-Holland, Zuid-Holland, Zeeland, and Utrecht, the Catholics according to the census of 1960 formed 25 to 32 percent of the population, and in Gelderland Catholics totaled 40 percent. Only Groningen, Friesland, and Drenthe had a percentage of less than 10.[5] During the period of the Netherlands emigrant lists, 1835–1880, Catholics formed about 20 percent of the emigrants, or 11,300 persons; thus they were underrepresented. However, we should not conclude that Catholics were less inclined to emigrate than the Protestants.

Viewed from a regional perspective, national borders did not separate any more than did provincial borders. The first emigrants during the 1840s were small groups of Catholics from the German border region of Westphalia who had experienced intensive contacts with their co-religionists across the border.[6] The Seceder emigration movement also came from the same eastern part of the Netherlands.

What was the relation between Seceders and Catholics? We may assume that in the regions where they lived in close proximity, they customarily avoided each other, at least in daily activities. But their leaders shared the same concerns. Both groups suffered under the reign of William I (1813–1840) from oppression in matters of religion and church governance because of William's interfering church policy. The religious orders, for instance, were not allowed to admit new members after 1815. We know that periodicals such as the *Catholijke Nederlandsche Stemmen* and the Calvinist *De Reformatie* referred to each other and that Catholic newspapers like *De Tijd* and *De Noord-Brabander* sympathized with the colonization plans of the Seceders and reported on their emigration. Even during the reign of William II (1840–1849), when the official policy towards the churches was far more permissive, the Protestant establishment on the local level showed as much arrogance as before. Nevertheless, in most newspapers and reports, emigration was referred to in relationship to economic concerns, to poverty, and the lack of future opportunities. Even for those who gave as a reason for emigration "lack of religious freedom" (these were all Protestants), economic motives were fundamentally very important.[7]

Only in the appeal of the Catholic emigrant leader, Christiaan Verwayen of Nijmegen, do we find a trace of a religious motive, but it was mixed with other motives. In the emigration literature, the story of this secretary of the Nijmegen Catholic Emigration Committee is generally well known, but recently new documentary materials have been discovered that show the relevance of local history. This former seminarist, after completing his law studies at the University of Utrecht, established himself as an attorney in his hometown of Nijmegen. Here he became an opposition leader against the Protestant establishment that dominated Nijmegen, even though the great majority of the inhabitants was Catholic. Verwayen presented the king with a petition concerning the discrimination against Catholics in civil positions. He also wrote a leaflet to defend his fellow Catholic townsmen against a court's magistrate who had published a very insulting pamphlet about Catholic pilgrimages to Kevelaar (in Germany). Three times Verwayen had difficulties because he did not respond to a call to enlist in the citizen militia. Between 1843 and 1845 he edited *De Batavier*, a radical weekly newspaper. Then he laid plans for a cigar factory. But in 1846 he decided to emigrate and founded a committee to stimulate others to do the same.[8]

All these activities indicate that Verwayen was unsuccessful or ineffective in his ventures. Thus in 1847 he left for America to find his fortune. He planned to found a colony under the name "Disabdera," which means "Away from Abdera." The city of Abdera in ancient writings meant a city of ignorance or stupidity. To

Verwayen, Nijmegen was this city. Verwayen and his group of one hundred persons from the Nijmegen region left from Antwerp and arrived in New Orleans, enroute to their intended destination of Iowa. What happened to him and his fellow travellers afterwards is not yet known.

In 1848 a much larger group of Catholics emigrated under the leadership of the Dominican Father Theodorus van den Broek and settled in the Fox River region in Wisconsin (the following section recounts more about this well-known emigration). Most of the 200 emigrants of Van den Broek's group came from the eastern part of Noord-Brabant. In 1850 a secular priest, Gerardus van den Heuvel, chaplain in the municipality of Boekel in the same area of Noord-Brabant, emigrated to the Fox River Valley with another 200 emigrants. There is no evidence that discrimination of Catholics played any role in this emigration movement.

The fact that priests sometimes played a leading role in the Catholic emigration was not unusual. They were the leaders in a rural society and were the trusted guides when it came to such important decisions as emigration. Often they had contacts overseas or had been abroad themselves and thus they were a source of information. For example, the Norbertine, Gerlacus van den Elsen, who was very well-known in Noord-Brabant as a founder of the farmers co-operative, the "Noord Brabantse Christelijke Boerenbond," had a brother in the Norbertine settlement (now St. Norbert Abbey) in De Pere, Wisconsin. The first Norbertines arrived in De Pere from the "Abdij van Berne" in Heeswijk, Noord-Brabant, in 1893. The brother of Gerlacus, Mathias, wrote several times about the opportunities for farming in the state of Wisconsin and in 1906 Gerlacus paid a visit to the United States to gather first hand information. He wrote the members of the co-operative a series of letters published in the organization's weekly newspaper. Later these letters were published in a book under the title "Twintig brieven uit Amerika" [Twenty Letters from America].[9]

P. Hollenberg, the biographer of Gerlacus van den Elsen, commented on the lack of enthusiasm for emigration displayed in his letters. "It is clear that after having observed the conditions among the lumbermen and pioneer farmers, Van den Elsen's opinions concerning emigration were reserved. Only for those farmers who suffered the most from poverty did he approve of emigration. In general he remained cautious and warned about economic hardships and lack of spiritual guidance especially for those who emigrated as single individuals."[10] The generally more reserved attitude of the Dutch clergy was only abandoned after the Second World War.

The major emigration regions in Noord-Brabant, according to the official Netherlands records, were the northeastern and northwestern areas. The remainder of the province had little or no overseas emigration. The differences between these two areas are striking: the northeast is sandy soil, Catholic in religion, and the emigrants went mostly to the Fox River region in Wisconsin; the northwest is clay soil, Protestant in religion, and the emigrants settled mostly in Michigan and Pella, Iowa. H. P. Scholte, the founder of Pella, had been a minister in the northwestern area of Noord-Brabant, in the communities of Doeveren, Genderen, and Gansoyen (1833–1836). C. Smits referred to this area as "a heart of the Secession-movement, just like Ulrum in Groningen."[11] However, in the bordering area, "Het Land van Heusden," where the Secession also had substantial support, only a few persons emigrated. From there, however, many families settled in the Haarlemmermeer polder, which was reclaimed in 1853.[12] These regional differences show that it is very important to become familiar with local history in both area of origin and area of destination in order to establish a clearer picture of the emigration movement as a whole.[13]

The Role of the Church

In the Old World and the New, churches and their ministers had a central function. The often impressive, usually neo-Gothic church buildings in every town and village still form the material expression of the great sacrifices that were made to maintain church property and functions. Besides the religious role, the church was also in charge of education, poor relief, care of the sick and elderly, training of priests, and missionary service. Thus, until the 1960s at least, the Catholic church in the Netherlands was very influential in the whole scope of social life. The relationship between laymen and clergy, order brothers and sisters (nuns) was very intensive and the innumerable Catholic organizations on all levels served an important function.

In Catholic emigration history very little use has been made of the diocese, parish, and monastery records. These archives and other collections of sources, such as the many publications of missionary orders, contain a wealth of information and often have the advantage of being inventoried and described in great detail. These sources provide all kinds of information about church life and even genealogical information, as in the official registers of baptisms, marriages, and burials and the special "In Memoriam" cards that Catholics customarily print. Letters, reports, and portraits also form part of the collections.

These sources illuminate the global character of the Catholic church, as is evident in the life of Theodorus van den Broek, who was born in Amsterdam in 1783. After he had been a Franciscan friar for a few years, he became a Dominican in 1817. The Dominicans had a so-called "Engels College" [English College] in Bornhem near Antwerp since 1658. After the papal dissolution in 1773 of the Societas Jesus, the Order of the Jesuits (this order existed from 1773 to 1814 only in White Russia), this college also attracted young men from Maryland in America to receive their training. One of the college's students, Dominic Fenwick (1762–1832), became the founder of the Dominican order in America, which was concentrated in Springfield, Kentucky, and Somerset, Ohio.

In 1820 Van den Broek had become pastor of the Dominican parish in Alkmaar, Noord-Holland. The church and the rectory were in ruinous condition and had to be repaired. Van den Broek was forced to contribute from his own family resources. He finally decided to leave Alkmaar, because he did not feel comfortable there any more. In the meantime, Fenwick, who had become bishop of Cincinnati, Ohio, and other Dominicans were urging Van den Broek to go to the mission field in America.[14]

Father Van den Broek left for America in 1832.[15] His missionary experience is told in his brochure "Reize naar Noord-Amerika" [Voyage to North America] (1847)[16] and in a letter to

De Godsdienstvriend (1843), a church periodical in the Netherlands, and in a report written in 1840 that is addressed to his superior in the Netherlands.[17]

In 1835 Van den Broek moved to Little Chute, Wisconsin,
twenty-two miles south of Green Bay, where he built a church
and a rectory and worked among the Indians and a few white settlers. He soon decided that Little Chute would be an ideal place
for a Dominican convent and nunnery. He created land for agriculture and claimed that his farm could support at least six
priests, so he asked permission to found a monastery.[18] The few
Dominicans in the Netherlands at that time could not react positively, but Van den Broek again referred to his plans concerning a
Dominican monastery in a letter in 1848, addressed to all Dutch
Catholics, asking financial support for his mission.[19] In 1847 he
returned to the Netherlands and in 1848 he brought three ships
with emigrants to America. Most of them came from northeastern Noord-Brabant. A few years later, Van den Broek gladly
accepted a plan from the Crosier Fathers in the same region in
Noord-Brabant to found a Crosier convent at Little Chute. He
was happy to be assisted by more priests, but most probably was
disappointed by the fact that these priests were not Dominican
brothers. The connection between the Crosier Fathers and the
Dominicans, however, had already been established in Noord-Brabant. Around 1840 they both had convents in the community of
Uden and their student priests trained there at the same insti-
tutes. In 1841 the bishop of Nashville, Tennessee, the Dominican Richard P. Miles, visited that region and received a very
hearty welcome.[20]

These facts help explain why so many inhabitants from the
isolated region of Uden emigrated to Wisconsin. By following Van
den Broek and other missionary-priests, the emigrants from
Noord-Brabant preserved much of their culture and values. Thus,
although I agree with those who see emigration as a response to
socioeconomic hardship, the role of the church was also very important in channelling the migration. Nevertheless, the part of
Dutch Jesuits in the making of the Catholic Church of America is
underestimated in American historiography. Even in the three
volumes of Gilbert Garraghan, *The Jesuits of the Middle United
States*,[21] they are not identified as Dutch but as Flemish or Bel-

gian. Thus it is necessary to consider their influence as a new illustration of the worldwide character of the Catholic church and the consequences for Catholic emigrants, who in this instance, were "emigrants for God."

In the early years of the nineteenth century, there was only one bishop in the United States, John Carroll, a former Jesuit and bishop of Baltimore. Carroll did everything in his power to draw priests from Europe to the American mission field. He remained close to the prior of the small Jesuit mission in Maryland, Antonius Kohlmann, who in 1803 had spent some time with Adam Beckers, pastor of "De Krijtberg," an old Jesuit church in Amsterdam. Beckers promised him support and financial aid, and as a result of this connection five former Jesuits left for the United States in 1806–1807, but they were not Dutchmen.[22] Karel Nerinckx, a Flemish missionary, organized the recruitment of priests on a large scale during some trips to Europe (1815–1817 and 1821), in collaboration with laymen like P. J. de Nef, a businessman, school leader, and politician from Turnhout in Belgium.[23] Nerinckx, who was not a member of the Jesuits, brought twenty-two missionaries or candidate-missionaries to America, and sixteen of them joined the Jesuits in Maryland.[24] Among them was Peter de Smet, later nicknamed by the Indians "the Great Black Robe."[25] Beginning in 1826, many Dutch Jesuits went to the United States. There were sixty-three in all by 1885.[26] They mostly worked in the Missouri district of the order and established their base at Florissant near St. Louis. Since 1829, the general superior of the Jesuits worldwide was a Dutchman, Johannes Roothaan, and he ordered in 1830 that all the Dutch Jesuits or candidate-Jesuits coming to the United States should go to Missouri.[27] The most famous among the Dutch Jesuits in America was Arnold Damen, who traversed the western territory and finally settled in Chicago. There an avenue and a bridge were named in honor of him, "Damen Avenue" and "Damen Bridge," because he performed pioneering work in developing the city.[28]

Of the sixty-three Jesuits from the Netherlands (excluding Belgium, which became independent in 1830), forty came from the province of Noord-Brabant.[29] To understand this remarkable phenomenon, we have to pay attention to the "presidenten" (directors) of the two major seminaries of the secular clergy in that province, particularly Antonius van Gils and Jacques Cuyten of the diocese (before 1853, vicariate) of 's-Hertogenbosch. Van Gils, the founder and first president of the major seminary and a former professor at the University of Louvain, had in 1808 been in touch with a wine merchant in Louvain, Jozef Peemans, who was interested in supporting the mission in the United States and who had induced Karel Nerinckx to go there.[30]

His successor, Jacques Cuyten who was president from 1837 until 1884, was a personal friend of Peter de Smet. American prelates often sent requests for new recruits to Cuyten or visited him in Noord-Brabant. After 1857 many of his students went to the "American College" in Louvain, which was a special institute for the training of American priests. From 1857 until 1898, eighty Dutch priests studied there.[31] Thus the presidents Van Gils and Cuyten promoted the American mission among their students and many joined the orders or became secular priests in the United States.

In the episcopal archives at 's-Hertogenbosch, there are fifty letters addressed to Cuyten from his students and others in America.[32] One tells about the Dutch emigration to America; it is written by Joannes van de Luytelaar in 1854 and reports on his appointment as pastor to a 400-member Dutch Catholic parish in Cincinnati, which he claimed was the only Dutch Catholic parish in America. In 1857 Van de Luytelaar returned to the Netherlands to raise funds for his Cincinnati parish.[33] There were more so-called Dutch churches but few were predominantly Dutch. Even the Dutch Calvinist colony of Pella, Iowa, boasted a Catholic church in 1869 with a priest who understood Dutch, but most of the parishioners were Irish-Americans.[34] Scholars recognize that many Dutch priests worked among their countrymen, but especially in the first generation there were not enough even to meet the need for confession.[35] In total, 213 missionary-priests originating from the Netherlands worked in the United States prior to 1900.[36] An American in 1874 characterized the Belgian and Dutch missionaries in these words:

> Strong and muscular in body, frank and open in character, ready to accomodate themselves in the customs of their country, remarkable for their practical good sense and gifted

with more than ordinary facility for acquiring a knowledge of English, they formed in the early days and now still the thews and sinews, the bone and marrow of the catholic clergy of America.[37]

In contrast to the orthodox Calvinist groups, there was no Dutch Catholic "ethnic church" among the immigrants. Identification with their Dutch origin was not a matter of church and religion for the Catholic immigrants. Nevertheless, Dutch Catholics played an important role in the growth of the Catholic church in the United States in the nineteenth century. The influence of priests, both secular and regular, on those who stayed behind must have been considerable. In every Catholic family in the Netherlands there was a lively interest in the mission fields. This likely encouraged a number of them to emigrate on the basis of information they received about America from the missionaries.

Conclusion

Studying the emigration history of a small country with a relatively very small number of emigrants to the United States, the tendency to generalize might be stronger than in the case of typical emigration nations. In fact, however, the story of backgrounds in the Old World and adaptation in the New World is always very complicated, and recognizing the many differences (periodical, regional, religious differences, for instance) we will stay more in touch with reality. Comparison of different groups of emigrants can help to make clear this reality.

Two of these groups, the Orthodox Calvinists and the Roman Catholics, who together during the last century numbered approximately one-half of all Dutch emigrants, had in common a strong alliance to their churches. In the process of emigration this provided a supportive environment; and like the Orthodox Calvinists, who had themselves seceded from the official church, it strengthened the initial motivation. But in the process of adaptation, these Calvinists and the Catholics went different ways: the former group going on as an ethnic group around an ethnic church, the latter group in a very short time totally integrating in a church that was essentially not different for all the nationals. This is the main reason that it is not easy to find the traces of Dutch Catholics in contrast with the Calvinists who have a strong motivation to study their heritage.

Notes

1.   H. A. V. M. Van Stekelenburg, "Rooms-Katholieke Landverhuizers naar de Verenigde Staten," *Spiegel Historiael* 12 (Dec. 1977), 681–689; and "Tracing the Dutch Roman Catholic Emigrants to North America in the Nineteenth and Twentieth Centuries," in Mark Boekelman and Herman Ganzevoort, eds., *Dutch Immigration to North America* (Toronto: Multicultural History Society of Ontario, 1983), 57–83.

2.   For a comparison of emigration patterns among religious groups, see Robert P. Swierenga and Yda Saueressig-Schreuder, "Catholic and Protestant Emigration from the Netherlands in the 19th Century: A Comparative Social Structural Analysis," *Tijdschrift voor Economische en Sociale Geografie* 74 (1983), 25–40.

3.   Frank Thistlethwaite, "Migration from Europe Overseas in the Nineteenth and Twentieth Centuries," *XIe Congrès International des Sciences Historiques, Stockholm 1960, Rapports V, Histoire Contemporaine* (Göteborg-Stockholm-Uppsala: Almquist & Wiksel, 1960); 32–60; Maldwyn Allen Jones, *American Immigration* (Chicago: University of Chicago Press, 1960); Philip Taylor, *The Distant Magnet: European Emigration to the USA* (New York: Harper and Row, 1971), 27; J. Potter, "The Economic Context of Migration," in Rob Kroes (ed.), *American Immigration, Its Variety and Lasting Imprint* (European Contributions to American Studies), 1 (Amsterdam: Amerika Instituut, Universiteit van Amsterdam, 1979), 19–20.

4.   J. A. De Kok O.F.M., *Nederland op de breuklijn Rome-Reformatie: Numerieke aspecten van Protestantisering en Katholieke Herleving in de Noordelijke Nederlanden, 1580–1880* [Holland on the Fault Line of Rome and the Reformation: Numerical Aspects of Protestantization and Catholic Revival in the Northern Netherlands, 1580–1880] (Assen: Van Gorcum, 1964), 57, 256.

5.   De Kok, *Nederland*, 8.

6.   The importance of this cross-border stimulation for emigration recently has been demonstrated by G. H. Ligterink, *De Landverhuizers, Emigratie naar Noord-Amerika uit het Gelders-Westfaalse grensgebied tussen de jaren 1830–1850* [The Emigrants: Emigration to North America from the Gelderland-Westphalian

Borderland Between the Years 1830–1850] (Zutphen: De Walburg Press, 1981).

7. P. R. D. Stokvis, *De Nederlandse Trek naar Amerika, 1846–1847* [The Dutch Migration to America, 1846–1847] (Leiden: Universitaire Press, 1977), 202–207.

8. Alard Beck, "De Batavier, Staat- en Letterkundig Weekblad" [The Batavian, Political and Literary Weekly], (unpublished study, Roman Catholic University, Nijmegen, n.d.).

9. Gerlacus Van Den Elsen, *Twintig Brieven uit Amerika* [Twenty Letters from America] (Helmond: Stoomdrukkerij J. de Reijdt, 1907).

10. Petrus Hollenberg, "Gerlacus van den Elsen O.P., Emancipator van de Noordbrabantse Boerenstand, 1853–1925" [Gerlacus van den Elsen: Emancipator of the Noord-Brabant Peasantry, 1853–1925] (Ph.D. dissertation, Roman Catholic University of Nijmegen, 1956), 195.

11. C. Smits, *De Afscheiding van 1834, Derde Deel, Documenten uit het archief van ds. H. P. Scholte, bewaard te Pella, Iowa, U.S.A.* [The Secession of 1834, Volume 3, Documents from the Dominie H. P. Scholte Archive, located at Pella, Iowa, U.S.A.] (Dordrecht: J. P. van den Tol, 1977), 11, 15.

12. A. Noordam Sr., in *Oud Nuus*, ed. *Stichting Oud-Aalsmeer* [The Old Aalsmeer Foundation] (1979), nr. 3: 23–35.

13. Examples of local studies are few, but see H. J. Prakke, *Drenthe in Michigan* (Assen: Van Gorcum, 1948); G. Ligterink, *Landverhuizers*; Yda Saueressig-Schreuder, "Emigration, Settlement, and Assimilation Among Dutch Catholic Emigrants in Wisconsin, 1850–1905" (Ph.D. dissertation, University of Wisconsin, Madison, 1982); G. C. P. Linssen, "Limburgers naar Noord-Amerika" [Limburgers to North America], *Economisch en Sociaal Historisch Jaarboek* 35 (1972): 209–225.

14. *De Godsdienstvriend* 13 (1824): 147–152.

15. Frans H. J. Doppen, "Theodoor J. van den Broek, Van Missionaris tot Emigrantenleider: De vroege geschiedenis van een Katholieke Nederlandsche Nederzetting in Little Chute, Wisconsin, USA" [Theodoor J. Van Den Broek, From Missionary to Emigrant Leader: The Early History of the Dutch Catholic Colonization in Little Chute, Wisconsin, USA], an unpublished study (Gainesville, Florida and Utrecht, 1982) makes clear that Van Den Broek was not exact in the dates of his own life. In several original sources there is also a variation in years. Thus Henry S. Lucas in "De reize naar Noord-Amerika van Theodorus J. van den Broek, O.P." [The Journey to North America of Theodorus J. Van Den Broek], *Nederlands Archief voor Kerkgeschiedenis* 41 (1956), 100, understandably mistates the year of departure as 1830.

16. Lucas, "Reize naar Noord-Amerika."

17. A. Meijer O.P., *Gedenkboek van de Dominicanen in Nederland, 1803–1910* [Memorial Volume of the Dominicans in the Netherlands, 1803–1910] (Nijmegen: Kloosterman, 1912), App. XXIII, 541–544; *De Godsdienstvriend*, 51 (1843): 257–263.
18. Meijer, *Gedenkboek*, XXIII, 541–544.
19. Meijer, *Gedenkboek*, XXIV, 544–547.
20. *De Godsdienstvriend* 46 (1841): 303.
21. Gilbert J. Garraghan S.J., *The Jesuits of the Middle United States* (3 vols., New York: America Press, 1938).
22. L. Van Miert, "Some Historical Documents Concerning the Mission of Maryland, 1807–1820," *Woodstock Letters: A Record of Current Events and Historical Notes Connected with the Colleges and Missions of the Society of Jesus* (Woodstock, Md.: Woodstock College, 1872–1969), XXX (1901), nr. 3., 333–352, gives information about the five missionaries: the Belgians Francois Maleve and Jean Henry; the German Adam Britt; and Karel Wouters, a Belgian, and Jan Beschter from Luxemburg.
23. K. [Carolus] Schoeters S.J., *P. J. de Nef, 1774–1844, Een katholiek van de daad, een groot vaderlander, een weldoener van Amerika* [P. J. De Nef, 1774–1844; A Catholic of Action, a Great Fatherlander, a Benefactor of America] (Louvain: Davidsfonds, 1948).
24. Schoeters, *P. J. de Nef*, 65–75; William J. Howlett, *Life of Rev. Charles Nerinckx, Pioneer Missionary of Kentucky and Founder of the Sisters of Loretto at the Foot of the Cross* (Techny, Ill.: Mission Press, 1915); Joseph A. Griffin, *The Contribution of Belgium to the Catholic Church in America, 1523–1857* (Washington: Catholic University of America, 1932).
25. About Peter De Smet, see Hiram M. Chittenden and Alfred T. Richardson, eds., *Life, Letters and Travels of Father Pierre-Jean de Smet S.J., 1801–1873* (4 vols., New York: F. P. Harper, 1905); Eugene Laveille, *Le Père de Smet, 1801–1873* [Father De Smet, 1801–1873] (Liege: H. Dessain, 1913). Peter De Smet's books are: *Letters and Sketches, With a Narrative of a Year's Residence among the Indian Tribes of the Rocky Mountains* (Philadelphia: M. Fithian, 1843); *Oregon Missions and Travels over the Rocky Mountains in 1845–46* (New York: E. Dunigan, 1847); *Western Mission and Missionaries: A Series of Letters* (New York: E. Dunigan and Brother, 1863); *New Indian Sketches* (New York: D & J Sadlier, 1863).
26. F. Van Hoeck S.J., "Nederlandse Jezuieten in de Verenigde Staten" [Dutch Jesuits in the United States] *Het Missiewerk, Nederlands Tijdschrift voor Missiewetenschap* 1 (1949): 47.
27. Schoeters, *P. J. de Nef*, 208.
28. Joseph P. Conroy S.J., *Arnold Damen S.J.: A Chapter in the Making of Chicago* (New York: Benzinger Brothers, 1930).

29. Lodewijk H. C. Schutjes, *Geschiedenis van het Bisdom 's-Herto- genbosch* [History of the Bishopric of 's-Hertogenbosch] (5 vols.; 's-Hertogenbosch: C. N. Teulings, 1870–1876), II, App. XII, 296–301, gives information about many of them. See also Van Hoeck, "Nederlandse Jezuieten," 47; he mentions 50 from Noord- Brabant, but they did not all come from that province.

30. Schoeters, *P. J. de Nef*, 43–48; H. J. Allard S.J., *Antonius van Gils en de kerkelijke gebeurtenissen van zijn tijd* [Antonius Van Gils and the Church Events of His Time] ('s-Hertogenbosch: Mosmans, 1875), merely mentions the contacts with Carroll.

31. J. D. Sauter, *The American College of Louvain, 1857–1898* (Ph.D. dissertation, Roman Catholic University of Louvain, 1959), App. B. List of alumni and students, 205–245.

32. Jacques Cuyten Papers, Groot-Seminarie, 186a, Episcopal Ar- chives, 's-Hertogenbosch.

33. Andreas J. J. M. Van Den Eerenbeemt, *De Missie-actie in Neder- land (1600–1940)* [The Mission Movement in Holland 1600–1940] (Ph.D. dissertation, Roman Catholic University of Nijmegen, 1945), 226; gives the best available information about the Dutch missionaries, including a list with their names and particulars; for Van De Luytelaar see *De Tijd*, Jan. 31, 1857.

34. Jacob Van Der Zee, *The Hollanders of Iowa* (Iowa City: Iowa State Historical Society, 1912), 278.

35. H. S. Lucas, *Netherlanders in America* (Ann Arbor: University of Michigan Press, 1955), 29–34, 213–225, 444–445, 471–528; Jacob Van Hinte, *Nederlanders in Amerika* (2 vols., Groningen: P. Noordhoff, 1928), I, 187–195; II, 102–106, 280–281, 295–308, 418.

36. Van Den Eerenbeemt, *De Missie-actie*, 180.

37. Van Den Eerenbeemt, *De Missie-actie*, 69, quoted from *Woodstock Letters*, Jan., 1874.

4. The Labor Market in Dutch Agriculture and Emigration to the United States

Hille de Vries

In the years 1878 to 1895, the Netherlands experienced a severe and sustained agricultural depression. These years also witnessed heavy overseas emigration by the Dutch to the United States. Was this a causal or coincidental connection? The answer to this question is not readily apparent.

The first argument against a causal link is the fact that all European countries were influenced by a sustained drop in agricultural prices caused by the strong sudden growth of grain production in the United States. Yet as Table 4.1 shows, they had different rates of emigration.[1] Far fewer Dutch emigrated than English or Germans. Also fewer Netherlanders emigrated in the 1880s, during the depths of the agrarian crisis, than in the prosperous decade prior to the First World War. In the 1880s an average of 5,271 emigrants per year departed, compared to 6,291 in the 1905–1914 period.[2]

As far as the Netherlands are concerned, then, the agrarian depression cannot be labelled as the reason for the emigration. Any push movement due to one single cause is refuted by the figures. On the other hand, it is possible that the agricultural situation may have had an incidental influence on the emigration. The acute increase in the emigration of the Dutch in the years 1880 and 1881, when incomes continued to drop sharply as a consequence of the agricultural crisis, is an indication of this.[3]

Adjustment of Agriculture in the Netherlands after the Eighties

Dutch agriculture and the rural population did not respond to the crisis by migration. There was neither a mass emigration nor a mass movement from the countryside to the towns since the pace of industrialization was too slow to absorb excess workers. The Dutch population thus found itself in a dilemma. Either they must protect their own agriculture by levying high tariff duties on the import of grain, in particular from America, or they must modernize their agriculture in accordance with the new competitive situation.

The farmers chose the latter course. They adapted their methods by working with fewer farmhands, by mechanization, and by specializing in products of which the price dropped relatively little (oats, barley, potatoes, pulses, and sugar beets). Seen as a whole, agriculture also reaped a few advantages from the drop in grain prices, since this resulted in a drop in the price of cattle fodder. In areas of mixed farming (the eastern and southern sandy areas), this led to a shift from arable farming to dairy farming.

As a result, farmers in the Netherlands exerted little pressure for tariff protection. Representatives of the agricultural organizations were well aware of the disadvantages of protection: "We Netherlanders, in particular, are small and somewhat modest users of land, but we work fruitful ground and thus are a productive nation. Because our cattle, our pigs, our horses, our dairy produce, our vegetables, our fruit, our flowers, we need the export market and thus we must surely be able to see that there is no greater foe imaginable to us than protectionism. . . . Or should we be as naive as the German Agricultural Union, and believe that when closing our own borders we could open up those of our neighbors?"[4]

Table 4.1. Immigration to the U.S.A. from the Netherlands, England, and Germany by Decades, 1830–1920

	Netherlands totals	England and Wales totals	Germany totals	Netherlands[a] Percentage	England[b] and Wales percentage	Germany[c] percentage
1831–1840	1,412	7,665	152,454	0.5	0.5	5.2
1841–1850	8,251	33,393	434,626	2.8	1.8	13.6
1851–1860	10,789	253,444	951,667	3.4	13.3	27.6
1861–1870	9,102	226,590	787,468	2.6	10.6	20.6
1871–1880	16,541	444,337	718,182	4.4	18.3	16.6
1881–1890	53,701	657,320	1,452,970	12.6	23.9	30.7
1891–1900	26,758	215,557	505,152	5.6	7.0	9.5
1901–1910	48,262	405,481	341,498	8.8	11.8	5.6
1911–1920	43,718	263,051	143,945	6.9	7.1	2.2

Source: B. R. Mitchell, European Historical Statistics, 1450–1970 (New York: Columbia University Press, 1975), 27–34; W. F. Wilcox and I. Ferenczi, eds., International Migrations, Volume I, Statistics (New York: National Bureau of Economic Research, 1929), I, 376–393.
[a] Average population calculated from the years 1839, 1849, 1859, 1869, 1879, 1889, 1899, 1900, 1910.
[b] Average population calculated from the years 1831, 1841, 1851, 1861, 1871, 1881, 1891, 1901, 1911.
[c] Average population calculated from the years 1834, 1840, 1852, 1861, 1871, 1880, 1890, 1900, 1910.

Royal Commissions on Emigration

The agricultural crisis made a deep impression in the Netherlands. As early as 1886 the government set up a royal commission to investigate the situation and make suggestions by which the authorities could advance agriculture. The accent lay on the second point. Therefore the government issued a number of directives, of which the most important were to stimulate agricultural education; organize scientific research to improve agricultural methods; adopt legal measures against corrupt practices in the butter trade; and stimulate better animal-breeding methods.[5]

Twenty years later, in 1906, when agriculture shared a boom period, another government commission was set up, this time to investigate the economic structure of independent agriculturists and agricultural laborers. One cannot posit any causal connection, yet these commissions of 1886 and 1906 both came at a time when relatively many Dutchmen emigrated to America. It is also noticeable that this emigration received considerably less stress in the report of the 1886 commission during the agricultural crisis than in that of the state commission of 1906, when times were good. In 1886 it was not the number of those leaving the country that aroused the anxiety of the commission, but their status as rural folk who, after all, "form the backbone of the nation."[6] The commission of 1906, by contrast, dealt in detail with the migration of the rural population, both within the country and outside of it, and even devoted a separate section of the report to it.[7] This commission extensively studied the economic structure of the Dutch countryside and recommended better housing for the rural population, social insurance for agricultural workers, and land for laborers and small holders. Thus, the agricultural commissions connected overseas emigration to the agricultural situation, notably the agrarian crisis, and to the structure of the total Netherlands rural economy.

The State Commission on Unemployment, a few years later, considered emigration to America in even more detail. The commission built on the report of the state commission of 1906 and expressed its opinion that "a very great deal of the trans-oceanic migration comes from the countryside."[8] With regard to the emigration of farmers and their sons, the commission made an indirect connection by noting that the problem of lack of work for laborers was relieved when they emigrated. Moreover, after a few years of hard work in the land to which they have emigrated, they tried to become independent farmers. Emigration meant that they would not influence the future percentage of unemployment in the homeland.

Among emigrants, dependent workers were more numerous than independent workers. They consisted of agricultural workers and farm laborers; educated non-farm laborers; and experienced laborers such as construction workers, building tradesmen, and casual laborers. These three groups are, according to the commission, predominantly from the countryside: "That the overseas emigration is of greater significance for the countryside than for towns and industrial areas becomes obvious if Dutch emigrants leaving from Dutch harbors are grouped according to their urban or rural origin. In 1911 there were 2,638 emigrants, of whom less than 900 came from towns, and about 1,800 from the countryside." This also explains the phenomenon that for so many the final aim of their emigration was not to work in their original trade but to work in agriculture. "They cherished the aim, after a year or more, of becoming landowners for which governments and land companies often provided an all too easy opportunity."

The commission assumed that the driving force of emigration was sustained to a considerable degree by the American "pull." It was not, however, primarily the industrial market but agricultural conditions that caused this pull. One important aim of emigration was the goal of achieving, sooner or later, the status of independent farmer. In the eyes of the commission this perspective related closely to the general employment situation in Dutch agriculture, for both wage earners and self-employed agricultural workers. The commission reported "that the proportion of the total from town occupations, compared to the rural ones, changes to the detriment of the latter if farming prospers in the land of emigration."[9] This is a striking illustration of the fact that Dutch agriculture was being pushed to the periphery by the American center.

Structural Changes
in Rural Migration

The hypothesis that emigration to America was mainly connected with structural developments in the countryside is also supported by regional historical research. In 1971, I illustrated this with regard to the Frisian sea clay municipality of Oostdongeradeel.[10] In this northern municipality, the migratory activity of single migrants, both within the country and abroad, had already attained a structurally higher level in 1875–1879, whereas during the agricultural depression, mobility increased somewhat but not to the extent of the seventies. The number of solitaries emigrating to America from Oostdongeradeel between 1880 and 1900 rose from 23 percent to 64 percent. This was primarily due to the greater share of migrants among laborers' sons and daughters and among farm hands, both male and female. The effect of the agricultural crisis also became visible in the emigration of families, which was very high in the periods 1880–1884 and 1890–1894 but dropped quickly thereafter. The growth of the number of solitary emigrants, however, was constant and therefore seems to be of a more structural nature.[11] M. L. Samson, in his study concerning the municipality of Wisch in the Achterhoek region of Gelderland discovered the same tendency in the emigration to Germany.[12]

Unofficial observers also connected the emigration to structural factors. J. Maurer of Haarlem, who was employed in the agricultural cooperative movement of Noord-Holland, published several lectures in 1912 under the title "The Dutch Farmer Faced with Emigration."[13] In Maurer's opinion the Dutch emigration at the start of the twentieth century was not insignificant compared to that of other European countries. During the period 1907–1909, the Dutch emigration rate per 1,000 population was midway between countries with very high rates, such as Italy and

Norway, and countries with minimal emigration, such as France and, in those years, Germany. Dutch emigration was also very geographically widespread. Most of the emigration, however, was from the agricultural provinces of Friesland, Groningen, and Zeeland, where in a number of municipalities there was a very high concentration of emigrants. (Table 4.2 compiled from J. Maurer.) By contrast, only a few people emigrated overseas from the southern provinces. The emigration from Noord- and Zuid-Holland was slightly higher. It is striking that about half the large towns

Table 4.2. Average Annual Number of Emigrants and Rate per 1,000 Inhabitants from Selected Netherlands Provinces and Muncipalities, 1906–1910

Provinces	N	Rate
Friesland	350	1.0
Oostdongeradeel	30	3.2
Westdongeradeel	18	2.3
Barradeel	20	2.8
't Bildt	17	2.1
Groningen	500	1.8
Bedum	18	6.8
Beerta	27	6.8
Finsterwolde	17	6.0
Leek	16	2.7
Zeeland	350	1.5
Yerseke	60	15.7
Biervliet	20	8.8
's Heer Arendskerke	13	4.0
Noord-Holland	700	0.6
Amsterdam	350	0.6
Zuid-Holland	550	0.5
Rotterdam	270	0.6
Noord-Brabant	150	0.2
Eindhoven	3	0.1
Tilburg	38	0.2
Limburg	40	0.1
Maastricht	11	0.1
Venlo	37	1.4

Source: J. Maurer, *De Nederlandsche boer tegenover de landverhuizing; Een tweetal lezingen* (Haarlem, ca. 1912).

were represented in the stream of emigration. In the west of the Netherlands, emigration thus had a far less rural character than it did in the north and in Zeeland.

The reason for emigration, according to Maurer, was primarily economic. Landownership was unequal, there were too many small holdings, and trade and industry were in crisis. Maurer's attention to the structural causes is evident in his classification of the emigrant stream. There was first the needy, many of whom returned after a year or two. But others, who found work as agricultural workers in America and hoped to become independent farmers, persevered. Many of these, Maurer suggested, had not worked in agriculture in their homelands. These emigrants persevered because they "are encouraged by their right to the land which, while very small at the outset, excites and gives hope, and heartens." Maurer suggested that a number of these agricultural workers who tried to become independent farmers had not emigrated for economic reasons, such as lack of work, but rather because of poor social conditions, such as a strong patriarchal relationship between farmer and agricultural worker.

The second group of emigrants, the less-well-off, left with 1,000 to 2,000 guilders. They included many crofters and market-gardeners who did not have enough land in the Netherlands and hoped for a new life across the ocean. The timing of their departure was sometimes dependent on the state of trade. For example, said Maurer, "the malaise in 1910 in Langendijk [Noord-Holland], the tulip crash in the bulb fields, have caused many to emigrate to the United States."

In the third group, the well-to-do, are the farmers with capital who somehow managed to earn a living by traditional agriculture. They refused to adopt to market gardening and found themselves "to be declining in their position and therefore prefer to leave."

Maurer's observations clearly show that emigration to America was closely allied to the structure of the Netherlands countryside. To consider this connection more closely, it is necessary to chart the propensity to emigrate over a time period longer than that of the agricultural crisis of the 1880s, preferably to the First World War. It is also important to differentiate regionally the occupational composition of the emigrant stream in order to determine if regional differences in economic structure affected emigration rates.

The Regional Pattern
of Emigration

Emigration is only a part of international migration. Dutch emigration within Europe was greater than overseas migration, although the proportion was not the same in each of the eleven provinces. E. W. Hofstee argued that the nature of the agricultural business in a particular area was related to emigration.[14] In the provinces of Friesland, Groningen and Zeeland, the extent of overseas emigration prior to the First World War equalled the total migration loss abroad. In all three provinces, largely composed of sea clay soil, specialized agriculture was the main activity and it was market-oriented. Zeeland and Groningen mainly had arable farming; in Friesland there was arable farming in the north and dairy farming in the southwest. The internal migration from these provinces was strongly negative, and there was a net migration loss.

After 1870 employment in agriculture stagnated, especially in areas of heavy grain production. In Zeeland the situation was worse due to the loss of modder as a cash crop. Inhabitants of these provinces who planned to leave the country had little alternative but to emigrate to America, especially if they only had agricultural skills. Apart from the eastern provinces, these families of farmers and agricultural laborers had little experience in working in the cottage industry. During prosperous years in agriculture (1850–1875) they had grown accustomed to a relatively high level of income, which was now threatened by the agricultural crisis. For emigrants from these areas, who were for the most part working in agriculture, departure for America was a way to continue in farming.

The eastern provinces of Drenthe, Overijssel, and Gelderland had a comparatively slight net migration loss, either during the agricultural crisis or in the years around 1900. There was a net migration loss with foreign countries, but this did not coincide with emigration overseas. For these areas migration across the border into Germany was more important. In the period 1880–1910, this continually resulted in a small net migration loss of approximately 1 per 1,000, primarily from laborers who sought work in industry, agriculture, or the peat trade.[15] Agriculture in these provinces had a less specialized and market-oriented character. There was a strong tradition of subsistence farming, supplemented by cottage industry. The job perspective for these emigrants was thus broader than agriculture alone.

The two southern provinces of Noord-Brabant and Limburg showed a picture similar to that of the eastern provinces. They had a small, usually negative internal migration loss and only a very slight migration overseas. Limburg, in particular, had a considerable foreign migration loss to Germany, where many laborers found work in industry or in the mines. As the land in Limburg is sandy, farms were mostly mixed, devoted to general farming and dairying.

Farmers in the three central provinces of Noord-Holland, Zuid-Holland, and Utrecht specialized mainly in dairy farming, with the exception of the sea clay area of the Zuid-Holland islands, where arable farming took first place. Foreign migration was at a low ebb—less than 1 per 1,000—and showed no relationship with emigration. From these provinces, oriented toward trade and shipbuilding, emigration was to Germany, Belgium, and the Dutch East Indies.

A Regional Survey of Emigration 1880–1909

The documentation to study Dutch overseas emigration after 1880 is not as complete as in the earlier period, but published figures are available in the yearly government agricultural reports and after 1900 in the annual census bureau's report "Trends of the Population." The figures included in Appendix 4.A1 portray the general picture.[16]

There is no apparent connection between the extent of Dutch emigration to non-European countries and internal migration, and certainly there is no one-sided push movement. Those

who migrated within the country were pulled to the western provinces, where they were mostly prepared to take non-agricultural
occupations. A second noticeable point is the strong regional difference. The lion's share of emigration to countries outside Europe came from the two northern provinces and Zeeland, with a
lesser number from Noord- and Zuid-Holland, particularly in the
early twentieth century. In the three agricultural provinces, emigration was heaviest during the agricultural depression. It is also
noticeable to what small extent the population of the eastern and
southern provinces contributed to emigration overseas. Was it,
then, the geographic factor that finally carries weight? The overseas migration was indeed primarily supplied from provinces that
border on the sea. Of the inland provinces only Gelderland made
a substantial contribution.

There is a scarcity of information on the countries of destination because some tables in the Reports on Agriculture are in-
sufficiently specific. But the available figures show that for emigrants from the northern provinces and Zeeland, the United
States heads the list, but for those from other provinces, America
ranks second or third. Emigrants from the eastern provinces
mostly went to Germany, whereas emigrants from the southern
and western provinces preferred Belgium, the Dutch East Indies,
or Germany.

The considerable regional differences give rise to many
questions that cannot be solved without further research. The
global information on this point in Table 4.3 permits very general
conclusions. Among the emigrants from Friesland, Groningen,
and Zeeland, the agrarian element of agricultural laborers and
farmhands, both male and female, dominated. By comparison, the
much smaller stream from the three eastern provinces includes
many more independent farmers and non-agrarian workers, and
less laborers and farmhands. Finally, except for emigration from
the northern provinces, the occupational distribution is wide.
This fact gives rise to various questions. Did all these emigrants
seek an agrarian occupation in America? Are we concerned with
people from families who have been working outside agriculture
for more than one generation? Only detailed regional investiga-
tions can provide more information about this.

In summary, the agricultural sector dominated emigration

from the northern provinces and Zeeland, and it was directed for the most part towards the United States. Among emigrants from Drenthe and North-Brabant, by contrast, there were peat cutters; in Overijssel textile workers; in Limburg mineworkers; and in Noord- and Zuid-Holland, traders and diamond cutters in addition to day laborers and craftsmen.

The View of H. Blink

Emigration from the Netherlands to the United States has continued for several hundred years. It is therefore proper to emphasize long-term trends. More than half a century ago, the social geographer H. Blink illustrated this aspect in a magazine article.[17] Blink was, to the best of my knowledge, the first Dutch scholar to study emigration from the Netherlands. As a geographer and agrarian historian, he saw a close connection between emigration and the availability of farmland. Emigration was, in his opinion, a form of colonization, a movement in which the Dutch had participated for centuries. On the basis of a simple statistical analysis of the emigration figures for the period 1904–1913, Blink reached two important conclusions. In relating the extent of emigration overseas to total population size, he found that extensive emigration was not related to population density. In Groningen, Friesland, and Zeeland, the population density is lower than the average of the Netherlands as a whole. Blink indicated subsequently two factors that facilitate emigration—the occurrence in a particular district of much arable land and of large farms where many farm laborers live. In this group of workers overseas emigration is fairly frequent. The same applies to farmers' sons who live in areas where there is little new land brought under cultivation and no farms are subdivided, so there is little chance of them becoming independent farmers. Blink thus explained the relatively large emigration from Groningen, Friesland, and Zeeland, where there were large commercial farms, and the limited overseas emigration from North-Brabant, Limburg, Overijssel, and Gelderland, where there were many small farms.

The significant factor in Blink's approach is the way in

Table 4.3. Socioeconomic Characteristics of Overseas Netherlands Emigrants, by Heads of Household and Single People, per Province, 1880–1899

	Household heads	Total persons	Wealthy	Middle	Poor	Farmer	Servant living in	Laborer	Crafts	Other occ.	No. occ.
Groningen											
1880–1889	2,617	8,549	3.9	73.6	22.9	2.2	19.1	53.5	12.1	9.3	5.7
1890–1899	2,301	5,451	10.5	66.9	22.6	5.0	28.4	26.2	13.3	13.3	13.0
Friesland											
1880–1889	2,853	8,405	5.1	62.9	31.8	3.4	14.2	39.0	15.5	15.7	12.2
1890–1899	3,159	7,128	4.2	67.2	28.6	3.8	20.4	27.3	13.0	20.6	14.8
Zeeland											
1880–1889	2,109	7,019	6.1	66.8	27.1	3.8	68.8 }		12.9	5.7	8.8
1890–1899	1,797	4,681	9.7	62.8	27.5	2.1	65.9 }		12.6	8.2	11.2
Drenthe											
1880–1889	375	1,251	7.5	81.3	11.5	24.0	10.0	33.1	13.9	7.2	11.7
1890–1899	259	589	18.1	70.3	11.6	20.5	9.7	13.1	15.4	19.3	22.0
Overijssel											
1880–1889	552	1,687	14.2	66.9	18.5	20.4	8.1	30.0	15.8	12.8	10.9
1890–1899	328	722	31.2	61.8	4.3	19.3	3.4	10.5	20.0	27.5	19.3
Gelderland											
1880–1889	1,594	4,247	18.3	55.7	26.0	23.1	12.1	21.5	16.0	12.6	15.1
1890–1899	1,524	2,962	41.5	45.1	13.5	10.0	5.7	10.1	10.3	37.0	27.0

Utrecht											
1880–1889	178	398	31.6	47.7	20.7	14.4	1.7	6.3	19.5	28.7	27.6
1890–1899	519	849	31.0	64.2	4.2	2.1	2.9	2.1	17.1	45.9	29.9
Noord-Holland											
1880–1889	1,796	4,060	NA	NA	NA	10.6	4.6	21.8	31.2	10.1	21.8
1890–1899	1,468	2,762	NA	NA	NA	9.6	5.9	24.8	5.6	36.7	17.4
Zuid-Holland											
1880–1889	1,504	4,510	10.5	49.5	40.0	5.5	6.2	40.2	15.5	16.0	12.3
1890–1899	1,585	3,343	19.8	56.4	23.8	6.8	5.6	17.7	14.7	28.1	27.1
Noord-Brabant											
1880–1889	323	1,014	12.6	66.0	24.7	21.1	19.7	19.7	18.3	11.3	9.9
1890–1899	343	701	25.7	65.6	5.8	16.1	3.7	7.0	19.8	39.2	15.4
Limburg											
1880–1889	270	777	15.2	65.6	19.3	31.2	9.8	22.5	16.2	16.2	3.5
1890–1899	115	233	19.1	53.9	27.0	32.2	7.0	12.2	21.7	13.9	13.0

Source: Verslagen voor den Landbouw.

which he accentuates the regional differences among those people actively employed in agrarian work, both employees and self-employed. Such regional differences are noticeable in the numerical growth of the Dutch rural population. In the century 1830–1930 and considering only the *agrarian* municipalities, it is evident that some districts, for example, parts of Overijssel, Gelderland, and Noord-Brabant grew quickly between 1880 and 1930 but increased much less rapidly in the period 1830–1880.[18] The reverse is true of rural municipalities in the north of Groningen and Friesland, and in Zeeland, where population growth was more rapid before the year 1880 than after it. The possibility of finding work in these agrarian areas thus varied greatly. As far as agriculture is concerned, two factors that were already recognized by Blink, may be significant: the mechanization process and the size of the farms. Precise quantitative details about the mechanization of each agrarian area are not available, but the clay farming areas in the north of Groningen and Friesland and in Zeeland pioneered in mechanization and were in advance of the eastern and southern provinces.[19] The large internal migration losses in the northern provinces and in Zeeland are probably linked to their higher level of mechanization.

Farm Size and Number of Land Users as an Indicator of Job Opportunities

Table 4.4 provides data on farm size in the several provinces at four time periods from 1888 to 1921. First it appears that fewer farmers used 20 hectares (50 acres) or more land except for Groningen. Given this evidence, Dutch agriculture cannot be said to have more developed as a large-scale production in this period. And yet the decrease is not so great that the increase of small agricultural units can be fully accounted for by subdivision of the larger units. Second, the middle category of 10–20 hectares (25–50 acres) increased considerably in most provinces. Finally, the greatest growth occurred among the small land users, which is the largest category in all provinces. In the eastern and southern provinces their absolute number is overwhelmingly large.

These are situated in the sandy areas where new land was being cleared for cultivation on a large scale at that time. Relatively speaking, the growth in small farms was greatest (more than 100 percent) in Friesland, Drenthe, Zuid-Holland, and Zeeland. Purely from a statistical point of view, the small agricultural units dominated during this period.

The statistics of the number of farmers, for which we have few quantitative details, are also indicative. To some extent the number of land users may be considered as an indication of the potential number of employment opportunities for independent farmers that was available in a province at a given period. In this connection I would indicate two points that became clear in the previous analysis. First, in the eastern and southern provinces there had always been more opportunities for independent farmers than in the north and in Zeeland. The trend in the number of the small farmers, the category in which most new positions became available, is demonstrated in Table 4.5. This shows the number of small farmers per 10,000 of the population in 1880 and 1910. Second, relatively speaking, the number of opportunities for small land users grew most quickly in Drenthe and the three modern agricultural provinces of Groningen, Friesland, and Zeeland.

Table 4.5 also shows the figures on the number of emigrants leaving for non-European countries, calculated per 10,000 of the population for each province. Here again, the three provinces of Groningen, Friesland, and Zeeland supplied by far the highest number of emigrants to non-European countries.

How can the strong correlation between emigration and number of farmers be interpreted? As has already been said, we may assume that most people emigrating to America intended to work in agriculture. In the three provinces there was also a great preference for agricultural work, as is evident in the increase in the number of land users. This preference for agricultural work is not surprising, since there was hardly any industrial employment in these provinces, as compared with the three eastern provinces (turf cutting, textile, paper trade) and in Noord-Brabant and Limburg (textile and mining). In other words, emigration to America took advantage of the resistance of Groningers, Frisians, and Zeelanders to the industrial way of life.

Table 4.4. Users of Land with One Hectare (2.46 Acres) and More, per Province, 1888, 1904, 1910, and 1921

Province	Area in hectares	1888	1904	1910	1921
Groningen	1–10	4,238	5,040	7,264	7,651
	10–20	2,111	1,839	1,993	2,191
	20	3,229	3,327	3,612	3,545
Friesland	1–10	5,923	8,768	12,678	14,491
	10–20	2,197	2,313	2,314	3,100
	20	4,770	4,441	4,417	4,204
Zeeland	1–10	3,252	4,108	5,880	7,003
	10–20	1,153	1,105	1,186	1,439
	20	2,145	2,140	2,346	2,243
Drenthe	1–10	5,736	7,544	10,808	11,545
	10–20	1,846	2,245	2,634	3,048
	20	1,381	1,138	1,136	1,135
Overijssel	1–10	13,591	14,638	17,606	18,551
	10–20	3,924	3,555	3,306	3,579
	20	1,759	1,767	1,562	1,452
Gelderland	1–10	22,325	24,963	29,479	30,842
	10–20	4,351	4,153	4,111	4,612
	20	2,312	2,172	2,486	2,229
Utrecht	1–10	2,469	2,610	3,025	3,278
	10–20	1,361	1,548	1,591	1,848
	20	1,724	1,578	1,733	1,587
Noord-Holland	1–10	7,209	9,269	10,192	12,240
	10–20	3,679	3,405	3,429	3,661
	20	2,960	2,876	3,268	2,800
Zuid-Holland	1–10	5,458	8,162	9,737	11,715
	10–20	3,260	3,254	3,507	3,813
	20	3,978	3,934	4,356	3,959
Noord-Brabant	1–10	23,553	24,520	26,029	26,277
	10–20	4,074	4,361	4,994	5,257
	20	1,293	1,210	1,629	1,704
Limburg	10–10	14,923	17,860	18,364	17,929
	10–20	2,048	2,019	1,756	1,961
	20	626	695	747	730

Table 4.4., continued.

Province	Area in hectares	1888	1904	1910	1921
The Netherlands	1–10	108,677	127,491	151,059	161,522
	10–20	30,004	29,797	30,821	34,509
	20	26,197	25,278	27,292	25,588

Source: *Verslagen en mededelingen van de Directie van de Landbouw,* no. 3: "Het grondgebruik in Nederland" ('s-Gravenhage: 1935).

Table 4.5. Increase in the Number of Users of Land (1–10 Hectare) Compared with the Total Number of Emigrants per 10,000 Population, 1890–1909

	Land users 1888	Land users 1910	Percentage increase	Rank[a]	Foreign emigration 1890–1909	
					N	Rank[a]
Groningen	155	221	66	8	365	9
Friesland	177	353	179	10	370	10
Zeeland	163	253	90	9	430	11
Drenthe	439	624	183	11	73	4
Overijssel	460	460	0	4	63	3
Gelderland	436	461	26	7	121	7
Utrecht	112	105	−6	3	85	5
Noord-Holland	87	92	6	5	139	8
Zuid-Holland	57	70	13	6	111	6
Noord-Brabant	462	418	−45	1	44	2
Limburg	584	553	−32	2	24	1

Source: Figures from Table 4.4 and Appendix 4.A1.
[a] Spearman's rank correlation: $1 - \dfrac{420}{11(121-1)} = 0.682$.

The increase in the number of land users was not solely a consequence of the division of large farmsteads into smaller ones. The extension took place primarily in the number of small units, without the number in the larger categories being proportionately reduced (Table 4.4). Rather, the total area of cultivated land increased due to land clearance (Table 4.6).[20]

The fluctuation in land clearance generally reflected the agrarian business cycle. Private large landowners and government authorities also took the initiative in stimulating land clearance. The most noticeable feature of Table 4.6 is the sharp drop during the years of the agricultural depression and the steady increase at the beginning of the twentieth century, which is a trend that co-incided with agricultural land prices. This increase in farmland prices and farm rents continued after the First World War, even when farm prices plummeted. This perplexing development in-dicated that farmers' sons continued to prefer farming to non-agricultural pursuits, which in turn created excess demand for farms despite low crop prices.[21]

Government policy after 1900 also consistently promoted the small family farm unit as good social policy, because it made citizens independent, discouraged social class divisions, and en-couraged capital formation by thrifty yeoman.[22] The government encouraged a gradually urban movement out of agriculture and tried to discourage emigration, although it did not explicitly con-demn it. Small independent farmers with a little land (a *"plaatsje"*) would be less mobile than farm laborers.

Conclusions

The agricultural crisis of the last quarter of the nineteenth century led to intensive adjustments in Dutch society that lasted longer than the depression era and had long-term social and eco-nomic ramifications. Dutch agriculture was part of an interna-tional market and specialized primarily in dairy and bacon pro-cessing. Rural society was gradually opened up especially in the inland provinces in the East and South, because of the increas-ing contact with other parts of the country and changes in agri-cultural and trade techniques. This modernization resulted in an increasing surplus of rural laborers. Modern agricultural methods produced more food with less people than actually of-fered themselves for the labor market. It was under these eco-nomic conditions that emigration overseas took place in the last quarter of the nineteenth century and the first quarter of the twentieth century.

Table 4.6. Average Annual Area of Land Cleared
in the Netherlands, by Selected Periods, 1840–1894

Years	Land area
1840–1856	4,365 ha. (10,787 acres)
1857–1863	3,710 ha. (9,168 acres)
1864–1873	3,102 ha. (7,666 acres)
1881–1886	1,451 ha. (3,586 acres)
1892–1894	1,092 ha. (2,699 acres)
1897–1901	2,210 ha. (5,461 acres)
1902–1906	3,962 ha. (9,791 acres)
1907–1911	7,031 ha. (17,375 acres)
1913–1915	7,621 ha. (18,833 acres)
1917–1920	4,541 ha. (11,222 acres)

Source: *Verslagen voor den Landbouw.*

The uneven regional distribution of emigration is also an important quantitative characteristic that demands a qualitative explanation. Compared to the period before 1880, Friesland and Groningen came strongly to the fore after 1880, and the position of Overijssel and Gelderland as emigration provinces is considerably less important. It is only in Zeeland that emigration is maintained at a high level. The occupational distribution of the emigrants also needs further study. Within each region, occupations in the sending area must be compared with the occupations of immigrants in America.

Before the First World War the policy of the Netherlands government with regard to emigration was limited largely to being an intermediary in the border area with Germany. The government had a passive attitude with regard to emigration overseas. To the extent that it supported small holders, it indirectly sought to limit emigration overseas of farmers and agricultural laborers by providing plausible alternatives for these traditionally emigrant-minded groups.

Appendix 4.A1. Internal Migration and Emigration from the Netherlands to Countries Outside Europe, by Five-Year Periods, 1880–1909

	Internal migration Surplus						Emigration outside Europe					
	1880–1884	1885–1889	1890–1894	1895–1899	1900–1904	1905–1909	1880–1884	1885–1889	1890–1894	1895–1899	1900–1904	1905–1909
Groningen	−2,803	−3,596	−2,321	−4,690	−6,390	−5,897	4797	3752	4235	1216	2819	2662
Friesland	−15,421	−9,873	−12,447	−15,348	−7,739	−8,798	4595	3810	5224	1904	2202	3277
Drenthe	−999	−326	−132	−197	+1,024	−135	870	378	356	229	240	257
Overijssel	−125	−3,115	−1,810	+1,483	−900	−575	1411	276	507	215	489	897
Gelderland	−1,551	+975	+2,596	+1,338	−3,070	+2,460	2684	1563	1847	1115	1534	2349
Utrecht	+2,672	+1,183	−498	−1,625	+1,995	−2,845	158	240	315	534	399	877
Noord-Holland	+30,884	+14,924	+16,275	+15,183	+13,800	+1,595	1693	2367	1607	1155	3654	7025
Zuid-Holland	+9,764	+10,617	+16,649	+18,412	+20,672	+24,357	1455	3055	2038	1305	3435	5973
Zeeland	−4,076	−2,982	−3,923	−6,219	−6,416	−5,073	3461	3558	3775	906	2089	2740
Noord-Brabant	+2,159	+337	−3,995	−2,250	−4,697	−4,352	561	453	433	268	609	1118
Limburg	+721	+1,756	+1,755	+3,300	+2,824	+3,938	622	155	202	31	84	364

Sources: For internal migration surplus, H. ter Heide, *Binnenlandse migratie in Nederland* ('s-Gravenhage: 1965), bijlage 6. For emigration outside Europe, figures for 1880–1900 are from *Provincial Verslagen* [Provincial Reports and *Verslagen voor den Landbouw* [Reports of Agriculture]; figures for 1901–1909 are from *Bijdragen tot de algemene statistiek van Nederland, Nieuwe Volgreeks*, Central Bureau voor Statistiek [Compilation of the General Statistics of the Netherlands, New Series, Central Bureau for Statistics].

Notes

1. B. R. Mitchell, *European Historical Statistics, 1450–1970* (New York: Columbia University Press, 1975), 27–34; W. F. Willcox and I. Ferenczi, eds., *International Migrations, Volume I, Statistics* (New York: National Bureau of Economic Research, 1929), I, 376–393. I would like to thank H. Van Bruggen, student assistant in the department of economic history at the State University of Leiden, for her help in collecting and computing the statistical data.

2. Averages calculated from H. S. Lucas, *Netherlanders in America: Dutch Immigration to the United States and Canada 1789–1950* (Ann Arbor: University of Michigan Press, 1955), 641.

3. Hille De Vries, *Landbouw en bevolking tijdens de agrarische depressie in Friesland, 1878–1895* [Agriculture and Population During the Agrarian Crisis in Friesland, 1878–1895] (Wageningen: H. Veenman en Zonen, 1971), 79.

4. C. J. Sickesz Van De Cloese, "De Nederlandsche landbouw en de malaise: Eenige opmerkingen naar aanleiding van het Kamerdebat over de motie Dobbelman" [Dutch Agriculture and the Depression: A Few Remarks in Relation to the Debate in the House of Representatives Concerning the Dubbelman Motion], *De Economist*, 1 (1895): 623.

5. *Verzameling van adviezen door de Landbouwcommissie* [Compilation of Advice by the Agricultural Commission] (Koninklijk Besluit, 18 September 1886, no. 28) ('s-Gravenhage: 1891).

6. W. H. Vermeulen, *Den Haag en de landbouw: Keerpunten in het negentiende-eeuwse landbouwbeleid* [The Hague and Agriculture: Turning Points in Nineteenth Century Agriculture Policy] (Assen: Van Gorcum, 1966), 72.

7. *Rapporten en voorstellen betreffende den oeconomischen toestand der landarbeiders in Nederland* [Reports and Proposals Concerning the Economic Condition of Rural Laborers in the Netherlands] ('s-Gravenhage: 1909), 45–66.

8. *Staatscommissie over de werkloosheid* [State Commission for Unemployment] (Koninklijk Besluit, 30 July 1909, no. 42) IX. *Eindverslag* [Final Report] ('s-Gravenhage: 1914), 561–564.

9. Ibid., 567–568.

10. De Vries, *Landbouw*, 122, 187.

11. The numbers of singles expressed as a percentage of the total number of heads of household and single individuals emigrating from Oostdongeradeel to North America are, by 5-year periods: 1880–1884, 23 percent; 1885–1889, 47 percent; 1890–1894, 60 percent; 1895–1899, 64 percent (De Vries, *Landbouw*, 185).

12. Mike L. Samson, *Population Mobility in the Netherlands*

1880–1910: A Case Study of Wisch in the Achterhoek (Uppsala: Universitatis Upsaliensis, 1977), 121.

13. J. Maurer, *De Nederlandsche boer tegenover de landverhuizing: Een tweetal lezingen* [The Dutch Farmer Facing Emigration: A Couple of Lectures] (Haarlem: Author, ca. 1912), 32–33.

14. E. W. Hofstee, "De functie van de internationale migratie" [The Function of International Migration], *Tijdschrift voor Economische en Sociale Geografie* 40 (1949): 10–22.

15. *Algemeen overzicht van den oeconomischen toestand der landarbeiders in Nederland* [General Overview of the Economic Condition of Rural Laborers in the Netherlands] ('s-Gravenhage: 1908), 171ff.

16. The original data for the graphs, published by E. W. Hofstee in "De functie," have never been released.

17. H. Blink, "De Landverhuizing uit Nederland" [Emigration from the Netherlands], *Vragen van den dag* 30 (1915): 177–194.

18. W. Steigenga, "Eenige opmerkingen omtrent de bevolkings-toename op het Nederlandsche platteland" [A Few Remarks Concerning Population Increase in the Dutch Countryside], *Tijdschrift voor economische geografie* 34 (1943): 115, 117.

19. Johannes M. G. Van Der Poel, *Honderd jaar landbouwmechanisatie in Nederland* [One Hundred Years of Agricultural Mechanization in the Netherlands] (Wageningen: H. Vreeman, 1967), 151, 195, 213.

20. H. Blink, *Woest gronden, ontginning en bebossching in Nederland voormaals en thans* [Virgin Land, Clearing and Reforestation in the Netherlands Then and Now] ('s-Gravenhage: H. Mouton, 1929), 48.

21. C. H. J. Maliepaard, "De Nederlandse landbouw" [Dutch Agriculture], in Pieter B. Kreukniet, ed., *De Nederlandse volkshuishouding tussen twee wereldoorlogen* [The Dutch National Economy Between the Two World Wars] IX (Utrecht: Het Spectrum, 1952), 58ff; Verslag over den Landbouw in Nederland over 1927, in *Verslagen en mededelingen van de Directie van den Landbouw 1928*, [Reports and Communications of the Board of Agriculture 1928] no. 2, LXII; Atc Sevenster, *Het bevolkings- en emigratievraagstuk in Nederland en in den Nederlandschen landbouw* [Population and Emigration Problems in the Netherlands and in Dutch Agriculture] (Wageningen: H. Veenman en Zonen, 1930), 81, 82, 88.

22. *Rapport over den sociaal-economischen toestand der kleine boerenbedrijven in Nederland gevolgd door voorstellen ter verbetering van den bestaanden toestand* [Report on Socioeconomic Conditions Among the Small Farm Operators in the Netherlands Followed by a Proposal for Improvement of the Present Condition] ('s-Gravenhage: 1937), 314; "Rapport betreffende

den oeconomischen toestand der kleine boeren en de maatregelen om daarin verbetering te brengen" [Report Concerning the Economic Condition of the Small Farmers and the Steps Taken to Improve Them] in *Rapporten en voorstellen betreffende den oeconomischen toestand der landbouwers in Nederland* [Reports and Proposals Concerning the Economic Condition of Farmers in the Netherlands] ('s-Gravenhage: 1912), 184–197; "Verstrekking van grond aan landarbeiders: Overzicht van de Buitenlandsche Wetgeving betreffende de bevordering van het kleingrondbezit" [Providing Land for Farm Laborers: An Overview of Foreign Laws Concerning the Promotion of Small Land Ownership], in *Bijlagen van verschillende aard behoorende bij de Rapporten en voorstellen betreffende den oeconomischen toestand der landarbeiders in Nederland* [Appendices of Different Sorts Pertaining to the Reports and Proposals Concerning the Economic Condition of Farm Laborers in the Netherlands] ('s-Gravenhage, 1909), 105–141; *Rapporten en voorstellen landarbeiders* [Reports and Proposals for Rural Laborers] (1909), 221–228.

PART TWO

Community Development and Family Migration

5. Dutch Catholic Immigrant Settlement in Wisconsin

Yda Saueressig-Schreuder

In analyzing European emigration and settlement in the United States, emphasis has traditionally been given to economic factors in both the Old and the New World.[1] Decline in subsistence in Europe and employment opportunities or land availability on the American frontier—the major "push" and "pull" factors in the emigration movement in the mid-nineteenth century—are usually considered the main factors in the emigration movement and settlement process, and social relationships are often overlooked.[2] This study, by focusing on individual emigrant households, will demonstrate that family contact and information exchange played a significant role in the choice of initial settlement in the New World.

A few years ago, research conducted among nineteenth century Swedish immigrants has clearly demonstrated the importance of family and kin in the emigration process and settlement choice on the midwestern frontier.[3] Robert C. Ostergren and John G. Rice first introduced the concept of diffusion in the emigration process and described the rural midwestern Swedish immigrant settlement as a "community transplanted" suggesting close ties between local communities on both sides of the Atlantic.[4] Usually, census records, church records, or population registers, as well as marriage records and records of other vital events, form the principal sources of information in emigration and immigrant settlement research. However, the quality of these demographic data sources differ substantially from one group to another. Swedish demographic data sources are of exceptional quality and allow for individual family level links to be analyzed. Dutch historical demographic records are equally suitable for analysis of family and kinship links between Old World areas of origin and New World areas of destination and form a good data source for emigration research.

A term frequently used in this kind of emigration research is "chain migration." Chain migration assumes contact between initial settlers in areas of destination in the New World and family members, relatives, neighbors, and friends left behind in the Old. Information about employment, availability of land, and social conditions in the New World, channeled through these contacts, often stimulated further emigration from particular source areas and led to clustering of regional, local, and sometimes kin groupings in immigrant settlements in the New World. In addition, this process of migration implies some kind of self-generating effect once initial immigration and settlement has taken place.

Households from three municipalities in northeast Noord-Brabant were considered in the analysis of the migration pattern and frontier settlement process (Figure 5.1). The municipalities include Uden, Zeeland, and Boekel, in the area of heaviest concentration of emigration from the southern provinces in the mid-nineteenth century. Almost all the emigrants were Catholic and many of them settled in the Fox River Valley in east-central Wisconsin. Initial settlement of Dutch Catholic immigrants in the area had followed the initiative of Father Theodorus van den Broek, a Dominican priest-missionary who had lost his Indian parish at Little Chute to the federal Indian removal program in the 1840s.[5] Emigration from Noord-Brabant to the Fox River Valley in Wisconsin continued throughout the second half of the nineteenth century and into the twentieth century. The study will concentrate on the period 1848–1870 when emigration was heaviest and the emigration flow was primarily directed towards the Wisconsin frontier (Figure 5.2).

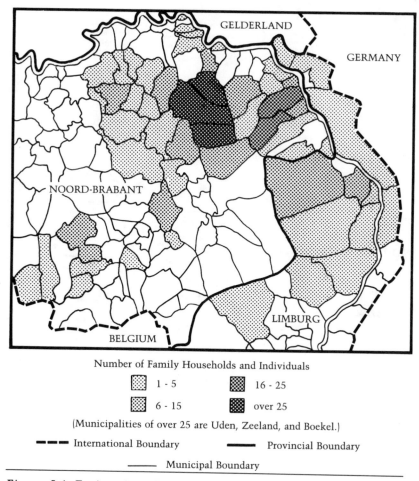

Number of Family Households and Individuals

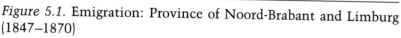

<figure>

	1 - 5		16 - 25
	6 - 15		over 25

</figure>

(Municipalities of over 25 are Uden, Zeeland, and Boekel.)

- - - International Boundary   ▬▬ Provincial Boundary

─── Municipal Boundary

Figure 5.1. Emigration: Province of Noord-Brabant and Limburg
(1847–1870)

Source: Dutch emigrant records, province of Noord-Brabant, 1847–1870.

Sources and Methodology

In order to analyze the patterns of emigration and the frontier settlement process, several sources were used. First, Dutch
emigrant records or *Landverhuizerslijsten* were examined to establish the place of residence (municipality of origin) in the

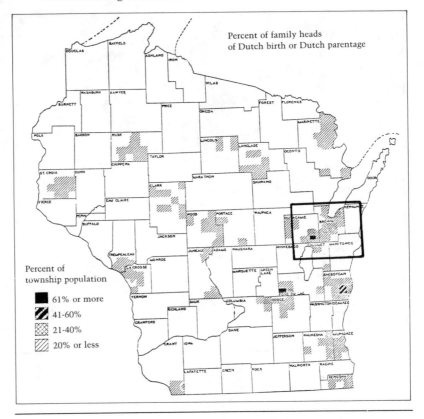

Figure 5.2. Dutch Immigrant Settlement in Wisconsin

Source: *Retabulated 1905 State Census of Wisconsin*, G. W. Hill, Department of
Rural Sociology, University of Wisconsin-Madison.

Netherlands.[6] Since the Dutch emigrant records were composed
of information obtained from municipal registers, population registers or *Bevolkingsregisters* could be used to determine household composition and the names of both spouses.[7] In addition,
marriage records provided information on the places of birth and
names of the parents of both spouses. Since the population registers formed the basis for the emigrant registration as well as the
main register in which all vital events were recorded, a direct link
between the three sources could be established. The sources together, aided sometimes by information obtained from birth and

death records, permitted tracing family links, including in-laws, through two or three generations. Finally, by linking emigrant records with U.S. population census records, initial place of residence in Wisconsin could be determined.[8] The study covers three census years (1850, 1860, and 1870), and the total number of census-linked households was 93, or 37 percent of the total of 251 emigrant households listed in the emigrant records and population register for the three municipalities.

On the basis of the linked record sources, kinship diagrams of emigrant households were drawn (Figures 5.3, 5.4, and 5.5). Each solid dark symbol identifies one emigrant household or individual found in the population census of Wisconsin for Outagamie or Brown county.[9] The outlined symbols identify emigrants who appeared in the population register but were not identified in the census registers. Lines between symbols indicate family relationships of the first order (brothers, sisters, sons, daughters, and parents). During the early years (1848–1850), a large majority of the emigrants chose as area of destination the Fox River Valley. In later years, especially after 1865, destination was more diverse.[10] The diagrams of the migration pattern among emigrants from the three municipalities show that a new wave occurred every two or three years (1848, 1850, and 1853, in the case of Uden). Considering time involved in information exchange and travel, two or three years seems a reasonable time for new emigration to take place.

Kinship and the Process of Emigration

In as far as "push" factors are concerned, a subsistence crisis in agriculture and a decline in rural industry may be considered the main economic reasons for emigration. Northeast Noord-Brabant was a backward and rather isolated part of the Netherlands in the mid-nineteenth century. The area was mostly devoted to small-scale farming and cottage industry such as shoemaking and linen and woollen industry which employed farm labor during the off-season. During the second half of the nineteenth century, the handicraft production was replaced by factory production and

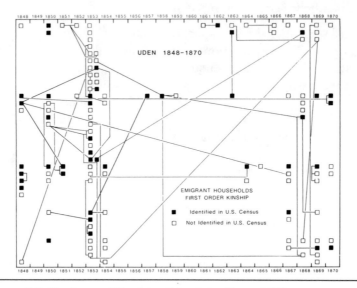

Figure 5.3. Emigrant Kinship, Municipality of Uden

Sources: Dutch emigrant records, population registers, and marriage records, municipality of Uden, 1848–1870.

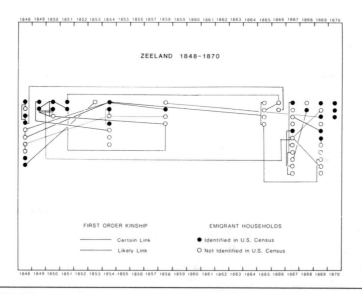

Figure 5.4. Emigrant Kinship, Municipality of Zeeland

Sources: Dutch emigrant records, population registers, and marriage records, municipality of Zeeland, 1848–1870.

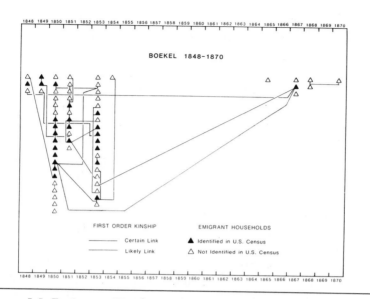

Figure 5.5. Emigrant Kinship, Municipality of Boekel

Sources: Dutch emigrant records, population registers, and marriage records, municipality of Boekel, 1848–1870.

since farming was mostly small-scale and of a subsistence kind, it did no longer provide a living for the growing population. Since the introduction of the potato crop in the early nineteenth century, landholdings had been divided repeatedly, reducing the average farm to a size of five to eight hectares by mid-century. Increasingly, family households had become dependent on potato cultivation and additional income had to be secured from home spinning and weaving, and shoemaking. When the potato disease struck in 1845 and 1846 and a simultaneous decline in the traditional rural industry occurred as a result of the introduction of manufactured cotton textiles, subsistence in the area was severely undermined.[11]

Emigration was one response under these circumstances. The large number of departures for 1853 were most likely the result of deteriorating subsistence conditions in the source area. Local municipal reports for Uden show a decline in linen weaving and other home industries, as well as increasing poverty among small subsistence farmers in the area.[12] According to local tax assessment records and social status classifications in the emigrant records, many of the emigrants of that year were of lower socio-economic status. Relatively few were identified in the 1860 U.S. census records, which may indicate that they had moved elsewhere. While many of the 1853 emigrants had direct or indirect links with earlier emigrants, far fewer had links with later emigrants, suggesting that the group had not established itself as well as earlier immigrants and that continuing emigration depended in part on the success or failure of predecessors.

The pattern of emigration shows distinct fluctuations with high rates prevalent during the late 1840s and early 1850s. A significant drop in emigration occurred in the late 1850s and early 1860s during a period of economic depression (1857–1858) and the Civil War (1861–1865) in the United States (Figure 5.6). Simultaneously, conditions in the Netherlands improved somewhat as the linen textile production revived briefly during the 1860s when the cotton industry was constricted by the limited supply and high prices of raw cotton from the United States during the Civil War period. Some Dutch immigrants returned to the Netherlands in 1857, and in 1858 a decline in emigration was observed by Dutch officials.[13] After a ten-year lapse, emigration resumed from the municipalities of Uden and Zeeland. In both cases kinship links could be established with earlier emigrants.

Sometimes return visits to the Netherlands triggered a new wave of emigration. Thus, for instance, Martinus Jansen from the municipality of Uden returned to the Netherlands for a visit in 1863 after a ten-year stay in Wisconsin. In 1864 he reported his second departure to Wisconsin, and during the next five years, several emigrants from Uden followed. Arnold Verstegen from the municipality of Zeeland is another example. He came to Wisconsin in 1850 and paid his first return visit to the Netherlands in 1861 at the start of the Civil War. Although the war apparently delayed emigration, his second return in 1865 resulted in another wave of emigration from the municipality of Zeeland.[14]

Part of a family or household often emigrated first to be followed by other members later on. Sometimes one son might emigrate while the parents followed; in other instances the reverse was the case. Among spouses it was rather common for the husband to lead the way and for the wife to depart a year later. Temporary stop-overs were sometimes made in Boston, New York,

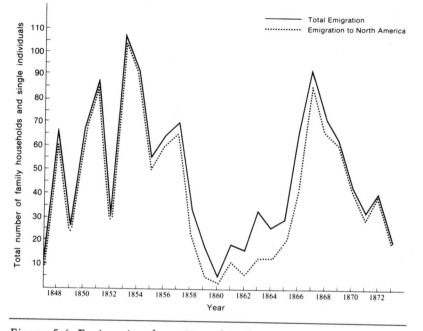

Figure 5.6. Emigration from Noord-Brabant

Source: Dutch emigrant records, province of Noord-Brabant, 1848–1872.

Philadelphia, and Buffalo; cities along the route to the Midwest.[15]

In the earlier years (1848, 1850, and 1853), most emigrants left in larger groups, while later emigration was generally in the form of individuals or households travelling in small groups. The population registers established the exact date of departure, which demonstrated that these years formed mass migrations. Among the 35 emigrant households reported for 1850 from the three municipalities, 27 left in April and recorded as date of emigration either April 18, 19, or 20 (municipality of Uden), and April 20 (municipality of Boekel). Among the emigrants leaving in 1853 from Uden, a large majority left in March of that year. Emigration after the Civil War more often involved individual households, as is evidenced from the wide diversity in month of departure. It is suggested that emigration during the later years was of a chain migration type, with individuals joining family in the United States.[16]

From this pattern of migration, we would expect settlement

to take place in some kind of clustered fashion. If emigration was channeled through kinship, initial settlement would also most likely occur along kinship lines, assuming that newcomers were aided in employment and housing by relatives and friends. Under frontier conditions, with ample availability of land and little in the way of institutional support, we might therefore see a strong concentration of immigrant settlement derived from particular locales in the Netherlands.

Kinship, Emigration, and the Settlement Process

The state of Wisconsin experienced rapid development during the middle decades of the nineteenth century. As western lands were opening up and being made accessible to East Coast and foreign markets, towns abounded with activities in road construction, canal building, and other sorts of commercial and local industrial activities. Agricultural development followed, and within fifteen years of settlement, Wisconsin had become specialized in wheat production. Prior to the Civil War, most of the transportation was overland and along water routes. As transportation routes developed, the state became more and more accessible to new settlers. Among these settlers were immigrants from northwestern Europe. European immigrants usually settled on the land. Small, often church centered immigrant communities evolved which continued to attract immigrants from the same source areas in the Old World for several decades. In time, members of the original group might move on to the western frontier or to the nearby industrial centers, but newcomers often continued to be drawn to the older settlements where they would find relatives and friends from their own villages in the Old World.

That emigration and settlement were part of the same process, which involved contact between relatives in areas of origin and areas of destination, has been clearly demonstrated in the Swedish case. Using birthplace information for Lutheran church members, Ostergren established that midwestern Swedish immigrants in rural settlements often originated from the same parishes in Sweden.[17] Social cohesion was usually maintained

despite geographical mobility, and group networks were often re-
stored after fragments had initially broken off. At the end of the
nineteenth century, Swedish immigrant communities were
found in several midwestern and Great Plains states, and a string
of settlements could usually be traced back to particular source
areas in Sweden.

Irene Hecht has also observed the existence of group migration and settlement in the case of Dutch Catholic immigrants in
Oregon.[18] Dutch immigrants had settled there after 1875 and had
come directly from Wisconsin. The occurrence of a hereditary genetic skin disease among members of the group established the
Oregon community as a genetic isolate.[19] Using family reconsti-
tution techniques in reconstructing kinship systems, her study
revealed that members of the group had been closely related prior
to migration to the Oregon frontier and that many originated
from several related families in the Netherlands.

The kinship data from the municipalities of Uden, Zeeland,
and Boekel permitted reconstruction of initial settlement and
kinship patterns among Dutch immigrants in Wisconsin for the
three census years 1850, 1860, and 1870. It appeared that initial
Dutch settlement concentrated in Kaukauna township (Little
Chute) and Holland township, with only a few immigrants living
in other townships along the Fox River. The Little Chute immigrant concentration represented mostly emigrants from other
municipalities in Noord-Brabant. In fact, there were no Uden residents among the Little Chute settlers and only two emigrant
families from the municipality of Zeeland. Uden and Zeeland residents, instead, concentrated in Hollandtown, while emigrants
from the municipality of Boekel formed a more scattered group.
During the next few decades, settlement becomes more dispersed, with a growing number of Dutch settlers concentrating in
Scott and Freedom townships in 1860 and De Pere township in
1870.[20] Overall, Dutch immigrant settlement focused on the Fox
River and expanded toward the lower end of the valley (Green
Bay) after the Civil War (Appendix 5.A1).

The distribution of initial settlement suggests that migration from the same municipality was not strictly directed to one
particular immigrant settlement in the Fox River Valley. Instead,
emigrant families from different municipalities lived inter-

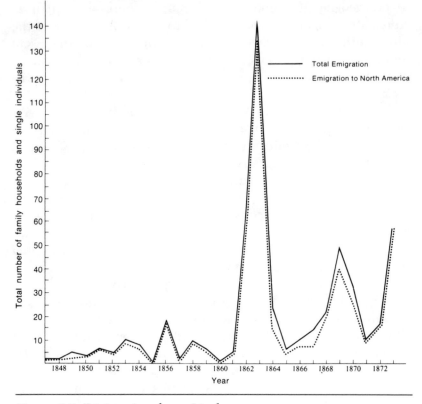

Figure 5.7. Emigration from Limburg

Source: Dutch emigrant records, province of Limburg, 1848–1872.

spersed. Newly arriving immigrants after the Civil War concentrated in the De Pere area in the lower end of the Fox River Valley. Most of these immigrants derived from the province of Limburg. Large scale emigration from Limburg did not start until after 1860, and thus migration was not necessarily directed by New World sources of information derived from relatives or neighbors (Figure 5.7). The Fox River Valley thus developed two slightly separated Dutch immigrant settlement clusters. While immigrants from the province of Noord-Brabant were interspersed among immigrants from the province of Limburg in the lower part of the Valley, no Limburg immigrants settled among the original Noord Brabant settlers in Kaukauna township.[21]

    While Dutch immigrant settlements in the Fox River Valley

did not demonstrate a clear relationship to regional or municipal origins, kin relationships, on the other hand, were quite important in the settlement process. By tracing immigrant kinship networks and by analyzing immigrant settlement, it was possible to isolate kin-group clusters among township populations (Figure 5.8).

Both Holland township and Scott township received a disproportionate share of emigrants from the municipalities of Uden, Zeeland, and Boekel. Both townships were settled by Dutch immigrants prior to 1850. The Hollandtown settlement was founded alongside Little Chute in 1848 and continued to attract immigrants from the three municipalities until the Civil War. The Scott township settlement started somewhat later and developed alongside the Convent of the Holy Cross, established in 1857. The majority of Dutch settlers in both townships were farmers and farm laborers. In the case of Holland township, many were of well-to-do socioeconomic background; the Scott township settlers were generally less well-to-do. Both settlements stagnated in their growth after the Civil War.[22]

The diagrams show lateral as well as vertical links. Not only did family units related through kin emigrate in the same year and settle alongside each other in particular townships, but later arrivals also followed kin in their choice of settlement. This pattern was most prevalent among Hollandtown settlers. In fact, very few unrelated immigrant families resided there. In Scott township, the pattern was less distinct; however, several links existed among immigrant families. While no other immigrant settlements were analyzed in a similar fashion, it is likely that in more regionally heterogeneous immigrant settlements kingroups also acted as the building stones of frontier society.

Summary and Conclusions

Like the Swedish demographic data sources, Dutch sources are exceptionally detailed and rather unique for emigration and immigration research. By focusing on individual emigrant households, it was possible to analyze the social interactive aspects of the emigration movement and settlement process among a group

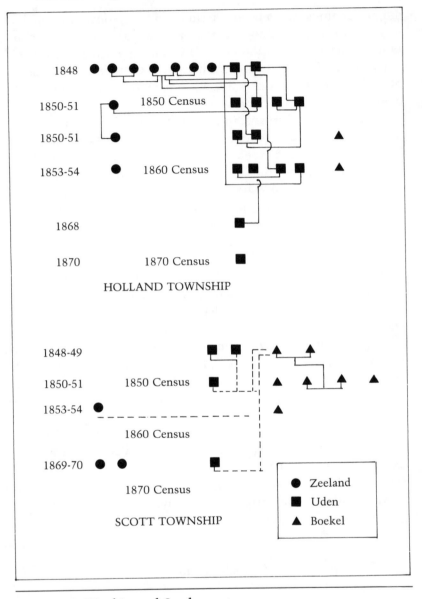

Figure 5.8. **Kinship and Settlement**

Source: Linked data set.

of Dutch Catholic immigrants in Wisconsin. First-hand knowledge about conditions in the United States obtained through contacts with friends, former neighbors, and relatives who had emigrated earlier, was a significant factor in the decision to emigrate. In nineteenth century society, personal letters and in particular return visits from earlier emigrants formed the main sources or information.

At the local scale, the volume and timing of emigration showed short-term emigration waves separated by two or three years, which can be explained by the time it took for information to be exchanged. The ten-year lapse or long-term wave from the mid-1850s to the mid-1860s can best be explained by the economic and political conditions in the United States. During the economic depression and Civil War period, prospective immigrants were discouraged from emigrating, and consequently a sharp drop in emigration occurred after 1857. The resumption of emigration after the Civil War again showed the significance of kin relationships in the emigration movement. However, mass migrations like those of the early 1850s were replaced by chain migration thereafter.

The findings suggest that kinship rather than regional or municipal origin formed the main factor in the settlement process. Whereas Dutch immigrant township populations were sometimes rather varied in geographical origins, kin or family relationship played a significant role in the choice of residence among newly arriving immigrants. Lack of institutional support and unfamiliarity with the new environment in general, probably explain why family relationships were so important. As new immigrants arrived, they were most likely assisted by other family members in finding housing and work and in purchasing farmland. Thus, proximity in residence would not seem totally surprising.

Since this aspect of the emigration movement and settlement process has so often been overlooked, the implications have never been fully considered. For instance, Oscar Handlin described the immigrant as *The Uprooted*, implying that social cohesion was lost as soon as the New World was reached. The pattern analyzed here suggests a very different immigrant experience. Instead of being uprooted, newly arriving immigrants usually were taken in by members of the same community or family group, and we may assume that traditional patterns of conduct were carried on for some time.

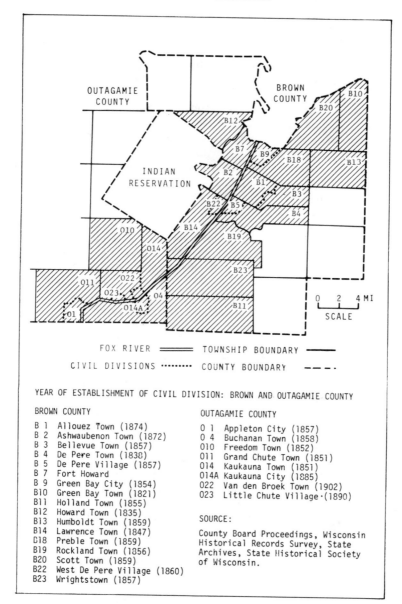

FOX RIVER ═══ TOWNSHIP BOUNDARY ────

CIVIL DIVISIONS ·········· COUNTY BOUNDARY ──── ·

YEAR OF ESTABLISHMENT OF CIVIL DIVISION: BROWN AND OUTAGAMIE COUNTY

BROWN COUNTY

B 1   Allouez Town (1874)
B 2   Ashwaubenon Town (1872)
B 3   Bellevue Town (1857)
B 4   De Pere Town (1838)
B 5   De Pere Village (1857)
B 7   Fort Howard
B 9   Green Bay City (1854)
B10   Green Bay Town (1821)
B11   Holland Town (1855)
B12   Howard Town (1835)
B13   Humboldt Town (1859)
B14   Lawrence Town (1847)
B18   Preble Town (1859)
B19   Rockland Town (1856)
B20   Scott Town (1859)
B22   West De Pere Village (1860)
B23   Wrightstown (1857)

OUTAGAMIE COUNTY

0 1   Appleton City (1857)
0 4   Buchanan Town (1858)
010   Freedom Town (1852)
011   Grand Chute Town (1851)
014   Kaukauna Town (1851)
014A Kaukauna City (1885)
022   Van den Broek Town (1902)
023   Little Chute Village ·(1890)

SOURCE:

County Board Proceedings, Wisconsin
Historical Records Survey, State
Archives, State Historical Society
of Wisconsin.

Appendix 5.A1. Township and Reference Map, Brown and Outagamie County, Wisconsin

Source: County Board Proceedings, Wisconsin Historical Records Survey, State Archives, State Historical Society of Wisconsin.

Notes

1. See, for instance, Brinley Thomas, *Migration and Economic Growth: A Study of Great Britain and the Atlantic Economy* (London: Cambridge University Press, 1954).

2. For a critique of Thomas's study, see Sune Åkerman, "Theories and Methods of Migration Research," in H. Runblom and H. Norman (eds.), *From Sweden to America: A History of the Migration* (Minneapolis: University of Minnesota Press, 1976), 19–75.

3. See, for instance, Sune Åkerman, Bo Kronborg, and Thomas Nilsson, "Emigration, Family, and Kinship," in Rob Kroes (ed.), *American Immigration, Its Variety and Lasting Imprint* (European Contribution to American Studies, I, Amsterdam, 1979), 32–47.

4. John G. Rice and Robert C. Ostergren, "The Decision to Emigrate: A Study in Diffusion," *Geografiska Annaler* 60, Ser. B. (1978): 1–15; and Robert C. Ostergren, "A Community Transplanted, the Formative Experience of a Swedish Immigrant Community in the Upper Middle West," *Journal of Historical Geography* 5, No. 2 (1979): 189–212.

5. For a brief description of the Dutch Catholic immigrant settlement in the area, see Henry S. Lucas, *Netherlanders in America: Dutch Immigration to the United States and Canada, 1789–1950* (Ann Arbor: University of Michigan Press, 1955), 213–225, 522–528.

6. Swierenga's lists were used in this study. See Robert P. Swierenga, *Dutch Emigrants to the United States, South Africa, South America, and Southeast Asia, 1835–1880: An Alphabetical Listing of Household Heads and Independent Persons*, (Wilmington, Del.: Scholarly Resources, Inc., 1983).

7. For a discussion about the population registers, see Mike L. Samson, *Population Mobility in the Netherlands, 1880–1910: A Case Study of Wisch in the Achterhoek* (Uppsala, Acta Universitatis Upsaliensis, 1977), 44–46, 115–116.

8. For a general discussion about problems of record linkage, see E. A. Wrigley (ed.), *Identifying People in the Past* (London: Edward Arnold, 1973). For a discussion about linkage techniques used in this study, see Robert P. Swierenga and Harry S. Stout, "Dutch Immigration in the Nineteenth Century, 1820–1880: A Quantitative Overview," *Indiana Social Studies Quarterly* 28 (Autumn 1975): 14–15; and Robert P. Swierenga, "Dutch International Migration Statistics, 1820–1880: An Analysis of Linked Multinational Nominal Files," *International Migration Review* 15 (Fall 1981): 445–470.

9. See Appendix 5.A1 for a reference map of township names in Brown and Outagamie counties.

10.   Evidenced from the fact that relatively fewer emigrants were iden-
      tified in the United States censuses of the research area.
11.   The two best documented studies on the potato disease in the
      Netherlands are M. Bergman, "The Potatoe Blight in the
      Netherlands and Its Social Consequences," *International Review
      Social History* 12, No. 3 (1967): 390–431; and E. Terlouw, "De
      aardappelziekte in Nederland in 1845 en volgende jaren" [The Po-
      tato Disease in the Netherlands in 1845 and Following Years] *Eco-
      nomisch en Sociaal Historisch Jaarboek* 34 (1971): 263–308. For a
      discussion about the development of the textile industry in the
      area, see H. F. J. M. van den Eerenbeemt, *Ontwikkelingslijnen en
      Scharnierpunten in het Brabants Industrieel Bedrijf, 1777–1914*
      [Structural Development of Brabant's Industrial Enterprise,
      1777–1914] (Bijdragen tot de Geschiedenis van het Zuiden van
      Nederland, 40, Tilburg: 1977).
12.   See the annual *Gemeente Verslagen* [municipal reports] of Uden,
      1851–1855.
13.   According to the *Verslag van de Toestand der Provincie Noord-
      Brabant* [Annual Report of the Province of Noord-Brabant] ('s-Her-
      togenbosch, 1857), three emigrants returned to the Netherlands
      within a year of their departure. The annual report for 1858 ex-
      plains the decline in emigration from the province as the result of
      deteriorating economic conditions in the United States and im-
      proved conditions at home.
14.   Arnold Verstegen's visits are recorded in a number of letters sent to
      in-laws in the Netherlands during the period 1850–1880. See Mat-
      thias van den Elsen (ed.), *Letters of Arnold Verstegen* reprinted in
      the *Annals of St. Joseph* 55 (1943), and 56 (1944).
15.   Place of birth of children in the census records revealed which
      states had been stop-over places along the route to Wisconsin. Evi-
      dence from immigrant letters reported more specifically where
      members of the group had stayed behind. Among the initial emi-
      grants, arriving on the ship *Libra*, three of the eighteen households
      remained in Boston. See letter written by Verboort, from Washing-
      ton County, Oregon, dated November 23, 1897, printed in *De Gids*,
      Dec. 20, 1897.
16.   These findings very closely correspond to those for Långasjö in
      southern Småland (Sweden). Åkerman et al., "Emigration," 43.
17.   See, for instance, Robert C. Ostergren, "Prairie Bound": Migration
      Patterns to a Swedish Settlement on the Dakota Frontier," in Fre-
      derick C. Luebke (ed.), *Ethnicity on the Great Plains* (Lincoln,
      Neb.: University of Nebraska Press, 1980), 73–92; and Rice and
      Ostergren, "Decision to Emigrate," 1–15.
18.   Irene W. D. Hecht, "Kinship and Migration: The Making of an Ore-
      gon Isolate Community," *Journal of Interdisciplinary History* 8
      (Summer 1977): 45–67.

19. *Isolate* is a term used by human geneticists referring to a small, closed population in which gene frequencies are different from those found in the general population.

20. Some of the older settlements no longer attracted large numbers of new immigrants after 1860. The explanation for this pattern can probably be found in the shifting employment opportunities and the decreasing availability of land. Different directions in settlement can also be traced through local internal migration among earlier immigrants and their offspring, as documented record-linkage cases have demonstrated.

21. The immigrants from the province of Limburg all derived from the northern municipalities bordering the emigration concentration area in the province of Noord-Brabant. Among residents from the municipalities on the east side of the Peel and the municipalities of northern Limburg there were probably quite frequent contacts.

22. For a detail description of the founding of Hollandtown, see Scott Vandehey, *Wooden Shoes West: A Saga of John Henry van de Hey* (n.p., 1979), 32–38.

6. Dutch Immigrant Neighborhood Development in Grand Rapids, 1850–1900

David G. Vanderstel

The Dutch immigrants who followed the leadership of Albertus C. Van Raalte to western Michigan in the late 1840s settled in the "unpopulated regions of the interior" between the Kalamazoo and Grand rivers. It was there that Van Raalte envisioned "settlements of thousands and thousands on both rivers" where his people could "cultivate the land, find a livelihood, and deliver their families from the misery of a land and a society [The Netherlands]" that was perishing. Because of his enthusiastic dedication to the colonization effort, Van Raalte urged his co-leader, Reverend Anthonie Brummelkamp, to shepherd others to "this good land of freedom." "It is of first importance," wrote Van Raalte, "to live together [for] 'in unity there is strength.' In this there are a lot of advantages, in everything we need each other."[1]

Beginning with the initial settlement of Netherlanders in western Michigan, the state legislature approved several internal improvement projects to accommodate these new inhabitants and to assist in the development of their colonies. Influential local businessmen foresaw the commercial benefits from the new immigrant population and actively sought to attract the Dutch to the banks of the Grand River, which flowed through the growing

125

village of Grand Rapids. Despite his own efforts, the prominent lawyer and land agent John Ball failed to convince the immigrants to make their homes in the village, claiming that Van Raalte "wished to have his people settled by themselves [since] there were too many other settlers in Grand River."[2]

Markets and employment opportunities were the primary motivations for contact with the village of Grand Rapids during the early years. Immigrants traveled from the Holland *Kolonie* [Colony] to sell their goods and to secure provisions and supplies that were either substantially less expensive or unavailable in their fledgling community. Meanwhile, as a consequence of economic necessity in the late 1840s, children and young adults journeyed to Grand Rapids to search for jobs as laborers, domestics, and apprentices, thereby becoming the first Dutch residents of the village. These young workers returned home regularly with "ground meal, pork, meat, articles of clothing, pieces of furniture or even money as wages or compensation" to supplement their families' incomes and to inject valuable capital into their settlements near Lake Michigan.[3] The increased interaction between the *Kolonie* and the newly incorporated city attracted more immigrants to the young urban community and convinced them to establish their homes and associations in the Grand River valley.

The press avidly followed the steady growth of the Dutch community in Grand Rapids. In September of 1849, the *Grand Rapids Enquirer* reported "our streets have been 'taken by the Dutch.' The Hollanders have resorted here in uncommon numbers and their ox teams have made quite a caravan."[4] *De Sheboygan Nieuwsbode* of Sheboygan, Wisconsin, also observed the rapid development of the Dutch colonies in western Michigan. "Suffice it to state that in Grand Rapids there are fully one hundred Dutch families," announced the paper in 1853. Furthermore, there are "a large number of young men and young women serving as hired help or as domestics, so that the total Holland population of that city may confidently be estimated at more than 600 persons."[5]

During the following years, there were numerous indications of the expansion and maturation of the immigrant community. In 1857 Leendert D'Ooge, a prominent Dutch realtor and resident of Grand Rapids, told *Nieuwsbode* readers that there were several storekeepers and clerks who understood and communicated in the Dutch language and who served as economic and cultural intermediaries in the mixed community.[6] As the city experienced rapid growth in succeeding decades, influenced in part by the attraction of wood-related and other industries, the new demand for skilled craftsmen, machine operators, and general laborers enticed the Dutch from surrounding rural regions and directly from the Netherlands. Thus, the nucleus of a Dutch community, which was established by 1850 with the employment of the first immigrants in general labor and public works projects, expanded to such a degree as to make the Dutch a prominent segment of the Grand Rapids population during the latter half of the nineteenth century.

At the turn of the century, there were over 11,000 Dutch-born individuals in the city of 87,565 people, constituting nearly one-half of the entire foreign-born population. Consequently, Grand Rapids stood in second place behind Chicago in the number of Dutch-born residents. However, the Dutch-born segment of Grand Rapids's total population (13 percent) was the highest of any American city with a population exceeding 25,000.[7] But, why were such large numbers drawn to the city? Proximity of the Dutch colonies and the economic and occupational incentives were partly responsible. More importantly, the Dutch were brought together by the ethnocultural community maintained through chain migration, the transplantation of institutions, and communications with friends and families. By 1900 the Dutch had established twenty-three churches, twelve newspapers, Christian schools, various associations, and twelve distinct neighborhoods in the city. The fusion of these factors provided the incentives necessary to attract the Dutch to Grand Rapids and to perpetuate their community in that new location.

Concepts of Neighborhood

The experiences of immigrants in American cities have led historians and sociologists to produce studies regarding ethnic residential concentrations, which have provoked controversy and generated scholarly debates. For years, the dominant theory in urban immigrant studies was the "concentric zone model" advanced in the 1920s by Robert E. Park, Ernest W. Burgess, Louis Wirth, and others constituting the Chicago School of urban studies. According to their arguments, the city possessed five distinct zones, ranging from the central business district and areas of transition to the suburban commuter zone. Ethnic groups were forced, due to their lack of money and skills, to cluster in centralized transitional sections where abandoned structures provided cheap housing close to sources of unskilled labor. As the residents acquired skills, wealth, and a greater familiarity with American society, they would leave the old residential cluster (or ghetto), move through the various zones, and eventually scatter among the general population in the suburbs.[8] Ten years later, Paul F. Cressey also claimed that immigrant populations followed predictable patterns of residential movement through the city by advancing steadily toward the suburbs and by leaving vacant old housing for newly arrived immigrants.[9]

In the late 1960s, Sam Bass Warner Jr. and Colin Burke challenged the assumptions of their predecessors. They argued that most nineteenth century cities were not developed enough to possess a large stock of abandoned housing that would accommodate the immigrants and create a centralized ghetto. Previous research, they asserted, had not shown an awareness of or sensitivity towards the "forces other than city size and ethnic mix [which] have been at work in each city to produce considerable variations in their residential patterns."[10] Furthermore, historical and sociological work on ethnic communities had suffered seriously as a result of the strong negative connotation of the "ghetto" as proffered by Oscar Handlin in his book *The Uprooted.* Finally, Warner and Burke noted that the theories of the Chicago School implied that immigrants would settle in random fashion if they were not so pervasively affected by poverty and social disorientation. Such assertions disregarded the importance of these population clusters, which served positively to sustain the immigrants by providing cultural affinity and familiar values.[11]

What the earlier studies and many recent works obviously overlook is the meaning of "neighborhood." Theodore Caplow and Robert Forman defined a neighborhood as a cluster of families or households with a sense of local identification and unity within a physical setting. "Where the neighborhood and the interest group coincide, there will be a high degree of association. . . . 'Homogeneity' is of crucial importance in group formation," they claimed.[12] Kathleen Conzen wrote that a neighborhood "results from the intersection of area with personal characteristics" and is influenced by family cycles and the congregational instincts of the area's constituency.[13] Finally, Suzanne Keller concluded that a "neighborhood contains inhabitants having something in common [shared activities, experiences, values, loyalties]. . . . This gives them a certain collective character, which affects and reflects people's feelings about living there and the kinds of relationships the residents establish."[14]

The Dutch in western Michigan, whether in the Holland *Kolonie* or in the developing urban center of Grand Rapids, tended to reside in relative isolation with their fellow countrymen. This was apparent in the Dutch neighborhoods which arose throughout the city. What encouraged these concentrations? Did the settlements possess distinguishable characteristics? How important was the Netherlands–Grand Rapids connection in determining residential patterns? These are some of the questions which must be addressed in order to understand Dutch immigrant neighborhood development in the city of Grand Rapids during the last half of the nineteenth century.

Characteristics of Dutch Immigrant Neighborhoods

The fifty-three Dutch households enumerated in the 1850 census did not share common provincial origins and did not cluster with their own kind as would be expected in a new immigrant settlement. However, as Grand Rapids expanded from four square miles to encompass over twenty square miles by century's end and as the number of Dutch residents steadily increased, immigrant concentrations became more noticeable in the city, primarily in the northwest and southeast sections (Table 6.1). The northwest part of Grand Rapids showed the only growth over

Table 6.1. Distribution of Dutch Households in Grand Rapids, Census Years 1860–1900 (Percentages)

Sector of Grand Rapids	1860	1870	Gain/loss	1880	Gain/loss	1900	Gain/loss	1860–1900 gain/loss
#1 Southwest (east of river)	22.7	29.3	+6.6	29.2	−0.1	22.0	−7.2	−0.7
#2 Northeast	25.0	25.8	+0.8	24.5	−1.3	17.9	−6.6	−7.1
#3 Southeast	37.0	35.0	−2.0	28.4	−6.6	32.5	+4.1	−4.5
#4 Northwest	10.2	7.1	−3.1	12.6	+5.5	22.4	+9.8	+12.2
#5 Southwest (west of river)	5.1	2.7	−2.4	5.3	+2.6	5.1	−0.2	0
Total N	216	631		1325		5259		

Source: Population Schedules for the Federal Manuscript Censuses for 1850, 1860, 1870, 1880, and 1900, hereafter referred to as the Grand Rapids Dutch Data.
Note: The 1850 distribution of 53 Dutch households is not obtainable since the city was not divided into wards at the time of the enumeration and since both city and federal records do not list place of residence.

forty years, whereas the Netherlanders residing in the southeast section constituted the largest Dutch concentration in the city (Figure 6.1).

The early population clusters spawned offspring neighborhoods in later years as a result of two principle factors: the clustering of new immigrants near the fringes of original settlements and the propagation of new church congregations, which met the spiritual and social needs of those experiencing the urbanization of Grand Rapids and the threats of Americanization. Each Dutch neighborhood possessed certain characteristics to distinguish it from the others in the city, such as provincial origins, years of emigration, occupations, among others. Hence, the neighborhood was not merely an aggregate of Netherlandic people residing on adjacent city blocks. Rather, it was a population concentration bound by some principle or common reference by which most of the residents distinguished themselves within the city.

Even though each Dutch neighborhood in Grand Rapids could easily be characterized as a "little Holland" because of the concentration of immigrant households and Dutch institutions, it would be more precise to identify each cluster as a "little Zeeland," "little Groningen," or "little Overijssel," thereby affirming the provinciality of the particular settlements (Table 6.2). Cultural homogeneity was purposeful among the Dutch. The names of towns established within the Dutch colony of western Michigan suggest the exclusive and intentional clustering of provincial and *gemeente* [municipality] populations. As these Netherlanders moved into the urban setting, established their households, and attracted fellow countrymen to their neighborhoods, they brought their local and provincial identities with them.

Nineteenth century Grand Rapids was a provincially oriented Dutch settlement with Zeelanders and Groningers comprising the predominant groups. Despite a proportional decline from the first period of migration, Zeelanders constituted nearly 40 percent of the Dutch households in the city (Table 6.3). They tended to emigrate from specific municipalities, namely Dreischor, Oud Vossemeer, Goes, Zierikzee, Oosterland, Sint Philipsland, and Ouwerkerk, most of which were located in the northern part of the province. As a result of changing migration patterns in the latter years of the century, other provincial groups formed a

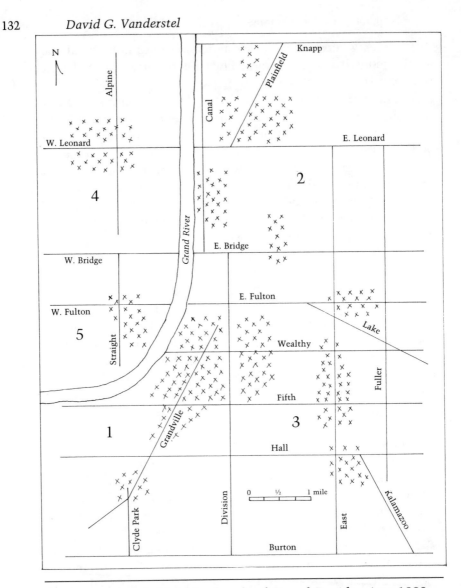

Figure 6.1. Dutch Neighborhoods of Grand Rapids, circa 1900

larger proportion of the Dutch population, most notably in the newer settlements at the city limits. Groningers, who emigrated in greatest numbers from Grijpskerk, Ulrum, 't Zandt, and Groningen, increased their representation in the city from 10 percent in 1850 to 25 percent by 1900. Their appearance in the latter decades coincided with the formation of such outlying neighborhoods as Grandville–Clyde Park, Oakdale Park, and Wealthy–East. Only in the case of the West Fulton neighborhoods of 1860 to 1880 did another provincial group—Overijsselers—comprise a majority of a neighborhood population. Although the Dutch demonstrated, in many cases, a proclivity for emigrating by their home villages, their settlement patterns in Grand Rapids did not indicate that devotion to locality. Instead, the Dutch formed neighborhoods according to broader provincial origins, which continued to attract immigrants of similar backgrounds during the later years of Dutch migration.

The periods during which the Dutch emigrated also affected their settlement patterns in Grand Rapids (Table 6.4). Through the 1870 census, the northwest sector of Grand Rapids possessed the largest proportion of new Dutch immigrants. By the 1880 enumeration, there were new migrations into the outlying residential areas of West Leonard–Alpine, Plainfield–East Leonard, and Wealthy–East streets. Twenty years later, only in three neighborhoods did immigrants from older periods of migration (1845–1879) constitute a majority of the households—West Fulton–Straight, 53 percent; North College–East Bridge, 73 percent; South Division–Lafayette, 81 percent. The latter centrally located neighborhood also possessed the highest concentration of immigrants from the 1845–1859 migration (27 percent). Of the four new residential districts founded after 1880—Fulton–Lake, Oakdale Park, Grandville–Clyde Park, and Knapp–Wartrous —an average of 68 percent of those households had emigrated during the last two decades of the century.

Considering both year of migration and region of settlement in the city, the Dutch established their households in a concentric pattern based upon the year of their arrival in the city. Families of earlier migrations tended to remain in the older established neighborhoods near the center of the city. In contrast, recent immigrants settled toward the suburban areas in recently annexed

Table 6.2. Provincial Origins of Dutch Heads of Household by Neighborhood of Settlement in Grand Rapids, 1850–1900

Neighborhood by census year	Provinces (%)											Total N linked
	Drenthe	Friesland	Gelderland	Groningen	Limburg	Noord Brabant	Noord Holland	Overijssel	Utrecht	Zeeland	Zuid Holland	
1850												
City	—	5	10	10	—	5	—	14	—	33	24	21
1860												
#1 Southwest	—	3	13	17	—	—	10	—	3	40	13	30
#2 Northeast	7	—	7	3	—	—	3	3	—	67	10	30
#3 Southeast	2	7	2	—	—	—	2	13	—	69	5	55
#4 Northwest	—	15	15	—	—	—	—	8	—	46	15	13
#5 Southwest	—	—	—	—	—	—	—	57	—	43	—	7
Total	2	5	7	4	—	—	4	10	1	59	9	135
1870												
#1 Southwest	5	2	14	28	—	1	5	5	1	30	7	109
#2 Northeast	1	8	7	9	—	2	6	1	1	51	15	118
#3 Southeast	5	6	4	16	—	—	2	5	2	50	9	163
#4 Northwest	3	—	9	15	—	—	3	6	—	61	3	33
#5 Southwest	—	15	8	—	—	—	—	46	—	23	8	13
Total	4	5	8	17	—	1	4	6	1	45	10	436

1880

#1	Fulton-Grandville	4	7	14	23	—	1	3	8	1	33	6	437
#2	Plainfield	3	6	—	3	—	—	4	—	—	61	27	33
	Canal-Division	2	3	8	5	—	—	8	2	—	64	12	124
	North College	—	17	8	17	—	—	—	—	—	42	4	12
#3	Wealthy-East	—	2	2	85	—	—	—	2	—	10	—	59
#4	West Leonard-Alpine	3	14	10	5	2	—	2	2	—	50	13	62
	West Bridge	3	9	15	33	—	—	—	9	—	27	3	33
#5	West Fulton-Straight	—	—	24	7	—	—	—	31	3	31	3	29
	Total	3	7	11	22	—	—	2	7	1	39	8	789

1900

#1	Fulton-Grandville	7	7	24	34	—	—	2	5	—	16	4	278
	Clyde Park	3	10	3	64	—	—	—	3	—	15	3	39
#2	Plainfield	—	10	1	9	—	1	1	1	1	59	16	132
	Canal-Division	1	11	8	19	—	1	4	1	1	43	8	88
	North College	3	6	15	9	—	—	6	—	—	54	6	33
	Knapp-Wartrous	—	30	—	—	—	—	—	—	—	40	30	10
#3	Division-Lafayette	1	7	7	26	—	1	5	8	2	40	3	155
	Fulton-Lake	1	2	8	8	—	1	1	1	—	60	17	167
	Wealthy-East	2	8	8	53	—	1	3	4	—	17	5	189
	Oakdale Park	10	7	—	43	—	—	—	20	—	10	10	30
#4	West Leonard-Alpine	3	20	14	15	2	—	3	1	—	43	9	312
#5	West Fulton-Straight	3	6	18	13	—	1	—	19	1	32	6	78
	Total	3	10	10	25	—	1	2	4	—	36	8	1511

Source: Grand Rapids Dutch Data; Robert P. Swierenga, *Dutch Emigrants to the United States, South Africa, South America, and Southeast Asia, 1835–1880* (Wilmington, Del.: Scholarly Resources Inc.. 1983).

Table 6.3. Dutch Immigrant Households in Grand Rapids
by Province of Origin and Migration Period, 1845–1900

Dutch Province	Migration periods							
	1845–1859		1860–1879		1880–1900		1845–1900	
	N	%	N	%	N	%	N	%
Drenthe	13	2.5	54	3.9	3	0.6	70	2.9
Friesland	35	6.8	101	7.4	81	15.3	217	9.0
Gelderland	46	9.0	140	10.2	36	6.8	222	9.2
Groningen	30	5.9	375	27.4	159	30.0	564	23.4
Limburg	—	—	1	0.1	—	—	1	0.0
Noord-Brabant	3	0.6	5	0.4	12	2.3	20	0.8
Noord-Holland	20	3.9	44	3.2	12	2.3	76	3.1
Overijssel	37	7.2	80	5.8	10	1.9	127	5.3
Utrecht	5	1.0	6	0.4	4	.7	15	0.6
Zeeland	253	49.6	492	35.9	164	31.0	909	37.7
Zuid-Holland	68	13.3	72	5.2	48	9.1	188	7.8

Source: Grand Rapids Dutch Data; Swierenga, *Dutch Emigrants to the United States*.

sections. There, they found new housing that would accommodate their families away from the growing central city and where they could avoid the potential threat to their traditions and values from the older Dutch American population. Consequently, this residential behavior disproved the assumptions posited by adherents of the ghetto and population succession theories.

The Dutch entered Grand Rapids with predominantly unskilled labor backgrounds. Occupations such as *daglooner* [day laborer], *arbeider* [laborer], and *boerenknecht* [farm hand] were most common. Skilled craftsmen, such as smiths, tailors, carpenters, and furniture makers, and a few petty proprietors, mainly shopkeepers and farmers, were also among the early immigrant population. Manual labor, however, prevailed in all neighborhoods during the last decades of the century, but the extent of skilled, semiskilled, and unskilled employment fluctuated greatly. The Dutch in early Grand Rapids were basically unskilled laborers (62 percent) who found jobs performing physical and menial tasks in public works projects. By 1900 unskilled labor constituted less than one-fourth of the Dutch work force. In contrast, the degree of skilled labor increased from 30 percent in 1850 to 41 percent by 1900, which resulted from a greater demand for specialized, trained labor in the diverse areas of manufacturing, particularly furniture production. A small group of individuals (4 percent) held upper level nonmanual occupations—professional, proprietary, clerical, and sales—in 1850; however, by 1900, 22 percent of the Dutch heads of household reported such employment, primarily as shopkeepers, retail dealers, and neighborhood grocers.

During the earliest censuses, occupational characteristics of the Dutch neighborhoods fluctuated in response to industrial and residential changes in the city. By the 1880s, neighborhoods could be differentiated on the basis of their resident labor forces (Table 6.5). The North College–East Bridge and Fulton–Grandville neighborhoods of 1880 had the largest concentrations of white collar nonmanual workers. Twenty years later, sections of the North College–East Bridge and the South Division–Lafayette neighborhoods could be identified primarily with nonmanual workers and the well-to-do Netherlanders (or Dutch Americans). They also included the oldest segments of the Dutch population, the early arrival of which allowed them to enter the job market with little competition from others and to acquire the necessary experience for later advancements.

Elsewhere in the city, the "upper class" Dutch were primarily involved as petty proprietors. They resided throughout the settlements, managing stores to serve the immediate neighborhoods or operating small businesses in nearby commercial districts. Meanwhile, other settlements could be distinguished by their manual labor force. The Fulton–Lake neighborhood contained a large group of skilled furniture workers; unskilled manual laborers inhabited the Knapp–Wartrous settlement of the extreme northeast side. Thus, even occupation added to the character of the individual settlements. This did not occur, however, in an exclusivistic manner since all but one neighborhood (Knapp–Wartrous) had representatives in the various occupational categories. Therefore, Dutch neighborhoods did not necessarily acquire the reputations for being occupationally oriented residential locations. Rather, the occupational stratification and diversification

Table 6.4. Neighborhood Distribution of Dutch Heads of Household by Migration Periods, 1845–1900

Neighborhood by census year	Migration period												N
	1845–1849		1850–1859		1860–1869		1870–1879		1880–1889		1890–1900		
	N	%	N	%	N	%	N	%	N	%	N	%	N
1850													
City	19	100											19
1860													
#1 Southwest	8	33	15	63	1	4							24
#2 Northeast	8	31	18	69									26
#3 Southeast	17	37	29	63									46
#4 Northwest	3	30	7	70									10
#5 Southwest (w. river)	4	57	3	43									7
Total	40	35	72	64	1	1							113
1870													
#1 Southwest	19	19	22	22	48	48	10	10					99
#2 Northeast	11	10	35	31	62	54	7	6					114
#3 Southeast	31	19	48	30	73	45	9	6					161
#4 Northwest	1	3	5	16	24	77	1	3					31
#5 Southwest (w. river)	8	73	1	9	1	9	1	9					11
Total	70	17	111	27	208	50	28	7					416

1880

#1	Fulton-Grandville	48	10	70	15	130	27	205	43	20	4	473
#2	Plainfield	1	3	4	10	10	26	22	58	1	3	38
	Canal-Division	12	9	26	20	39	30	45	35	6	5	128
	North College	1	7	1	7	5	36	7	50			14
#3	Wealthy-East	1	1	—	—	23	33	33	47	13	19	70
#4	West Leonard-Alpine	4	6	3	5	16	25	37	58	4	6	64
	West Bridge	3	8	5	13	7	18	22	56	2	5	39
#5	West Fulton-Straight	6	17	6	17	6	17	17	49	—	—	35
	Total	76	9	115	13	236	27	388	45	46	5	861

1900

#1	Fulton-Grandville	12	2	22	3	69	10	160	24	267	41	125	19	655
	Clyde Park	1	1	2	2	9	7	13	11	58	48	38	31	121
#2	Plainfield	3	1	9	3	37	13	65	23	131	46	37	13	282
	Canal-Division	11	4	11	4	35	14	28	12	113	47	44	18	242
	North College	2	4	9	16	14	25	15	27	13	24	2	4	55
	Knapp-Wartrous	1	2	1	2	—	—	5	13	23	58	10	25	40
#3	Division-Lafayette	17	7	46	20	47	21	76	33	36	16	7	3	229
	Fulton-Lake	11	3	14	4	51	14	64	18	144	40	72	20	356
	Wealthy-East	7	1	13	2	52	10	104	19	253	47	106	20	535
	Oakdale Park	3	3	2	2	12	10	11	9	58	50	31	26	117
#4	West Leonard-Alpine	11	1	15	2	65	7	149	16	522	57	158	17	920
#5	West Fulton-Straight	10	7	8	5	17	11	45	30	59	39	13	9	152
	Total	89	2	152	4	408	11	735	20	1,677	45	643	17	3,704

Source: Grand Rapids Dutch Data; Swierenga, Dutch Emigrants to the United States.

Table 6.5. Grand Rapids Occupations of Dutch Heads of Household by Neighborhood of Residence, 1850–1900

Grand Rapids neighborhood by census year	Nonmanual (%)					Manual (%)				Actively employed (N)
	Profes-sional	High pro-prietary	Low pro-prietary	Clerical-sales	N	Skilled	Semi-skilled	Unskilled	N	
1850										
City	—	2	2	—	2	30	4	62	45	47
1860										
#1 Southwest	—	—	7	—	3	51	12	30	40	43
#2 Northeast	2	4	—	4	5	25	19	46	43	48
#3 Southeast	3	1	6	4	11	35	9	42	66	77
#4 Northwest	—	—	9	5	3	29	—	57	18	21
#5 Southwest (w. river)	—	—	9	—	1	9	27	55	10	11
Total	1	1	6	3	23	34	12	43	177	200
1870										
#1 Southwest	1	3	7	3	27	33	7	45	152	179
#2 Northeast	1	2	6	4	20	20	11	56	141	161
#3 Southeast	3	1	5	1	22	40	6	44	188	210
#4 Northwest	—	—	2	—	1	11	7	80	44	45
#5 Southwest (w. river)	—	—	12	—	2	47	12	29	15	17
Total	2	2	6	2	72	31	8	50	540	612

1880										
#1	Fulton-Grandville	2	2	10	5	112	42	16	23	459	571
#2	Plainfield	4	—	4	—	4	13	11	67	42	46
	Canal-Division	—	1	6	2	16	29	22	40	167	183
	North College	5	—	20	—	5	30	25	20	15	20
#3	Wealthy-East	—	—	10	1	9	20	15	55	73	82
#4	West Leonard-Alpine	—	—	13	1	10	35	6	46	62	72
	West Bridge	—	2	8	2	6	53	14	20	43	49
#5	West Fulton-Straight	2	—	5	—	3	50	23	20	41	44
	Total	1	1	9	3	165	37	16	31	902	1,067
1900										
#1	Fulton-Grandville	2	3	11	4	146	44	15	21	581	727
	Clyde Park	—	—	10	3	15	53	16	18	101	116
#2	Plainfield	1	1	8	4	44	38	13	34	260	304
	Canal-Division	2	2	11	6	56	42	10	26	198	254
	North College	7	3	11	25	28	38	5	11	33	61
	Knapp-Wartrous	—	—	—	—	—	6	6	88	33	33
#3	Division-Lafayette	3	10	14	16	117	37	11	8	153	270
	Fulton-Lake	2	4	10	8	94	38	14	24	290	384
	Wealthy-East	1	3	16	6	144	32	14	28	406	550
	Oakdale Park	3	1	19	5	34	46	6	20	88	122
#4	West Leonard-Alpine	1	1	11	3	159	48	16	20	799	958
#5	West Fulton-Straight	1	2	9	7	30	45	17	19	129	159
	Total	2	3	12	6	867	41	14	23	3,071	3,938

Source: Grand Rapids Dutch Data.

of the Dutch neighborhoods demonstrated the opportunity for entering all levels of the city's economic structure, the capability of providing employment and internal services for their own people, and the ability to reside together in a neighborhood, despite one's economic status.

Characteristics of Dutch households offered yet another means by which to differentiate immigrant neighborhoods. Age of household heads was a major distinguishing factor which indicated the degree of maturity within the individual settlements. Citywide, the average age of the heads of Dutch families rose from thirty-six years in 1850 to forty-three years in 1900. The North College–East Bridge neighborhood had the oldest average age in 1900 (forty-eight years), while the South Division–Lafayette settlement averaged forty-six years. Both neighborhoods were long-established settlements, possessing characteristics of a more upper class constituency whose age and socioeconomic status contributed to the stability of the population. In other areas of Dutch concentration, the average age was in the low forties, particularly in the more recent Dutch neighborhoods.

Dutch families in 1880 and 1900 were essentially nuclear in nature (89 percent); however, particular neighborhoods could be distinguished on the basis of their resident family types (Table 6.6). Single individual households were twice as common in older neighborhoods than in the newer settlements on the city's outskirts. Nuclear families were present throughout the city, yet they had a slightly greater tendency to inhabit the more recently established neighborhoods of West Leonard–Alpine, Grandville–Clyde Park, and Oakdale Park. Extended families could be found in all Dutch settlements but were most common in neighborhoods established prior to 1880. These distributions indicated that the neighborhoods near the center of the city included an older group of people who exhibited a greater tendency to live in single individual or extended family situations. By contrast, new residential concentrations on the city's periphery consisted of a larger proportion of younger nuclear families.

The extent of home ownership characterized the level of economic success and the degree of residential stability within the Dutch settlements. Forty-eight percent of the Dutch households in 1900 owned their homes, though certain neighborhoods

Table 6.6. Dutch Family Types by Neighborhoods, 1880–1900

Grand Rapids neighborhood by census year	Family types			
	Solitary (%)	Nuclear (%)	Extended (%)	N
1880				
#1 Fulton-Grandville	3.3	87.7	9.0	578
#2 Plainfield	4.5	90.9	4.5	44
Canal-Division	3.8	84.7	11.5	183
North College	—	100.0	—	21
#3 Wealthy-East	2.5	89.9	7.6	79
#4 West Leonard-Alpine	1.4	90.3	8.3	72
West Bridge	2.0	96.1	2.0	51
#5 West Fulton-Straight	—	91.1	8.9	45
Totals	3.0	88.4	8.6	1,073
1900				
#1 Fulton-Grandville	3.1	86.4	10.6	784
Clyde Park*	1.5	91.5	6.9	130
#2 Plainfield*	.9	89.0	10.1	317
Canal-Division	2.6	89.1	8.4	274
North College	6.6	81.6	11.8	76
Knapp-Wartrous*	—	87.8	12.2	41
#3 Division-Lafayette	4.4	84.7	10.8	295
Fulton-Lake*	2.2	87.6	10.2	410
Wealthy-East*	2.5	89.7	7.8	592
Oakdale Park*	.8	91.9	7.3	124
#4 West Leonard-Alpine	1.8	92.4	5.8	1,011
#5 West Fulton-Straight	1.7	81.7	16.7	180
Totals	2.4	88.7	8.9	4,234
Neighborhood age:				
*1880–1900	1.8	90.5	7.7	2,625
pre-1880	3.2	85.8	11.0	1,609

Source: Grand Rapids Dutch Data.
Note: Asterisks indicate neighborhoods that emerged between 1880 and 1900; neighborhood names without asterisks indicate that those neighborhoods were formed prior to 1880.

were more conducive to that accomplishment (Table 6.7). Ownership was most common in the North College–East Bridge and South Division–Lafayette neighborhoods, where large concentrations of white collar workers and older immigrant families resided. However, 57 percent of the Dutch households in the Fulton–Lake neighborhood, a settlement of primarily furniture workers, and 57 percent of the Knapp–Wartrous area, whose residents were unskilled day laborers, owned their homes. These high rates among blue collar employees suggested that skilled and unskilled workers were able to save from their meager wages in order to purchase the small cottages on the fringes of the city. The lowest proportion of ownership occurred among the Dutch of the Canal–North Division area, where an absence of sufficient housing and the high concentration of industry discouraged long-term commitments to the area and resulted in higher instances of renting and greater residential instability.

Another assumption of the traditional ghetto hypothesis and population succession theory could be refuted by this evidence. If we agreed with the assertion that economic mobility

Table 6.7. Home Ownership among Dutch Heads of Household by Grand Rapids Neighborhoods, 1900

		Own		Rent		Total	
Neighborhood		N	%	N	%	N	%
#1	Fulton-Grandville	300	40.0	450	60.0	750	100.0
	Clyde Park	67	52.3	61	47.7	128	100.0
#2	Plainfield	142	46.7	162	53.3	304	100.0
	Canal-Division	101	39.3	156	60.7	257	100.0
	North-College	41	57.7	30	42.3	71	100.0
	Knapp-Wartrous	23	57.5	17	42.5	40	100.0
#3	Division-Lafayette	158	55.6	126	44.4	284	100.0
	Fulton-Lake	226	57.1	170	42.9	396	100.0
	Wealthy-East	277	48.6	293	51.4	570	100.0
	Oakdale Park	60	49.2	62	50.8	122	100.0
#4	West Leonard-Alpine	451	46.8	512	53.2	963	100.0
#5	West Fulton-Straight	85	49.4	87	50.6	172	100.0
	Totals	1,931	47.6	2,126	52.4	4,057	100.0

Source: Grand Rapids Dutch Data.

and home ownership were tied to residential location, then long-time residents would have moved from the core of the city into new residential suburbs to establish their homes. In actuality, the opposite occurred. Simply because a household experienced an improved economic status did not necessarily imply movement into the suburbs. Many of the well-to-do Dutch settled in areas immediately surrounding the central city, such as the present-day Heritage Hill district and the South Division—Madison—Wealthy area; whereas, new residential developments on the city's periphery were clearly settlements of manual laborers, petty proprietors, and recent immigrants.

The migration of Dutch families to Grand Rapids was by no means the last step in their geographical mobility since many experienced residential changes during their years in the city. The exact degree of mobility for the earlier decades is unknown since incomplete and imprecise records prevented the exact placement of households within the appropriate city blocks. Thus, the larger areal or ward units of the pre-1880 period obscure the degree of block-to-block movement that actually occurred within those areas.

Decennial mobility rates, based upon the federal manuscript census findings, indicated that 70 percent of the Dutch households who persisted between 1860 and 1870 remained in the same city ward, while one-fourth moved to another section, and 4 percent migrated into neighboring townships (Table 6.8). Residential stability was less common for the 1870–1880 persisters, as 59 percent of the households remained within the same areas during the course of the decade. The major change came with the sharp increase in the number of households leaving the city for

Table 6.8. Residential Mobility Rates of Persisting Dutch Heads of Household, 1860–1900

	1860	1870	1880
Number persisting to next census	96	362	624
Percent persisting in same sector	69.8	58.6	63.3
Percent persisting in other sector	26.0	29.6	26.1
Percent persisting to nearby townships	4.2	11.9	10.6

Source: Grand Rapids Dutch Data.

the surrounding townships. Between 1880 and 1900, there was a resurgence of residential stability within the larger ward areas which indicated the growing importance and solidification of neighborhood associations by that time.

Despite the general appearance of residential stability within the various sections of the city, it is possible to uncover greater restlessness among the Dutch households. Based upon residence according to grid cells (an area of approximately four square city blocks), 76 percent of the Dutch households persisting from 1880 to 1900 changed residential locations at some time between enumerations (Table 6.9). This contrasts drastically with the 63 percent stability achieved when considering the larger ward units. Yet, the changes of residence occurred primarily within the general vicinity of one's former residence and within the same neighborhood. Therefore, the Dutch exhibited a growing attachment to their particular neighborhoods. However, that attachment did not hinder them from seeking new housing elsewhere in the vicinity in order to accommodate their new family needs, social status, or ethnocultural and religious affiliations.

The Dutch neighborhoods were not founded or maintained solely on the basis of residential proximity, occupational similarity, or demographic factors. For life within the neighborhood to be meaningful for the residents, it had to be supported by a network of distinct institutions and associations, which would promote the common interests, values, and behavior of those people. Therefore, the neighborhood had to become more of a "community," claimed Robert Nisbet, through a "fusion of feeling and thought, of tradition and commitment, of membership and volition."[15] The ethnic or nationality identity was important for the foreign-born population since it served as an extension of the family unity and provided a "we-feeling" within the interactive network of supporting establishments and relationships.[16] Therefore, the ethnic identity as sustained by a visible system of institutions served a primary function: to provide a recognizable alternative for the immigrants to the dominant culture in order to undergird the cohesion of community in their adjustment to life in a new country.

The most important institutional establishment for the Dutch was the church. Since the First Reformed Church of Grand

Table 6.9. Proportion of Persisting Dutch Heads of Household
Demonstrating Residential Changes by Grid Cells, 1880–1900

Neighborhoods	Same cell		Different cell	
	N	%	N	%
#1 Fulton-Grandville	46	33.8	90	66.2
Clyde Park	—	—	2	100.0
#2 Plainfield	8	10.0	72	90.0
Canal-Division	16	34.8	30	65.2
North College	10	38.5	16	61.5
Knapp-Wartrous	—	—	1	100.0
#3 Division-Lafayette	42	33.6	83	66.4
Fulton-Lake	4	10.8	33	89.2
Wealthy-East	14	16.3	72	83.7
Oakdale Park	—	—	14	100.0
#4 West Leonard-Alpine	17	13.2	112	86.8
#5 West Fulton-Straight	19	42.2	26	57.8
Totals	176	24.2	551	75.8

Source: Grand Rapids Dutch Data.

Rapids was founded in 1840 by a group of non-Dutch Americans,
the pioneers of the Dutch influx immediately sought to organize
their own congregation, the Second Reformed Church, in order to
present the Gospel in their mother tongue. Appropriately, the
congregation became the center of the early Dutch community.
Frans Van Driele, alleged to be the first adult Dutch resident in
Grand Rapids, claimed that "we were all of one heart and one
mind. We recognized each other as truly being of the faithful."[17]
During the mid-1850s, as doctrinal conflicts grew within the congregation, members of the Second Reformed Church seceded to
organize the "True Protestant Reformed Church" (later known as
the Spring Street Christian Reformed Church), located at Ionia
and Island streets near Fulton Street. This church grew rapidly
since it served the heavily populated Dutch area of the city's near
southwest side. Reverend Peter Moerdyke, pastor of the First Reformed Church from 1873 to 1892, recalled that the Spring Street
Church ministered primarily to the new immigrant population
"before the 'swarming' of its members to form new churches in
different parts of the city."[18]

As new immigrant settlements arose toward the periphery of the city, resident members of the early Dutch churches became less willing to travel the long distances to worship and were more attracted to the idea of a neighborhood congregation. Likewise, recent immigrants wanted to continue to fellowship within churches that were more doctrinally true to their heritage and that often reflected their specific provincial origins. Because of their separation from the mutual support achieved through close congregational affiliations, these individuals organized committees, appealed to consistories, and overtured denominational classes to authorize the founding of new neighborhood churches. Besides the convenience of a neighborhood congregation, theological and cultural issues also inspired the formation of several church organizations, which illustrated the sensitivity of local constituents to particular doctrinal and social expectations within their church. Most common was the desire to establish an English-speaking congregation, intended primarily for the preservation of the younger generations for the Reformed Christian faith but also to assist in the assimilation of portions of the Dutch population. Many of the larger churches assumed the responsibility of organizing outreach ministries to serve the emerging neighborhoods of the city. Finally, disputes over doctrines and church practices led others to create new congregations. For example, the members of the East Street Christian Reformed Church who resided in the Fulton–Lake neighborhood, about one mile away from the church, expressed their opposition to the church's proposal to hold special group pastoral visitations for them instead of the traditional personal *huis bezoek* [family visit]. This proved again that neighborhood residents outside the immediate reach of the local church body did not want their faith to be compromised. Rather, they desired to possess their own local worshipping body with which they could more closely identify.

The other primary neighborhood institution was the Christian school. Prior to the Dutch migration, Van Raalte intended that "when a settlement is made, we shall be able to enjoy the privilege of seeing our children taught in Christian schools."[19] These words became a guiding force for those Netherlanders who established settlements in subsequent years. Consequently, Dutch Christian education began in Grand Rapids only seven

years after the first immigrants arrived. The school, housed in the
Second Reformed Church at its inception in 1855, educated immigrant children through the age of nine in primary instruction,
the Psalms, and the Dutch language. As a result of the schism in
that church, the school's leaders removed instruction to the
Spring Street Church in the heart of the large southwest side
Dutch settlement. The "Dutch school," as it became known
among Grand Rapids residents, educated children in accordance
with the covenantal responsibilities of their parents, perpetuated
Dutch culture, maintained instruction in the Dutch language,
and taught Reformed doctrines. With the increased settlement of
immigrant households during the last twenty years of the century, the Christian school movement flourished. Immigrants
opened schools in the Wealthy–East, Coldbrook, West Leonard–Alpine, and Oakdale Park neighborhoods, primarily as ex-
tensions of their local Christian Reformed Church congregations.
These institutional developments demonstrated the willingness
of Dutch residents to support such organizations in order to pass
on religious and cultural traits which were essential to perpetuate
the distinct Dutch presence in Grand Rapids.

The church, Christian schools, and other establishments
such as the press and voluntary associations helped to sustain the
common Dutch heritage shared by a growing segment of Grand
Rapids' population. Community-wide and within the separate
neighborhoods, these institutions functioned to promote a commonality in human relations among the Dutch. Most important,
however, they symbolized the religious beliefs and cultural values essential to the continuation of the Dutch settlements. Com-
menting on the significance of these factors in urban immigrant
life, Randall M. Miller and Thomas D. Marzik wrote that "religion was intertwined and imbedded in the psyche, the folklife,
the very identity of each immigrant. It gave meaning, a system of
moral values, self-definition and community to the immigrants.
It ordered their internal, private works and the world outside the
family. Thrown into close proximity with competing cultural
and linguistic groups in industrial and urban America, the immigrants turned to religion, the very bone and sinew of ethnicity, to
shore up communal ties."[20] As a central part of neighborhood
life, these institutions served as an important conduit for the

transmission of the ethnocultural and religious values that were the life blood of the individual neighborhoods and the growing Dutch community in Grand Rapids.

Conclusions

Settlement patterns of the Dutch immigrants in Grand Rapids did not adhere to the framework created by early and some contemporary urban theorists. Since Grand Rapids did not possess large quantities of old abandoned housing in the central city which could be passed on to incoming "lower class" immigrants, the Dutch could not have moved according to the predefined stages of the ghetto and population succession theories. Neither were the Dutch confined to one central immigrant enclave; rather, they inhabited most sections of the city, establishing their households in neighborhoods of predominantly Dutch, though often mixed, constituencies. Geographical and residential mobility by persisting households could not be characterized as "leap-frogging" or centrifugal in nature. On the contrary, Dutch inhabitants of the older sections tended to remain within the boundaries of the original neighborhoods. Recent arrivals from the Netherlands and other Dutch settlements of western Michigan were inclined to develop the fringe areas of existing neighborhoods or to establish new settlements on the city's periphery. Any residential transiency was essentially confined to the general vicinity of the former place of residence. Simply put, the Dutch possessed motivations other than economic or geographical reasons which influenced the formation of their settlements. Through these distinct settlements, the Dutch were able to preserve their particular kinship networks that were dependent upon family, municipality, denomination, and province.

It is difficult to uncover the precise motivations governing the residential choices of individuals within the city, although this has not prevented researchers from venturing opinions based upon generally accepted theories. Arguments posited by the Chicago School and economic determinists alike have emphasized residential developments in relation to the economic activities of the business and industrial districts of the city. Some cases of recent scholarship have argued that the factor most responsible for determining neighborhood location and choice of residence was one's place of employment. Essentially, these studies concluded that location of job opportunities and other economic considerations, such as the anticipated savings on transportation costs, were far more important in the residential decision-making process than were the promises of community founded upon shared culture, life style, and group consciousness.[21]

Even though it is true that residential patterns responded, in part, to economic factors, the formation of neighborhoods must not be accepted merely as an expression of occupational proximity and economic demands. For the Dutch who could be linked to both residence and place of employment in Grand Rapids, it was a common occurrence for these workers to travel two or more miles and even cross-town to work. This was especially true of those who inhabited the new neighborhoods on the city's outskirts. Thus, the Dutch neighborhoods were not simply individuals united by economic bonds but they were clusters of families sharing a common locality, bound by common provincial or *gemeente* origins, by year of migration, and by an ethnocultural homogeneity that was evident in the early Holland *Kolonie* and its secondary settlements.

There are scholars who have concluded that settlement by common origin occurred only within the initial wave of first-generation immigrants, whereas new social relationships and the effects of Americanization forced later immigrants to reorient their traditional behavior and attitudes to a more heterogeneous society.[22] However, others have emphasized cultural traditions and ethnocentricity as the ingredients to sustain a familiar life style in neighborhoods. "Propinquity would ease the formation of formal community organizations," concluded Kathleen Conzen, thereby "providing the threshold population necessary to support a wide range of services and activities which would further ensure the newcomer against the insecurity of his new environment."[23] This congregational affinity, characterized by national, provincial, and denominational affiliations, strengthened the Dutch identity in Grand Rapids and encouraged a local as well as a community-wide kinship network, which was central in the formation and preservation of their neighborhoods.

Neighborhoods were a central part of the lives of Dutch immigrant households in late nineteenth century Grand Rapids. For some segments of the population, these locations were places where families grew up, individuals interacted with others, residents received guidance from supportive institutions, and where distinct Dutch traditions and culture existed. For others, the ethnic neighborhood was, according to Milton Gordon, a temporary decompression chamber "in which the newcomers could, at their own pace, make a reasonable adjustment to the new forces of society, vastly different from that which they had known in the Old World."[24] Yet, the neighborhoods underwent noticeable alterations between 1850 and 1900: the demographic character of their constituents changed; provincial and *gemeente* origins fluctuated; occupational careers of the residents diversified in response to the maturation of the city; opportunities for the development of new residential areas emerged in response to the city's annexation of additional land; and institutions arose to meet the needs of the local populations. Each neighborhood was truly unique in its own right; nevertheless, all of them shared in a common Dutch heritage. The provincial, often clannish, behavior, strengthened by the immigrants' religious commitments and the communal visions instilled by their leaders, formed the core of their settlements and their distinct communities in Grand Rapids. Despite increased industrialization and urbanization of the city, the Dutch neighborhoods did not disintegrate, but they became more pronounced and more densely populated.

In conclusion, the residential behavior of the Dutch in Grand Rapids truly challenged the traditional views of immigrants in the American city. There was no evidence to indicate residential exclusion on the basis of their "Dutchness." Since the Dutch did not cluster in the city center and migrate to the suburbs, residential stimuli were certainly more complex than simple responses to economic opportunities and cheap housing. In 1847 Van Raalte had called for his followers to "live together" for in their unity they could experience strength. The Dutch made great strides in Grand Rapids during the last half of the century. They increased their numbers, became a major part of the furniture industry, and established a cultural and religious network in the city. Yet, the strength that they acquired was of a nonquantifiable nature. Even as the influx of immigrants received a certain boost from the economic and industrial developments of the city in subsequent decades, it was the greater assurance that the Dutch could reside together in neighborhoods and experience the fellowship sustained by familiar institutions and relationships which attracted them. Therefore, the Dutch sought their fellow Netherlanders, established their neighborhoods, and maintained distinct communities in Grand Rapids, thereby fulfilling the words of Van Raalte that "in everything we need each other."

Notes

1. Albertus C. Van Raalte, *Holland in Amerika; of de Hollandsche Kolonisatie in den Staat Michigan, Januari 30, 1847* (n.p., 1847). Translated from the Dutch by Rev. G. Vander Ziel under the title "Holland in America, of the Dutch Colonization in the State of Michigan, January 30, 1847," typescript (Grand Rapids: Colonial Origins Collection, Calvin College), 13, 19–23; Albertus C. Van Raalte, *Landverhuizing, of Waarom Bevoerden Wij de Volksverhuizing en Wel Naar Noord Amerika en Niet Naar Java?* (Amsterdam: Hoogkamer & Comp., 1846). Translated from the Dutch by Rev. John Ver Brugge under the title "Emigration, or Why We Promote the Emigration of People to North America and Not to Java?" typescript (Colonial Origins Collection, Calvin College), 34.
2. John Ball, *Autobiography of John Ball, 1794–1884*, compiled by Kate Ball Powers, Flora Ball Hopkins, and Lucy Ball (Grand Rapids: The Dean-Hicks Company, 1925), 170.
3. Dingman Versteeg, *De Pelgrim Vaders van het Westen. Eene Geschiedenis van de Worstelingen der Hollandsche nederzettingen in Michigan, . . .* (Grand Rapids: C. M. Loomis & Co., 1886). Translated from the Dutch by Rev. Wm. K. Reinsma under the title "The Pilgrim Fathers of the West: A History of the Struggles of the Dutch Colonies in Michigan, . . ." typescript (Colonial Origins Collection, Calvin College), 93.
4. *Grand Rapids Enquirer*, Sept. 19, 1849, 2.
5. *De Sheboygan Nieuwsbode*, Oct. 25, 1853, 2.
6. "Letter from Leendert D'Ooge," *De Sheboygan Nieuwsbode*, Apr. 28, 1857, 2.
7. U.S. Department of the Interior, *Twelfth Census of the United States, 1900: Population, Part I* (Washington, D.C.: U.S. Census Office, 1901), 796–797, 800–801.
8. Robert E. Park and Ernest W. Burgess, *The City* (Chicago: The University of Chicago Press, 1928).

9.   Paul F. Cressey, "Population Succession in Chicago, 1898–1930," *American Journal of Sociology* 44 (1938): 59, 61.

10.   Sam Bass Warner Jr. and Colin Burke, "Cultural Change and the Ghetto," *Journal of Contemporary History* 4 (1969): 185–187.

11.   Ibid., 173–187.

12.   Theodore Caplow and Robert Forman, "Neighborhood Interaction in a Homogeneous Community," *American Sociological Review* 15 (1950): 365–366.

13.   Kathleen Neils Conzen, "Patterns of Residence in Early Milwaukee," in Leo Schnore (ed.), *The New Urban History* (Princeton: Princeton University Press, 1975), 147.

14.   Suzanne Keller, *The Urban Neighborhood: A Sociological Perspective* (New York: Random House, 1968), 90.

15.   Robert Nisbet, *The Sociological Tradition* (New York: Basic Books, 1960), 47–48.

16.   E. K. Francis, "The Nature of the Ethnic Group," *American Journal of Sociology* 52 (1947): 399.

17.   Frans Van Driele, "First Experiences," in Henry S. Lucas (ed.), *Dutch Immigrant Memoirs and Related Writings* (2 vols., Assen, The Netherlands: Van Gorcum & Company, 1955), 1:338.

18.   Peter Moerdyke, "Churches and Religious Societies," in Albert Baxter, *History of the City of Grand Rapids, Michigan* (New York and Grand Rapids: Munsell & Company, 1891; reprint ed. Grand Rapids: Grand Rapids Historical Society, 1974), 335.

19.   Albertus C. Van Raalte, *Aan de Geloovigen in de Vereenigde Staten van Noord Amerika* (Amsterdam: n.p., 1846). Translated from the Dutch by Rev. John Ver Brugge under the title "To the Faithful in the United States of North America," typescript (Colonial Origins Collection, Calvin College), 6.

20.   Randall M. Miller and Thomas D. Marzik (eds), *Immigrants and Religion in Urban America* (Philadelphia: Temple University Press, 1977), xv.

21.   Caroline Golab, *Immigrant Destinations* (Philadelphia: Temple University Press, 1977); Eugene P. Ericksen and William L. Yancey, "Work and Residence in Industrial Philadelphia," *Journal of Urban History* 5 (1979): 178–179; Stephanie Greenberg, "Relationships between Work and Residence in an Industrializing City: Philadelphia, 1880," in William W. Cutler III and Howard Gillette Jr. (eds.), *The Divided Metropolis: Social and Spatial Dimensions of Philadelphia, 1800–1975* (Westport, Conn.: Greenwood Press, 1980); 162.

22.   Humbert Nelli, "Italians in Urban America: A Study in Ethnic Adjustment," in James F. Richardson (ed.), *The American City: Historical Studies* (Lexington, Mass.: Xerox College Publishing, 1972), 58–78.

23.   Kathleen Neils Conzen, *Immigrant Milwaukee, 1836–1860: Ac-*

commodation and Community in a Frontier City (Cambridge, Mass.: Harvard University Press, 1976), 148–149.

24. Milton Gordon, *Assimilation in American Life: The Role of Race, Religion and National Origins* (New York: Oxford University Press, 1964), 105.

7. Wealth Mobility in Pella, Iowa 1847–1925

Richard L. Doyle

The immigrants from the Netherlands who founded the community of Pella, Iowa in 1847 had two major motives for leaving their homeland. They had endured persecution for refusing to modify their religious beliefs to conform to those of the King's Church. More important, they suffered from a depressed economy in their native land, which was compounded by the failure of the potato crop. Some offered a religious interpretation as the cause of their economic distress but agreed that it was necessary to leave their homeland before their financial resources were depleted. Thus, these immigrants sought religious tolerance as well as economic opportunity in America.

These goals of their migration emerged when the Dutch immigrants, almost half of whom had been farmers in their native land, selected a site for their new settlement on the vacant Iowa prairie and named it Pella, or City of Refuge, after the city in TransJordan where early Christians had fled when Roman troops destroyed Jerusalem in 70 A.D. Pella was to be a colony where the immigrants could improve their economic situation, but it was also to be a colony where they would practice their religion, maintain their social values, and generally preserve their ethnic heritage.

The Prairie

To ensure the integrity of their colony, within six months after their arrival in Iowa the new settlers purchased 18,000 acres of prairie land lying between the Skunk and Des Moines Rivers in northeastern Marion County. When the first settlers arrived, these river bottoms were timbered and the trees were used for fuel, fencing and building materials. As this bottomland was cleared, however, the alluvial soil proved to be the most productive in the county. The region between the rivers is gently rolling upland prairie with enough slope to secure good drainage. Here the soil is developed on loess measuring five or more feet deep. The upper one to two feet contains a large amount of humus, making a rich, black, highly fertile top soil which can absorb and hold large amounts of water. Thus, the land which the Dutch farmers selected proved to be highly productive and suitable for general agriculture.[1]

The area around Pella also contained deposits of clay, limestone, and coal which served as the basis for extractive industry. This industry was of secondary importance, however, for the Pella community maintained an agricultural economic base through 1925. Over an extended period, the decision to emphasize farming helped the Dutch settlers to maintain their ethnic identity and affected the character and development of their colony.

The Growth of Pella

As Table 7.1 indicates, 1,057 individuals lived in the town of Pella and the surrounding rural area of Lake Prairie Township in 1850. Over the next twenty years, 1,526 new immigrants from the Netherlands settled in or near the Pella community. Americans, attracted by the local rail monopoly that Pella held between 1866 and 1875, also settled and invested in the Dutch community. Thus, by 1870, Pella's population had increased nearly fourfold to include 4,975 individuals. By that date, all but 1 percent of

Table 7.1. Population Growth and Ethnic Distribution in the Pella Community, 1847–1925

Year	Population of the Pella community		Dutch heads of household (%)	American heads of household (%)	Non-Dutch European heads of household (%)
	N	% Δ			
1847	945		92	8	
1850	1,057	11.9	91	7	2
1856	2,811	165.9	76	21	3
1860	3,391	20.6	73	26	1
1870	4,975	46.7	70	27	3
1880	5,076	2.6	75	22	3
1885	4,559	−10.2	82	15	3
1895	4,552	−0.2	82	16	2
1905	4,635	1.8	84	14	2
1915	4,667	0.7	83	15	2
1925	4,477	−4.1	86	12	2

Sources: G. A. Stout, Souvenir History of Pella, Iowa (Pella, Iowa: The Booster Press, 1922); Population Schedules for the Federal Manuscript Censuses for the years 1850, 1860, 1870, and 1880; Manuscript Censuses for the State of Iowa for the years 1856, 1885, 1895, 1905, 1915, and 1925.

the public domain in Lake Prairie Township had passed into private hands, and assessed land values exceeded ten dollars per acre, thus making it too expensive for most new arrivals or the sons of settlers already in Pella to purchase. This situation led some of Pella's residents to found a new Dutch colony in Sioux County, Iowa, and others to move beyond the boundaries of Lake Prairie Township to where cheaper land was still available.

Because of the depletion of the supply of farmland, rapid growth in Pella came to an end in 1870. Over the next decade, the population did show a modest rise but then entered a period of decline which lasted until 1895. Until near the end of this second period of Pella's development, farming dominated the local economy. In 1885, 53 percent of the work force was directly employed in agriculture, but by 1895, that proportion had fallen to 48 percent.

Although farming continued as the foundation of Pella's economy, the Dutch settlers began to place a greater emphasis on the urban sector of their work force. New jobs created by the modest business and industrial development that occurred after 1895 led to a very moderate rise in the population which was eventually checked by the economic depression of the early 1920s. By 1915, the proportion of Pella's workers employed in urban occupations had risen to 61 percent of the work force, only to fall slightly to 59 percent in 1925 as more urban than rural workers left the community during the post–World War I depression. Thus, the period between 1895 and 1925 marks a third stage in the development of the Dutch community.

The People of Pella

The significant feature of the change that occurred in Pella, especially after 1870, is that it was not dramatic. During the frontier period, rapid growth was expected, but after 1870, stability became the dominant feature of the Dutch colony. This stability can be seen not only in the lack of major changes in the population but also in the success that the Dutch settlers had in maintaining a homogeneous Christian community. As Table 7.1 indicates, in 1850, 91 percent of the heads of household in Pella were

Dutch, but because of interrupted migration from the Netherlands during the business panic of 1857 and the Civil War and continued American settlement in the community, that proportion fell to 70 percent in 1870. After 1870, the trend was reversed so that by 1925, 86 percent of Pella's household heads were of Dutch descent.

Furthermore, 86 percent of the heads of household in Pella in 1925 were affiliated with a Christian church. While this figure is somewhat less than the 94 percent level of church affiliation in 1895, the first year in which all household heads rather than only those who persisted in the community can be considered, it nevertheless represents a significant majority and demonstrates that the founders of the Dutch colony had indeed been able to transmit their religious values to their children and grandchildren.

The attitude which the people of Pella had toward their community is expressed most clearly in their lack of geographic mobility. Since more than half of the workers in other nineteenth-century communities usually left within ten years after they had arrived,[2] geographic persistence among Pella's workers provides another example of the essential stability of the Dutch community. Never more than 38 percent of all heads of household left Pella between any two consecutive census years through 1915, as Table 7.2 shows. Between 1915 and 1925, however, that proportion rose to 43 percent when workers sought opportunity elsewhere because of the depressed local economy. Largely, it was the non-Dutch residents who were most prone to move away. Among the Dutch heads of household who had settled in Pella, only 44 percent left the community before their death or before 1925. However, 80 percent of the Americans and 72 percent of the non-Dutch Europeans who had lived in Pella before 1925 eventually moved from the community.

Yet another example of the stable character of the Dutch colony was the reluctance of its workers to change jobs. Of all heads of household who had found employment in Pella prior to 1925, only 19 percent changed occupations during their average thirteen-year tenure in the community.[3]

Thus, social stability remained the hallmark of the colony which the Dutch immigrants had established on the Iowa prairie. Because these conservative farmers and craftsmen were slow to

Table 7.2. Percentage of Residents in the Pella Community Present in Consecutive Census Years

Years	1850	1856	1860	1870	1880	1885	1895	1905	1915	1925
1850	100	84	77	56	33	32	13	4	0	0
1856		100	85	60	41	38	19	7	1	0
1860			100	66	47	44	26	13	5	1
1870				100	62	54	33	19	8	3
1880					100	77	52	34	20	11
1885						100	66	44	27	15
1895							100	67	46	28
1905								100	68	44
1915									100	57
1925										100

Sources: Population Schedules for the Federal Manuscript Censuses for the years 1850, 1860, 1870, and 1880; Manuscript Censuses for the State of Iowa for the years 1856, 1885, 1895, 1915, and 1925.

change their habits does not mean, however, that they did not prosper. Of all the heads of household who worked in Pella before 1925, almost three-fourths were able to acquire property, and while they remained in the community they often saw the value of that property increase.

Prosperity in Pella

An indication of the prosperity of the Pella community can be gained by tracing the changes in the total wealth and in the median wealth held by a sample of the working population. Wealth is defined as the combined value of real and personal property identified in the Marion County tax lists converted to constant 1853 dollars to control for inflation.

Table 7.3 indicates that in the first period of Pella's rapid economic development from 1853 until 1871, the size of the work force increased by 232.6 percent, which was less than half of the 488.1 percent rise in the amount of wealth controlled by Pella's workers. Also during this period, the median wealth in the community rose by 84.1 percent, from $289 to $532, and the percentage of workers holding no property fell from 18.5 percent of the work force in 1853 to 15.7 percent in 1871.

In the second period, between 1871 and 1890, when farming almost totally dominated the local economy, the number of workers in Pella rose by 11.8 percent, but the total amount of wealth they controlled increased by 128 percent. Also by 1890, half of the workers in the community held property valued at $675. During this second period, however, the number of locally born young adults entering the work force for the first time increased. Because these young adults had had little opportunity to acquire wealth, the proportion of workers holding no property doubled. Most of these young workers, however, went on to acquire wealth as their tenure in the work force lengthened.

The years between 1890 and 1925 mark the third stage of development, when the people of Pella began to place greater emphasis on the business and industrial sector of their economy. Because of the demand for farm products which generated higher prices during World War I and the economic depression that fol-

Table 7.3. Wealth Controlled by the Work Force in Pella, Iowa, 1853–1925

Tax list years	Wealth in sample population ($)	Percentage of change	Median wealth ($)	Percentage of change	Individuals holding no wealth		Sample Worker population [a] (N)	Percentage of change
					N	%		
1853	71,532		289		17	18.5	92	
1871	420,699	488.1	532	84.1	48	15.7	306	232.6
1890	959,018	128.0	675	26.9	114	33.3	342	11.8
1925	1,078,414	12.4	1,183	75.3	62	16.1	384	12.3

Sources: Population Schedules for the Federal Manuscript Censuses for the years 1850, 1860, 1870, and 1880; Manuscript Censuses for the State of Iowa for the years 1856, 1885, 1895, 1905, 1915, and 1925; Marion County Tax Lists for the years 1853, 1871, 1890, and 1925.

[a] Retired workers are included in the sample population.

lowed the war, this was also a period in which the wealth of the Pella community and the size of its work force fluctuated. Nevertheless, between 1890 and 1925, Pella's work force increased in numbers by 12.3 percent, and the total wealth that workers controlled increased by 12.4 percent. Because unpropertied workers were quicker to leave the community during economically depressed times than were their property-holding counterparts, the proportion of workers holding no wealth fell to 16.1 percent of the work force. This exodus also led to a 75.3 percent increase in the median wealth from $675 in 1890 to $1,183 in 1925. While these figures on median wealth may seem very low today, it should be remembered that the median annual income in Pella in 1914 was only $575, while the median wealth in 1915 was $1,179. Thus, those at the midpoint of Pella's wealth structure in 1915 held property worth what their income would be over two years.

Wealth Mobility in Pella

Because it deals directly with individuals as well as the distribution of wealth in the community, a better way to gauge the economic success of Pella's workers is to divide the total wealth recorded in the tax lists for each tax year into ten equal parts or decile ranks and then measure the movement of workers over time between decile ranks.[4]

Table 7.4 displays a summary of mobility between wealth decile ranks for workers who persisted in the community during the inter-tax list periods. At least half and usually 60 percent of those workers experienced wealth mobility in each of the several periods between 1853 and 1925. The only exception was the short period between the 1886 and 1890 lists, when only 39 percent of the workers were mobile. However, if mobility is measured between 1879 and 1890, 58 percent of Pella's workers saw their economic status change. As would be expected, it was easier for Pella's citizens to improve their economic condition during the early years of rapid growth when public land was still available and the town held a regional monopoly on rail transportation. Between 1853 and 1860, 54.8 percent of Pella's workers moved up in

Table 7.4. Summary of Wealth Mobility between Decile Ranks in Pella, Iowa, 1853–1925

Years	Downward mobility			Mean distance moved (ranks)	Upward mobility			Mean distance moved (ranks)	Gross mobility		Persistence in rank		Persistence in community
	N	%	(%)[a]		N	%	(%)		N	%	N	%	N
1853–1860	9	10.7	(16.4)	1.3	46	54.8	(83.6)	1.4	55	65.5	29	34.5	84
1860–1871	27	17.9	(25.2)	2.0	80	53.0	(74.8)	2.7	107	70.9	44	29.1	151
1871–1879	80	31.5	(49.7)	1.7	81	31.9	(50.3)	1.6	161	63.4	93	36.6	254
1879–1886	69	27.5	(53.1)	1.5	61	24.3	(46.9)	1.8	130	51.8	121	48.2	251
1886–1890	38	12.6	(32.8)	1.1	78	25.9	(67.2)	1.5	116	38.5	185	61.5	301
1890–1904[b]	51	28.2	(43.2)	2.4	67	37.0	(56.8)	2.4	118	65.2	63	34.8	181
1890–1910	13	20.3	(29.5)	3.0	31	48.4	(70.5)	3.3	44	68.8	20	31.2	64
1904–1915	53	23.6	(39.0)	2.4	83	36.8	(61.0)	2.1	136	60.4	89	39.6	225
1910–1915	25	19.8	(29.1)	2.2	61	48.4	(70.9)	2.0	86	68.3	40	31.7	126
1915–1925	96	31.6	(50.8)	1.9	93	30.6	(49.2)	1.8	189	62.2	115	37.8	304

Note: Both employed and retired members of the work force are included.

[a] Percentages in parentheses show directional mobility as a proportion of gross mobility while all other percentages are proportions of persistence in the community.

[b] The 1904 Tax List is available only for the town of Pella, and the 1910 Tax List is available only for rural Lake Prairie Township.

wealth status an average of 1.4 decile ranks, while only 10.7 percent moved down an average of 1.3 decile ranks. As the growth rate slowed in the 1860s, the proportion of workers experiencing downward mobility rose to 17.9 percent. It was still relatively easy to acquire wealth, however. This is indicated by the fact that 53 percent of the work force gained an average of 2.7 decile ranks in wealth status.

As noted, very little public land remained in Lake Prairie Township after 1870, but the demand for farms continued to drive up land prices. As a result, some residents sold their farms and moved to neighboring townships or to Sioux County. This conversion of real property into cash, which is not included in the definition of wealth because of deficiencies in the data, probably inflated downward mobility rates during that time, although it is not possible to determine the degree to which this occurred. Nevertheless, during the 1870s almost one-third of the work force experienced downward mobility while almost an equal number improved their standing. These higher rates of downward mobility continued into the early 1880s, but between 1886 and 1890 this trend was checked because only 12.6 percent of the work force lost wealth status and 25.9 percent gained in wealth rank during these years. This second period in the development of Pella's economy saw a decline in the number of farmers who owned the land they worked. This was coupled with an increase in the number of farm tenants and sharecroppers. These changes tended to increase the rates of downward mobility and reduce the extent of movement between wealth ranks.

During the third period of development, when the local economic base began to shift toward manufacturing and when high farm prices brought increased prosperity to Pella, upward mobility rates again rose, as did the degree of movement between wealth ranks. Between 1890 and 1915, the proportion of workers experiencing upward wealth mobility ranged from 37.0 percent to 48.4 percent, and on average, these upwardly mobile workers gained between 2.0 and 3.3 wealth ranks. In that same period, the proportion of mobile workers who lost wealth varied from 20.3 to 28.2 percent, and these individuals, on average, saw their economic status decline from 2.2 to 3.0 decile ranks. During the decade beginning in 1915, a depressed economy led once again to an increase in the size of the downwardly mobile group. During this decade 31.6 percent of the work force lost an average of 1.9 decile ranks, while 30.6 percent gained an average of 1.8 decile ranks in wealth status.

Because the constant 1853 dollar value of property required to move up in decile rank increased between each of the tax list periods (except the one between 1915 and 1925), even those who held property but persisted in wealth rank usually saw the value of their property holdings go up. In general, then, at least two-thirds of Pella's workers saw an increase in their wealth during each of the tax list periods between 1853 and 1915.

Because of the low rate of geographic mobility in the Dutch colony, a number of workers are included more than once when economic mobility is computed between tax list years. Thus, a somewhat more accurate determination of the economic success that workers experienced while living in Pella can be obtained by comparing the wealth they held in the first tax list year after they arrived in the community with that which they held in the last tax list year before they left or died.

Not all of the workers who settled in Pella were without resources when they arrived. More than half of them held property in the first tax list after they entered the work force, and almost one-fifth were initially able to acquire enough property to place them above the tenth or lowest decile rank. However, as Table 7.5 indicates, 550, or 46.3 percent of the 1,187 workers in the sample of the work force, held no property in the first extant tax list after they arrived. Of this initially unpropertied group, 330, or 27.8 percent of the work force, never acquired property while they remained in the community. Thus, almost three-fourths of the workers did own property during their residence in Pella.

As the total wealth of the community increased between 1853 and 1925, 32.1 percent of the work force saw the value of their property rise but not fast enough to place them in a higher wealth decile ranking. Moreover, 29.8 percent of Pella's workers moved up an average of 2.2 decile ranks, while only 10.3 percent moved down an average of 1.9 decile ranks during their stay in the community.

From a different perspective, 40.1 percent of those who worked in Pella through 1925 experienced wealth mobility. Of

Table 7.5. Wealth Mobility between First and Last Tax List Years per Ethnic Group in Pella, Iowa, 1853–1925

Ethnic Group	No Wealth in first tax list		Persistence in no wealth category		Persistence in wealth rank		Downward mobility			Upward mobility			Gross mobility		Total
	N	%	N	%	N	%	N	%	(%)[a]	N	%	(%)	N	%	N
Dutch	449	49.8	254	28.2	255	28.3	89	9.9	(22.7)	303	33.6	(77.3)	392	43.5	901
Non-Dutch Europeans	18	58.1	12	38.7	6	19.4	4	12.9	(30.8)	9	29.0	(69.2)	13	41.9	31
Americans	83	32.5	64	25.1	120	47.1	29	11.4	(40.8)	42	16.5	(59.2)	71	27.8	255
Total	500	46.3	330	27.8	381	32.1	122	10.3	(25.6)	354	29.8	(74.4)	476	40.1	1187

[a] Percentages in parentheses represent the proportion of those experiencing mobility who moved up or down. Other percentages are proportions of the total number in the row.

this mobile group, 74.4 percent gained wealth status, while only 25.6 percent saw their property holdings diminish.

When the work force is divided according to ethnicity, the Americans were initially somewhat better off than either the Dutch or the non-Dutch Europeans. However, as Table 7.5 indicates, these latter groups experienced a greater degree of upward mobility over time than did their American neighbors. Part of this relative lack of success may have been due to a character trait of the Americans. Shortly after the Dutch arrived in Iowa, Hendrik Pieter Scholte, their leader, commented that the Americans "turn a nickel not over on the other side . . . before they spend it, and that makes dealings easier, sometimes too quick for the Hollander."[5]

However, age at entry into the work force as well as length of residence in the community were also important elements in economic success. The median age at entry was twenty-eight years for the Dutch, thirty-seven for the non-Dutch Europeans, and thirty-four years for the Americans. Members of these ethnic groups remained in the community for an average of seventeen, nine, and nine years respectively. Moreover, a large proportion of the Dutch workers were members of the second or third generations who had entered the work force as young adults. Thus, unlike the Americans or the non-Dutch Europeans, they had had little prior opportunity to acquire wealth in some other community that could be transferred to Pella. Yet since the Dutch remained in the Pella community for a longer time, they had greater opportunity to acquire property. Of those who initially held no property, nearly half of the Dutch, one-third of the non-Dutch Europeans, and almost one-fourth of the Americans acquired property while in Pella. Moreover, 33.6 percent of the Dutch, 29.0 percent of the non-Dutch Europeans, and only 16.5 percent of the Americans experienced upward mobility between wealth decile ranks while in the community. Thus, while approximately three-fourths of both the Dutch and the American workers in Pella held property, the proportion of Dutch workers experiencing upward wealth mobility was twice as great as that of their American neighbors.

In sum, the story of the Pella colony is one of achievement. The Dutch immigrants who founded the Pella community met and perhaps even exceeded the goals they had set for themselves. These transplanted Hollanders not only built the "city of refuge" they had envisioned but also found prosperity for themselves and for their descendants on the Iowa prairie.

Notes

1. B. L. Miller, "Geology of Marion County," *Iowa Geological Survey* 11, Annual Report, 1900 (Des Moines: Bernard Murphy, State Printer, 1901), 132.

2. In examples from midwest urban settings, only a minority of the work force remained in South Bend for any given decade between 1850 and 1880, while two-thirds of the "prime-age" males left Omaha during the twenty-year periods between 1880 and 1920. In Trempeauleau County, Wisconsin, the majority of residents were geographically mobile between 1850 and 1880, and the foreign-born were less likely to persist than native Americans. Minority persistence was also the pattern in Crawford Township in Washington County, Iowa and in Wapello County, Iowa in the 1850s and 1860s. In Grand Rapids, only 19 percent of Dutch heads of household remained between 1850 and 1860, and during the 1860s, 33 percent persisted. In Holland, Michigan, for the three decades between 1850 and 1880, respective persistence rates were 61, 61, and 55 percent.

    See Dean R. Esslinger, *Immigrants and the City* (Port Washington, N.Y.: Kennikat Press, 1975), 73; Howard Chudacoff, *Mobile Americans: Residential and Social Mobility in Omaha, 1880–1920* (New York: Oxford Univ. Press, 1972), 103; Merle Curti, *The Making of an American Community: A Case Study of Democracy in a Frontier County* (Stanford, Calif.: Stanford Univ. Press, 1959), 68; William L. Bowers, "Crawford Township, 1850–1870: A Population Study of a Pioneer Community," *Iowa Journal of History* 58 (Jan. 1960): 21–24; Mildred Thorne, "A Population Study of an Iowa County in 1850," *Iowa Journal of History* 57 (Oct. 1959): 321; David G. Vanderstel, "The Dutch of Grand Rapids, Michigan: A Study of Social Mobility in a Midwestern Urban Community, 1850–1870" (unpublished master's thesis, Kent State University, 1978), 67; Gordon W. Kirk, Jr., *The Promise of American Life: Social Mobility in a Nineteenth-Century Immigrant Community, Holland, Michigan, 1847–1894* (Philadelphia: The American Philosophical Society, 1978), 51–54.

3. Richard L. Doyle, "The Socio-Economic Mobility of the Dutch Immigrants to Pella, Iowa, 1847–1925" (unpublished Ph.D. dissertation, Kent State University, 1982), 206.

4. Because the dollar value of property within each decile rank varied from tax year to tax year, this approach measures relative wealth mobility within the community and not the absolute economic success of workers. Also, when wealth mobility between decile ranks is measured between each of the several tax list years, mobility rates demonstrate the ease or difficulty that workers had in improving their economic condition during the particular periods in the community's history. However, when mobility is measured between the first and last tax lists in which an individual worker appeared, mobility rates indicate the degree of success that workers experienced in acquiring wealth during their entire tenure in the community.

5. Hendrik Pieter Scholte, "Eene Stem uit Pella," [First Letter from Pella] (Central College Archives, Pella, Iowa, March, 1848), 36.

PART THREE

Religious and Cultural Adjustment and Conflict

8. Americanization in Reformed Religious Life

Elton J. Bruins

The Dutch Reformed Church in America was founded just nine years after the ecumenical Synod of Dort concluded its deliberations in 1619.[1] The West India Company had brought the first Dutch settlers to Manhattan in 1624 and encouraged the founding of the first church in 1628 by bringing the Rev. Jonas Michelius to serve the religious needs of the inhabitants of New Netherland. The pattern of theology, liturgy, and church order set by the Dort gathering was to be dominant for the church in the Netherlands and equally important for the Dutch churches established in America. The whole Americanization process of the Dutch immigrant churches in America must, in fact, be seen against the backdrop of Dort.[2] The settlers moving from the Netherlands to America between the early seventeenth century and the latter part of the nineteenth century wished to pattern their church life on that of the mother church in the Netherlands. Consequently, when the Americanization process of the American Dutch churches is measured or evaluated, the historian must first come to terms with the determination of the American churches to be true to the Dort patterns of church and religious life.

During the seventeenth and eighteenth centuries, Americanization really consisted of a forced adaptation to the American scene in spite of all the immigrants' best efforts to remain thoroughly Dutch in their approach to church life. Americanization

175

as adaptation to American denominational or revival patterns was to be avoided at all cost. The Dutch pattern of church life was regarded as the complete and perfect one, so any departure from that sacred path was out of the question. Americanization took place in the American Dutch churches mainly as a survival measure; the American Dutch church adapted to some aspects of the American scene lest it simply go out of existence as had the French Reformed Church.[3]

The determination to remain Dutch was simply assumed and successfully followed without question in the first period of the Dutch church in America, 1628 to 1664. Though the church experienced many trials in those years, it never wavered in its struggle to be a Dutch Reformed Church, transplanted from the Netherlands to Manhattan. Its trials were instead the directors of the colony, who were often difficult to deal with, and the perennially inadequate supply of ministers. Otherwise, during this early period the religious life of the Dutch settlers in America was not threatened by American faiths and religious groups. The Quakers, the Jews, and the Lutherans were banned from Manhattan and Long Island by the director, so the people in the New York colony who were Dutch could worship in the Dutch manner without any threat from "outsiders." In addition, because the church itself was supported by the West India Company and operated under the direct supervision of the Classis of Amsterdam, where the headquarters of the West India Company was located, there was no question about the use of the Dutch language because, of course, the language of the colony was Dutch. The first major threat to the Dutch church and its adherents in America was the loss of sovereignty over New Netherland to the English in 1664. It was at this time that Americanization began, for the Dutch churches had then to begin a long fight to remain Dutch and to resist the forces of Anglicization that now confronted them.

The first problem the Dutch church had was to become established in English eyes.[4] It did not want to be regarded as just another sect but as a church with rights. It finally won this struggle in 1696 when it received a charter making it virtually equal to the English church. There was no change in the ecclesiastical relationship with and control from the Netherlands, however. The

Classis of Amsterdam continued to support the Dutch churches in America with ministers, and even though English became the dominant language of the colonies of New York and New Jersey, Dutch remained the language of the home and church of the Dutch people in America.

The second problem began in the early part of the eighteenth century with the Reverend Theodore Frelinghuysen, a Dutch minister in New Jersey who had become acquainted and friendly with Gilbert Tennent, a Presbyterian minister in New Brunswick, New Jersey.[5] Their views of Christianity were very similar because Tennent, a Presbyterian, was also a Calvinist; as a result, Frelinghuysen allowed Tennent to preach in the congregations Frelinghuysen served in the Raritan valley. Complaints soon followed this action, and the Classis of Amsterdam was called upon to mediate in the difficulties and dissensions that followed in Frelinghuysen's congregations in New Jersey. The actual complaint is very indicative of the attitude of most of the members of the Dutch churches in the eighteenth century about remaining Dutch in all aspects of religious and church life:

> During these conjoint services of him and Frelinghuysen, he administers the Covenant Seals, mingling the English and Dutch language with each other in worship. Rev. Frelinghuysen preaches and Tennent prays and baptises; and then together they administer the Holy Supper. All this is further proof that he [Tennent] is a secundus [colleague]. Now, if those who belong in Dutch Churches persist in employing English dissenters, they depart from the Holland Church-Order and Liturgy: for these belong to the Dutch alone; and certainly they are nowhere in use among the English over here. We must, therefore, be careful to keep things in the Dutch way, in our churches, even as you also request and advise us, yea, admonish and beseech us. We have not therefore complained to you concerning that English Dissenter because of any departure from the pure administration of the Covenant Seals, but because of his departure from the Holland manner of administering these Holy Covenant Seals; and concerning the administration of them, according to his self-opinionated ways; for he is a stranger among us.[6]

Frelinghuysen saw cooperation with Tennent as no threat to the Dutch churches but only as a way to enhance religious life and deeper piety among his parishioners. The people who opposed Frelinghuysen saw him as a person who would endanger and change the Dutch ways of doing things in the churches and saw his action as an Americanization process that would damage the pure Dutch way of church life. What resulted was a long, bitter controversy that engulfed the Dutch churches in New Jersey and New York for much of the eighteenth century.

A third problem developed for the Dutch churches. Frelinghuysen and those who came to sympathize with his point of view believed that the Dutch churches in America needed to develop an organization which would enhance their effectiveness on the American scene. This issue was first raised in 1737, and reluctantly the Classis of Amsterdam gave its permission for an organization called the Coetus ("seetus") to be formed.[7] The proponents did not intend that this organization would help the Dutch churches to Americanize faster though its opponents thought it would.

The opposing party, which came to be known as the Conferentie, and the Coetus ministers both did things the Dutch way, following the order and pattern of Dort. The difference of opinion was over the question of some adaptation to the American scene. The Coetus ministers considered it necessary to adapt to the American scene to keep up with Dutch church members whenever they moved to new settlements. These ministers also wanted to develop some kind of educational system for ministerial recruits instead of sending them to Holland for training and ordination. The Conferentie was adamant in following the Dutch way precisely and doing everything according to the pattern of the previous century when New York was controlled by the Dutch government. The sad result of this difference of opinion was that the two parties in the Dutch churches in America were locked in a bitter struggle between 1747 and 1771.

Still another problem forced itself upon the Dutch churches. Although the two parties were fighting over the question of an American ecclesiastical organization, they did all their fighting in the Dutch language. Even after nearly a century of English control over New York and New Jersey, where the Dutch lived, none of the churches considered changing the language of worship to English. Only in 1762 did the New York congregation finally concede to pressure and bring an English-speaking Dutch Reformed minister from the Netherlands so that worship could be conducted in English for those who wanted English language services in the Dutch church. The reason for this concession was entirely practical: the Dutch churches were suffering considerable erosion in membership to the English churches because many young people could no longer understand Dutch and thus no longer wanted to worship in Dutch.

Further impetus towards adaptation to the American scene was provided by the independence of the American colonies. Prior to the Revolutionary War, the Classis of Amsterdam insisted on a mother-daughter relationship and formal ecclesiastical ties, as did all the American Dutch churches. The Classis of Amsterdam often bemoaned the number of headaches the quarreling American churches gave them, but there was no question about the authority of the Classis of Amsterdam in ecclesiastical affairs. Fortunately for the Classis and all the American churches, the rift between Conferentie and Coetus was healed in the Union Convention of 1771 so that by the time of the Revolution the American church was again united. During the Revolutionary War the Dutch churches were sorely tested. Most of the members and ministers were loyal to the American side. But many churches, particularly in New York, suffered damage. Some congregations were scattered, and several ministers had to flee because of the British occupation. The war, however, loosened the ties with the Netherlands, and when the war was over, the Dutch churches had entered a new day in spite of their ardent desire to remain Dutch in every respect if at all possible.[8]

The question of training and ordination of ministers was settled immediately after the war. John H. Livingston was appointed the first theological professor and with the approval of the whole church began to give theological instruction to recruits who upon completion of their studies were ordained in America by the American Dutch church. Since America had become an independent country, ties with the Netherlands were no longer practical nor desirous, so the supremely capable Livingston was called upon to draw up a constitution for the Dutch churches. But the new organizational pattern he constructed in 1792 for the American Dutch churches was simply the Dort church order modified for the American scene. The only change of the Dort order was a necessary adaptation in order that the Dutch churches might function more effectively on the American scene.[9] The anathemas were deleted from the canons. The Dutch language was already dropped by most churches by the time the new constitution took effect. Livingston also was charged with setting up the liturgy and hymnbook largely Dutch in style and direction. As the old Dutch church in New York and New Jersey stood on the threshold of the nineteenth century, it was now an American church—but an American Dutch church which had reluctantly adapted to the American scene in order to survive. It was still very much the Dutch Reformed Church with emphasis on the Dutch even though its congregants now worshipped in English and its ministers were trained and ordained in America. Indeed, the sense of Dutchness declined very slowly, its last gasp coming in 1867 when after years of pressure, the denomination finally dropped the word Dutch in its legal title and became known as the Reformed Church in America.[10]

The Church did pay a great price for its reluctant adaptation to the American scene. As the nineteenth century began, the Dutch Reformed Church was woefully understaffed because the old policy of training and ordaining men to the ministry in The Netherlands had stifled the development of an adequate supply of ministers. Consequently, when the West was opening for settlement and Dutch Reformed people were moving out of the East, the old church could not keep up with the demand for new churches. Overall, it failed to meet the challenge of the frontier. It was no match for the Baptists and Methodists, who had a ready supply of ministers and who thoroughly accommodated themselves to the American religious scene and could operate effectively within it. Thus, at this crucial time in the history of the American church, the Dutch Reformed Church, which served the Dutch, who made up one-fifth of the population of New York and one-sixth of the population of New Jersey, and which had been essentially a majority church, became a minority one.[11]

Yet, in spite of the slow adaptation to the American scene in the colonial period, some acculturation did take place in the religious life of the Dutch churches and their members—as indicated in part by the general acceptance of Freemasonry by many of the male members of the Dutch church. The order of Freemasonry came to America in the early eighteenth century and numbered Ben Franklin as one of its earliest members.[12] At first it was rejected by orthodox Christians, but by the end of the eighteenth century, it came to be widely accepted among Christian as well as non-Christian men.[13] But even the Freemasonry movement had been Americanized; for while in Europe a Mason was usually an agnostic, atheist, or freethinker, the Masons in America so syncretized their Enlightenment philosophy with Christianity that by 1800 a Mason in America was most likely also a Christian and saw no conflict between the two.

When the scandalous Morgan affair dominated the public scene in the later part of the 1820s and initiated a strong anti-Masonic movement in America, the True Dutch Reformed Church, which seceded from the Reformed Church in 1822, affirmed that no members of the True Dutch Reformed Church could belong to the Masons and joined the vigorous efforts of the anti-Masonic movement to fight the "evils" of Masonry.[14] The Dutch Reformed Church, still strongly orthodox and Dutch in its ways, remained tolerant of Freemasonry. There is no evidence whatsoever in the records of either the General Synod of the Reformed Protestant Dutch Church, as it was then called, or in the records of the Particular Synods of Albany and New York[15] that Masonry was an evil and should be condemned. The silence was, in fact, consent. The old Dutch church, which had now been in America for exactly 200 years, had inevitably absorbed some of the American public's attitude toward this secret society. Thus, in spite of the best efforts of the Dutch church to adapt as little as possible, there had been a certain acculturation of its members to attitudes and practices of the general American public. On the one hand, the church had adapted so slowly to the American scene that it lost the impact on America that it could have had. On the other hand, in spite of its efforts to remain Dutch, it simply had not been able to prevent some acculturation to American thinking and outlook.

The Americanization process for the mid-nineteenth century migration of Dutch people to America was of a different kind, due, in part, to the different circumstances of their coming.[16] The Dutch who settled in the Midwest under the leadership of the Reverend Albertus C. Van Raalte and the Reverend Hendrik P. Scholte came to America intentionally, not as servants of a West India–type company. The nineteenth century immigrants experienced difficult circumstances in the Netherlands and had little to lose and much to gain by coming to America. They came with the intention of becoming American citizens and of participating fully in the American dream of a good life with economic gains. Both Van Raalte and Scholte were pro-American and saw America as a kind of promised land where each would establish a colony that would be like a city "set on a hill." They did not intend a slow adaptation to American life and customs but immediately set about building colonies which were enterprising and vigorous. Both men moved about the country freely and had a wide range of interests.

When it came to the Americanization of their religious life and the religious life of many of their followers, a major factor prevented them from a rapid adaptation of their religious faith to the American scene. Scholte, Van Raalte, and many of their followers were Separatists, and—though the Separatists were a minority among the nineteenth century Dutch immigrants—the ideals of the Separatist movement of 1834 proved a dominant factor in how the immigrants of the nineteenth century dealt with religious affairs and lived the Christian life.[17]

Scholte and Van Raalte interpreted one Separatist ideal differently. Both shared the Separatists' belief that a return to Dortian principles of church life was necessary because the Reformed Church in the Netherlands had departed from that sacred norm, but Van Raalte did not desire complete independence for the local congregations as Scholte did. Scholte refused to join any American denomination after he founded Pella, Iowa. He insisted instead on the independence of the local congregation, and because most of his followers disagreed with him on this point, they soon came under Van Raalte's leadership in choosing a denominational affiliation. Van Raalte, too, wanted no part of the dictatorial, dominating kind of church that both he and Scholte had rejected in the Netherlands by joining Hendrik de Cock in his secession. But that did not mean that Van Raalte wanted a con-

gregational (and un-Reformed!) church polity in America. Van
Raalte had no questions about having an ecclesiastical organization on the American scene, and one reason for his coming had
been to make sure that the immigrants did not drift religiously in
America. In contrast to what had happened with the Dutch
churches in the seventeenth century, Van Raalte organized the
Classis of Holland (Michigan) in 1848, only one year after the settlement, encountering no objection from the mother church in
the Netherlands for doing so.[18]

Nor did Van Raalte's idea of separatism exclude an affiliation with the historic Dutch Reformed Church in America. When
Van Raalte and his people came to America in 1846 and headed
west, Dutch Reformed Church clergymen in New York City and
Albany proved especially kind and helpful both to him and his
followers and to many other Dutch immigrants going west. Two
of the clergymen, Thomas De Witt of New York and Isaac
Wyckoff of Albany, even spoke Dutch, so the new Dutch pastor
on American shores, Van Raalte, happily found Dutch Reformed
dominies who could speak the Dutch language and who were
conservative and orthodox in their theology, unlike so many ministers in the Reformed Church in the Netherlands. Through these
men, Van Raalte also became well acquainted with the Dutch Reformed Church in America and realized that the church and its
practices were completely agreeable to him. In 1849, Isaac
Wyckoff visited the Holland colony on behalf of the mission
board of the Reformed Church and invited the Holland Classis to
unite with the old Dutch Reformed Church in the East.[19] This
union was effected in 1850.

For the great majority of the Dutch immigrants this union
was both agreeable and beneficial. The concern of the eastern
Dutch churches for the needs of the immigrant churches was
manifested in many ways, through financial help in particular. In
succeeding years, Van Raalte made numerous forays among the
Dutch churches in New Jersey and New York and canvassed congregations, asking them to help finance his many projects in the
Holland colony. He got assistance for the inauguration of the Pioneer School which became Hope College, the primary institution
for the education of ministers for the immigrant churches in the
West. Van Raalte found the association with the old church in the

East most congenial and very helpful in fulfilling his vision for the new Jerusalem he was attempting to build on the eastern shores of Lake Michigan.

Because of his personal feelings and attitudes, Van Raalte encouraged the Americanization of religious life among the colonists. His concept of Americanization was not a reluctant adaptation to the American scene, which would have excluded the techniques of a Methodist revivalist by the name of Clapper, but neither was it a full and uncritical acceptance of American religious practices. The progressive element in the old Dutch church in the East had worked for a century before it got an American educational institution organized to train ministers. But Van Raalte got a school going within the first five years of the settlement. Nonetheless, despite his openness in encouraging Americans to come into the colony to help him build, Van Raalte always intended that his congregation would be the controlling factor of the community in a quasi-theocratic sense.[20]

Van Raalte's idea of Americanization was to bring about an accommodation to the American scene as soon as practically possible but to do so without losing sight of his ideal of moving the church "back to Dort." Thus, once he realized that insisting on the use of the Dutch language might undermine the more important parts of his program, Van Raalte insured that the pupils of his pioneer school and academy and later the college received the best possible training in the English language. Since no immigrant had the training or skill to teach in the academy or college, he imported Dutch Reformed clergy and laity from New York to staff the institution. In addition, Van Raalte helped the people of his colony obtain their American citizenship as quickly as possible after five years of residence in the new land. Further, the local paper, *De Hollander*, had English sections so that the people would be confronted with the necessity of learning English in order to be better Americans and become acquainted with the American scene. Yet Van Raalte's press for an accommodation to the American scene was not at the expense of religious piety or solid doctrine. He soon outdistanced Scholte by bringing the immigrant churches in Wisconsin and Illinois as well as all the Pella Separatists, except Scholte's own little congregation, into the Reformed Church orbit.

Van Raalte's concept of Americanization of religious life was soon challenged, however. Some of the Separatists feared Americanization and resisted Van Raalte's ideas and ultimately his leadership. The opposition became strong enough that in 1857 about 10 percent of the members of the Holland Classis left the Reformed Church and established what today is known as the Christian Reformed Church. Various reasons for the defection have been given, but they can best be summarized by saying that they display an extreme reluctance to adapt to the American scene. As much as Van Raalte and the leaders in the Classis of Holland felt that the old Dutch church in the East was the perfect home for them, this 10 percent disagreed. Gijsbert Haan, a vocal opponent of the union with the Reformed Church, had been in the East for a time and complained loudly that the Dutch Reformed churches were lax in many crucial Reformed practices such as regular preaching from the Heidelberg Catechism. His numerous complaints gave the impression to many of the western Michigan colonists that Van Raalte and the Classis had entered into the union too hastily, but the basic reason for the opposition of Haan and those like him was that they refused to accept the Americanization tendencies now becoming pronounced in the East. Even though the church in the East was sound basically, it was no longer very Dutch in ethos and outlook. It had become an American church, and no Dutch Separatist counterpart to the Michigan churches was to be found in the East. Haan complained that Van Raalte's ideas of Americanization would lead to the results of what he thought he witnessed in the eastern churches.[21]

The idea of complete separation from American society and very reluctant Americanization dominated the new Christian Reformed Church in its early years while the Separatist congregations united with the Reformed Church Americanized with some sense of accommodation. The Christian Reformed Church very soon began to make an issue over the matter of membership in the secret society. Doubtless this started with some of the immigrants who had stayed in the East for a time before coming West and learned that several Reformed Church ministers and laymen were members of the Masonic lodge. The Christian Reformed Church went on record, as had the Church of the Secession of 1822, that membership in the lodge and membership in the church were contradictory and hence unlawful. Of course, most of the separatist immigrants in the Classis of Holland and the Classis of Wisconsin of the Reformed Church felt the same on the issue, for they too had recently come from the Netherlands where no Christian would ever be a member of the lodge. The issue was soon joined with intensity. It was not that the Christian Reformed laity were against the lodge membership. The opinion was virtually unanimous among all serious Dutch Separatist Christians, whether in the Reformed Church or the Christian Reformed Church, that membership in the lodge was an evil thing. The issue rather was what should the denomination do. The Christian Reformed Church banned membership in the secret society as a synodical principle. On the other hand, the Reformed Church ruled that membership in the lodge was not to be condoned and was an unwise thing to do but concluded that it was a consistorial prerogative to deal with the issue. This was Van Raalte's position, too: the local consistory had to exercise proper discipline of lodge members to see that they lived good Christian lives.

The controversy, underway in force by 1868, that ensued was most unsettling. Deprived of Van Raalte's mediating presence because of his death in 1876, his own congregation decided in 1882 to break with the Reformed Church over the issue.[22] Other Reformed Church congregations joined the Christian Reformed Church during this controversy. The concept of very slow Americanization held by the Christian Reformed Church gained considerable ground. The Christian Reformed Church in the Netherlands, which in 1850 favored the union of the Classis of Holland and the Reformed Church in America, withdrew its support from Van Raalte's people and in 1882 gave it to the new Christian Reformed Church in America. Consequently, the Christian Reformed Church began to grow much more rapidly as many more immigrants joined it instead of the Reformed Church. Because the Reformed Church had not condemned Masonry and refused to disallow membership in it across the board, the Reformed Church appeared too Americanized to the mother church in the Netherlands. The strong spirit of Separatist-reluctant adaptation to the American scene now ruled the day for many Dutch immigrants in the West.

The strong separatist idea of the Christian Reformed Church was further enhanced by the Christian school concept developed in the Netherlands by Abraham Kuyper and the Doleantie movement which he began in 1886. The Doleantie group united with the Netherlands Christian Reformed Church in 1892, and when these people came to America and joined the new Christian Reformed Church here, there was a new press for a reluctant adaptation to the American scene in the guise of the Christian day-school movement. By this time the Reformed Church people had opted for public education with its attendant Americanization by accommodation principle. The Christian Reformed Church went clearly in the other direction. The Christian school movement ostensibly promoted a Reformed Christian education, but the Christian day-school movement also had an elective affinity with the separationist and reluctant adaptation principle of Americanization. The Christian day-school movement effectively reinforced a slow Americanization for many Dutch immigrants. By 1900, and certainly by the end of World War I, the Americanization process in the religious life of the colonists who had come to America in the middle of the nineteenth century had split into two different streams that influenced all their church life and practice. The Reformed Church in the Middle West began to Americanize according to the principles of accommodation and the Christian Reformed Church by following the reluctant adaptation principle.

Each principle brought its successes. The Christian Reformed Church appealed to immigrants of Doleantie background who insisted on the Christian school. The new immigrants were also very comfortable in the American Christian Reformed Church because it was almost identical with the church at home in the Netherlands out of which they had just come. The Psalms were sung and the services were always in Dutch, so there was a uniformity of church life in almost every detail. Those Dutch immigrants who wanted something different could join the Reformed Church, where the services would use both Dutch and English, where hymns would be sung as well as the Psalms, and where there was more tolerance for American ways and ideas. The Reformed Church published most of its religious literature in the English language, while the Christian Reformed Church used Dutch exclusively for nearly all of its publications. Depending on what a particular immigrant was looking for in religious life, both churches offered something distinctive and meaningful. After World War II, the Christian Reformed Church principle paid off when a new host of Dutch immigrants who came to Canada chose to affiliate with the Christian Reformed Church while the Reformed Church received only a handful. Because it had chosen to accommodate itself to America, the Reformed Church was identified with the Hervormde Kerk in the Netherlands, while the Christian Reformed Church here became completely identified with the Gereformeerde Kerk of the Netherlands.

The Americanization of religious life is no longer an issue in the Reformed Church; that is, it is no longer a Dutch immigrant church which must accommodate to the American religious scene. Its concerns now involve coming to terms with American evangelicalism and with the Methodistic tendencies of Norman Vincent Peale and the ideas of Robert Schuller. The Americanization of religious life in the Christian Reformed Church has become the question of how to adapt to America with much less reluctance than formerly.

Notes

1.   The most recent history of this church is Gerald F. De Jong, *The Dutch Reformed Church in the American Colonies* (Grand Rapids: Wm. B. Eerdmans, 1978).

2.   The major resource for understanding the Americanization of the Dutch Reformed Church is John P. Luidens, *The Americanization of the Dutch Reformed Church* (Ph.D. dissertation, University of Oklahoma, 1969).

3.   Many of the French Reformed congregations joined the Dutch Reformed Church, De Jong, *Dutch Reformed Church*, 63–65.

4.   Ibid., 54–55.

5.   For a definitive study of Frelinghuysen, see James Tanis, *Dutch Calvinistic Pietism in the Middle Colonies: A Study in the Life and Theology of Theodorus Jacobus Frelinghuysen* (The Hague: Martinus Nijhoff, 1967).

6.   Hugh Hastings (ed.), Ecclesiastical Records State of New York (Albany, N.Y.: J. B. Lyon Company, 1902), IV, 2587, as quoted by J. J. Mol, *Churches and Immigrants: A Sociological Study of the Mu-*

tual Effect of Religion and Immigrant Adjustment, Research Group for European Migration Problems, vol. 9, (May 1961), 23.

7.   De Jong, *Dutch Reformed Church,* 189–193.

8.   Luidens said: "Under the provisions of the Articles of Union of 1771, the Dutch Church had achieved an ill-defined but palpable state of semi-independence. The chaos of the Revolutionary years had given the appearance of a static or even retrogressive institution, but this was only illusory. Like all other American institutions, the Reformed Church was forced to move forward along the path of national independence which was opened by the final victory. In company with the other religious institution it had begun to modify its relationship to Europe at the coming of peace, but it was among the last to complete the process of separation by creating its own constitution and organizational structure," Luidens, *Americanization,* 308.

9.   These changes and adaptations are embodied in the Explanatory Articles. See Edward Tanjore Corwin, *A Digest of Constitutional and Synodical Legislation of the Reformed Church in America* (N.Y.: Board of Publication of the Reformed Church in America, 1906), v–lxxxvii. One change Livingston made was to blend the work of the elder and deacon into the function of a consistory member.

10. Gerald F. De Jong made a detailed study of the controversy that was involved with the change of name in his article. See "The Controversy over Dropping the Word Dutch from the Name of the Reformed Church," *Reformed Review* 34 (Spring 1981): 158–170.

11. Luidens, *Americanization,* 306.

12. David Freeman Hawke, *Franklin* (New York: Harper and Row, 1976), 44.

13. For a detailed study of Masonry in Connecticut, see Dorothy Ann Lipson, *Freemasonry in Federalist Connecticut* (Princeton, N.J.: Princeton University Press, 1977).

14. *The Acts and Proceedings of the General Synod of the True Reformed Dutch Church in the United States of America* (Hackensack, N.J.: June 1831), 10–11.

15. The Synod of New York then included the New Jersey churches. See the *Acts and Proceedings* of those bodies for the period of about 1825 to 1835.

16. The standard material on this immigration and its leaders is Henry S. Lucas, *Netherlanders in America: Dutch Immigration to the United States and Canada, 1789–1950* (Ann Arbor: The University of Michigan Press, 1955).

17. Robert P. Swierenga has clearly demonstrated that the Separatists or Seceders were a minority of the immigrants, although many of us were under the impression that they were in a majority. But he

also believes that they had a disproportionate influence in the Reformed churches in the Dutch immigrant communities. See his informative article, "A Denominational Schism from a Behaviorial Perspective: The 1857 Dutch Reformed Separation," *Reformed Review* 34 (Spring 1981): 172–185.

18. A very good picture of Van Raalte's organizational abilities are reflected in the *Classis Holland Minutes 1848–1858*, translated by a Joint Committee of the Christian Reformed Church and the Reformed Church in America (Grand Rapids: Wm. B. Eerdmans Publishing Co., 1950).

19. "Report," in Henry S. Lucas, ed., *Dutch Immigrant Memoirs and Related Writings* (2 vols., Assen, Neth.: Van Gorcum, 1955), I, 449–457. The report is an excellent description of the *Kolonie* in 1849.

20. See my article, "Albertus C. Van Raalte and His Colony," *Reformed Review* 30 (Winter 1977): 83–94, for Van Raalte's attempt to make Holland, Michigan, a theocratic community.

21. William O. Van Eyck discussed many of these issues in his miscellaneous papers, which were published under the title *The Union of 1850: A Collection of Papers By the Late Wm. O. Van Eyck, Esq., on the Union of the Classis of Holland with the Reformed Church in America: in June, 1850* (Grand Rapids, Mich.: Wm. B. Eerdmans Publishing Co., 1950).

22. The best discussion to date on this secession is Gerhard de Jonge, "Secession Movements," unpublished paper in the Kolkman Memorial Archives of Western Theological Seminary, Holland, Mich.

9. The Reformed Churches and Acculturation

James D. Bratt

The upsurge in American ethnic studies in the past twenty years has made the task of analyzing acculturation much more complicated, if also more stimulating. The method by which so much earlier scholarship proceeded—simply fixing the old country's cultural character, then America's, and then measuring a group's passage from the first to the second and calling it "progress"—has been challenged in whole and in every part. "Progress" now seems to have been neither so steady, but marked by generational ebb and flow; nor so unidirectional, but oscillating between New World and Old World poles; nor even progress at all. The models describing the process have changed. Definitions of American and European cultures have changed, notably in the direction of complexity. And the very concept of acculturation has opened to reveal multiple levels and components.[1]

Of all these, the change in models is most familiar. As to the ultimate *destination* of the acculturation process, an earlier shift from Anglo-conformity (i.e., immigrants should and would assimilate to an English-derived set of laws, language, and values) to melting pot (all ethnic traits would combine to produce a new American type unique to itself) has gone on to pluralism, emphasizing the persistence of ethnic groups and the enduring diversity of American culture.[2] Regarding the *character* of the process, just as the proto-American school (represented by Carl Wittke and popular in the 1930s), which deemed immigrants to have been

191

Americans "before they got off the boat," gave way to culture shock theories (notably, with Oscar Handlin in the 1950s), so the latter have given way to portraits of carry-over from Old World to New.[3] Whatever their predictive quality, the new models seem truer to the historical record. Yet they have problems of their own. Has all this scholarly sweat and toil come to no more than the formula, persistence amid change? Is not pluralism invoked far too quickly to "explain" or, subtly, to defuse differences in American society? Such considerations have given rise to a new order of questions. Granted that a multiplicity of ethnic groups exists, what is the network of relations among them and other blocs in society? What keeps them together and apart? And what is the historical course by which these relations have come into being?[4]

Other scholarly trends have been more diffusive. The cultures of the European sending countries no longer appear so monolithic, static, or reproachable; and in the field of American Studies, attempts to define *the* American character fell off sharply from the mid-1960s on, probably because the profound dissension of those years cast doubt on whether any such character existed.[5] At the same time, noble values have given way to a welter of commercialized images as America's distinctive substance. How does one gauge acculturation when the standard of measure is a fleeting set of pop figures? And how can one defend acculturation if Coke or J. R. Ewing or McDonald's is the United States's "real thing"?

Finally, two important theoretical confusions have come to attention. First, for many immigrants, especially those of the late nineteenth and early twentieth century era, immigration also entailed modernization: passage from a rural and more traditional social order to one more urban and industrial, officially secular and pluralistic. To designate all changes involved in this process as Americanization, therefore, is mistaken; any distinctively American traits must be sorted out from the generally modern.[6] Second, cultures have form as well as substance, values and ideas but also systems of interaction.[7] Students of acculturation should use both measures, but with regard to American ethnicity they have not consistently achieved the best balance of the two. Persistence of ethnic values, dispositions, and modes of family regulation, for instance, must be reckoned in conjunction with participation in the American system of denominationalism, non-confessional political parties, and "pragmatic" labor unions. But the latter must also be measured over against the former.

All of which might imply that traditional intellectual history has nothing to contribute to the subject. After all, that school is now ritually associated with the "consensus history" which ethnic studies have helped to demote. But actually, its approaches have helped uncover the complexity of immigrants' responses to the symbols of American civilization. Ethnic allegiance to such "American values" as progress, pragmatism, freedom, and fair play has not been unanimous, nor has it necessarily been deep, undivided, or exhaustive. The records of almost every ethnic group show marked ambivalence and many merely perfunctory salutes toward the ruling code words of the new homeland. Equally important, close examination of ethnic attitudes reveals that these code words can bear strikingly different meanings and connotations in one group than they do in another or in the cultural mainstream.[8] In ethnic groups there can lie beneath the Americanized surface another layer of ideas, attitudes, and symbols descendant, with modifications, from the European past. These mentalities have tones and colors of their own. They constitute latent world views which, coherently or in fragments, stand in alliance, confrontation, or duality with the "American" symbol network.

Religion and Americanization

My project on Dutch Reformed acculturation has not, unfortunately, worked all these considerations into a definitive account. Both interest and ability inclined me more toward culture-as-substance than toward culture-as-structure, and the two theoretical problems mentioned, along with the possibilities of pluralism-as-cliché, dawned on me only in midstream or near the far bank. This essay, then, is a progress report that implies its own agenda for future research.

The model I have come to is that of mosaic-in-motion, or a kaleidoscope.[9] Ethnic communities are the pieces of the mosaic;

larger American culture the field in which they are embedded; and pop culture the layer of wax over the top—shiny but transparent. What we must do then is get at this mosaic from underneath, for its pieces have a depth and an interior which surface looks cannot see but which are crucial to the understanding of each and of the whole. This at any rate is what I have tried to do with the Dutch Reformed piece of American society.

Of all the facets of acculturation mentioned above, I set out after one—determination of ethnic world view—and had two others forced upon me: cultural diversity in, and carry-over between, Old World and New. Through all the shocks and alterations—and these must not be underestimated—the Dutch Reformed guided their entry into American life by mentalities established in their European past. The pertinent questions concerning Americanization therefore turn out to be, what type of Americans did these people become? Who were their perceived friends and enemies in the new land and what were the criteria of determination? The language question becomes a "higher" language question, one quite basic but so often ignored. Granted the shift to English, what was the new tongue used to say?

The sources used to answer these questions are distressingly traditional, that is, literary. The distress being not only the social historian's but my own, I tried to overcome some of the elitist tendencies of the method by considering a wide range of artifacts: sermons as well as theological tomes, periodicals for the populace as well as for the professoriate, controversial broadsides and treatises on social and political matters, novels approved for holiday giving and the often first-rate fiction of the community's rebels. The range is also broad topically, countering another objection. Religion was the foundation and glue of the Dutch Reformed community, but that community long insisted on what scholars more lately have emphasized: that religion bears social, political, economic correlations and implications; that is, involves (in the Dutch Reformed slogan) every sphere of life. Since religion served as this community's medium of culture, we can well examine it for the tensions and processes of acculturation.

The group's very formula for Americanization reflected this fact. For all their disagreements on the pace and substance of change, everyone by the twentieth century agreed: We cannot remain Hollanders; we must remain Reformed.[10] The trouble arose when it came time to define exactly what the terms Reformed and American meant. It soon became obvious that the community contained several parties, each working from a different stream of the Dutch Reformed tradition and consequently having different perceptions of and different prescriptions for entry into American society. For the Dutch, Americanization first of all involved the deeper struggle for self-definition and went forward in the dynamics and resolution of group conflict.

The Four Mentalities

The tension in Dutch-America stemmed from two nineteenth century divisions in the Reformed churches in the Netherlands. The first had begun in 1834 when dozens of congregations seceded from the Hervormde Kerk (the national church) complaining of a centralized, state-controlled polity, liturgical laxity, and confessional liberalism. Drawing heavily on a century-old conventicle movement, the Secession embodied the fervent devotion and stringent orthodoxy of that tradition as well as its pietistic ethic. Defensive and individualistic in style, it urged separation from evil as a negative duty, and diligence, sobriety, and obedience as the positive.[11] The second division, the Neo-Calvinist movement, emerged around 1870 out of similar complaints against the national church. But Neo-Calvinists also criticized the Secession's passive, spiritualized attitudes and advocated instead a full-bodied, distinctive Christian witness in every sphere of society and culture.[12] Though the two movements merged ecclesiastically in 1892, differences of spirit and motive long persisted between them. Moreover, each camp developed internal conflicts of its own, pushing fragmentation even further.

Since Dutch immigration to the United States reached its largest scale (1880–1920) after all these events, the old country's divisions reappeared in the new. The western section of the Reformed Church of America (RCA) retained much of the character of its founder, Albertus C. Van Raalte, who represented that wing of the Secession oriented toward experiential piety and practical morality. This denomination came to attract an increasing percentage of Hervormde Kerk immigrants, and through its tie—especially via the education of its leadership—to a venerable American institution (the RCA East), was drawn more fully toward mainstream American Protestantism.[13] Since the latter laid greatest stress on religious experience (in the form of revivalism) and moral reform, and since in the nineteenth century it functioned (whatever the law) as a national church, the RCA West's new condition corresponded nicely with the character of both its Netherlandic origins and new clientele. Thus much of the RCA West's leadership brought to the Dutch community the vision of regnant Protestantism: rather genteel, optimistic, a bit condescending toward the ethnic past, convinced of the "Christian character" of the United States, and enthusiastic for the many early twentieth century crusades designed to enhance that character at home and spread it abroad.[14]

If this group followed the outward-looking possibilities of pietism, the rest of the RCA West and much of the Christian Reformed Church (CRC) embodied the Secession's tendency toward introversion. They shared the optimists' association of religion with the "spiritual" side of life but saw its present prospects quite differently. Modern times constituted not an opportunity but a threat for faith; the church was called not to move into the world but to attend to the faithful remnant. As much as a pietistic ethic, the spokesmen for this outlook stressed full and exact faithfulness to the Reformed creeds, qualifying them equally as Confessionalists. Through this double lens of caution, they viewed the American world skeptically, not so much because it was America as because it was "the world," and urged a slower pace of acculturation in order to preserve the Reformed doctrinal heritage. Confessionalist interpretations of public affairs revolved around two poles: the religious beliefs or personal character of the people involved, and the event's implications for the spiritual welfare of the faithful and the purity of public life.[15]

The Neo-Calvinists of Dutch-America, while also cherishing Reformed orthodoxy, decried such reductions as insulting the depth and breadth of the Christian faith and leading to the emergence by default of an ethic wholly inadequate to the modern order. A similar critique applied to the RCA professoriate. These had merely shifted concern for individual "souls" to the outside world, showing little critical rigor regarding either the institutional dimensions of public life or the quality of the Christian spirit that supposedly pervaded that life in America. But if the Neo-Calvinists wished to mount a witness both comprehensive and distinctively Christian, they disagreed radically among themselves over the direction that witness should take.

This conflict stemmed from the work of the movement's founder, Abraham Kuyper (1837–1920). Kuyper had propounded early in his career the doctrine of the antithesis—that the root motives ("principles") of Christians and unbelievers were diametrically opposed; that the spiritual quality of their respective actions were inevitably antagonistic, that Christians should therefore pursue their work in society from their own separate organizations. Later in life, but without diminishing the idea of antithesis, Kuyper had resurrected the doctrine of common grace—that God gave to all mankind grace which, while not "saving," enabled them to attain a remarkable measure of virtue and truth; that their achievements in technology, politics, scholarship, and art, though not motivated by faith, were to be cherished by Christians as gifts of God; that cooperation between believers and non-believers was therefore possible and necessary.[16]

Kuyper harnessed this contradiction to tremendous achievement, a feat his followers could not match. Thus the Kuyperians in the United States came to mirror the split in the ranks of the pietists. The Antithetical party emphasized the corruption (ideological and practical) everywhere present in the world, the negative or condemnatory purpose of Christian socio-cultural witness, and the need for separate organizations to protect the elect from contamination. They tended toward introversion, skepticism about America (not because of its Americanness but because it was "the world" at hand), and respect for the Netherlands where a model of proper Calvinism had been created.[17] Other Neo-Calvinists, in contrast, hoped to make a positive witness to the world, to realize some of the improvements which the Christian critique offered society, and to cooperate with people of other principles in achieving this goal. They were outward-looking, though with keener eye (as they thought) than their RCA counterparts. America, as "the world," was a field of Calvinistic opportunity, and Netherlandic models, though fully respected, were not to be automatically copied in the American context.[18]

Resolution: The 1920s

These mentalities underlie Dutch Reformed intellectual life to this day, but they were particularly predominant—indeed, almost all-absorbing—in the pre–World War I era. The coalitions between factions shifted, now joining the Kuyperians against the pietists, now the inward- versus the outward-looking. The great public issues of the day—women's suffrage, labor–capital conflict, Prohibition, and Progressivism—intensified the debate as they brought out the broader implications of theological differences. The controversy peaked in 1916 as these issues came to a head and as the United States moved toward involvement in World War I.[19]

The latter event proved momentous for the Dutch as for other American ethnic groups. In terms of factional strength, the Confessional and Antithetical groups, which for both parochial and farsighted reasons had opposed American entry into the war, lost ground in the CRC to the positive Calvinists. More importantly, the denomination as a whole came under severe attack from the RCA and from groups outside the community for its lack of "true Americanism." Under such pressure, all CRC factions agreed that the time had come to "enter fully into American life." But that required a decision as to which mode of entry, which perception of America, which part of the Reformed tradition would prevail. And after the wartime experience, the stakes seemed ultimate (the very survival of the denomination), unanimity essential.

The decision was made via the most severe ideological combat of Dutch-American history, a series of three heresy trials in the 1920s capped by a definitive ethical pronouncement. While Americanization on this level proceeded concurrently with the completion of the process in its more obvious sense, the two movements showed no simple correlation. By this time all parties had both Dutch- and English-speaking leaders, both Netherlandic and American born and educated, and used resources from both sides of the Atlantic. Everyone realized the key issue to be the "higher," not the "lower" language question.

The first heresy trial concerned the work of Harry Bultema, a CRC pastor in Muskegon, Michigan. The anxieties of World War I drove him, like many others, to Biblical prophecy for understanding. Bultema returned with an extreme premillenarian reading of the "signs of the times" and a dispensational understanding of Scripture and history.[20] As these constituted two of the principal tenets of American Fundamentalism,[21] Bultema represented one possible path of Americanization—coalesence with the new land's vast body of conservative, non-Reformed, largely Anglo-Saxon Protestants. Certainly abundant potential for such a step existed; the community merely needed to exaggerate, as had Bultema, some of its defensive pietistic inclinations. Bultema's strategy for the church also rang familiarly to Confessionalists: She should withdraw from error into the circle of the faithful, strengthening the righteous against the evil day. These very congruences, especially their political and cultural implications, turned both camps of Neo-Calvinists against Bultema. It was notable, therefore, that the CRC Synod of 1918 reproved him on confessional grounds narrowly defined (the only one of the synod's four 1920s pronouncements to take a strict construction) and showed sympathy with other elements of Bultema's vision.[22]

The other two heresy trials involved the issue of common grace, and for good reason. The doctrine not only differentiated the CRC's three mentalities but, as the tenet relating "the church" to "the world," constituted the prime theological metaphor for acculturation. True, in the first case, that of Ralph Janssen, chief positive Calvinist on the Calvin Seminary faculty, the Confessionalist-Antithetical prosecution insisted the problem was liberal tendencies, particularly Higher Critical approaches to Scripture. But Janssen so amply defended his position from recognized Reformed authorities as to make credible his claim that the prosecutors' denial of common grace forced them into a false supernaturalistic conception of revelation. To the more immediate point, it led them to exaggerate the separateness, the exceptionality of Old Testament Israel. The implications for the Dutch-American "Israel" were plain. Thus the 1922 Synod's demotion of Janssen signalled a check on his school's proposal for acculturation.[23]

The purging dialectic now advanced to take in some of Janssen's prosecutors, the Antithetical Calvinists. Their explicit denial of common grace put the issue once and for all at the forefront, and their absolutizing of the antithesis—with implications of increased institutional separation and severe philosophical critique of all the movements of the day, liberal and conservative—meant that another model of Americanization was on trial. The 1924 Synod's finding against their leaders, CRC pastors Herman Hoeksema and Henry Danhof, thus rebuffed the other side of Neo-Calvinism. It did not, however, restore the first. The synod's truncation of common grace to the purposes of "soul saving" and its warnings about the "abuses" the doctrine made possible (openings to "liberal theology" and "the sinful world") showed a Confessionalist construction.[24] This party's triumph was sealed in 1928 when the CRC Synod, fearful of the revolution in manners and morals underway (these were the "Roaring Twenties") in the society the church was now entering, officially prohibited three forms of "worldliness." The tactics of defensiveness, legalism, and symbolic representation of large structures and trends hardly bespoke Neo-Calvinism, and the sins specified—dancing, gambling, and theater attendance—constituted the old negative trinity of conventicle-Seceder piety.[25]

Stasis and Unsettlement: 1930–1960

Meanwhile, the RCA West was not negotiating a formula for acculturation but reconsidering it. The America it had joined around 1900 was, and was to have remained, normatively Protestant. But the 1920s' Modernist—Fundamentalist battle cast doubts on that Protestantism's orthodoxy, and the simultaneous sexual revolution, spirit of ballyhoo, and resistance to Prohibition did the same for its moral hegemony. The 1920s cost the RCA West leadership much of its confidence, yet saw no final battle between its outgoing and orthodox strains. The West instead opted over the next decades for a mainstream denominational strategy: skirting hard and fast theological definition, mandating coexistence for those differences which remained, and stressing above all institutional program. But this does *not* mean that the denomination took an entirely mainstream American Protestant character. On the two litmus tests of such churches, toleration of theological liberalism and enthusiasm for denominational mergers, the RCA failed, in large part because of Western resistance.[26] Through World War II, then, the RCA constituted a clear example of a denomination which had become *less* Americanized owing to the presence of a large ethnic bloc within it. It also showed European influences, in this case, the Secessionist instincts for orthodoxy and separateness, remaining potent even within that sector of an ethnic group most acclimated to the American environment.

The CRC in the same period followed what we might with caution call a Fundamentalist strategy. Rigorous theological self-definition, militant anti-Modernism, devout piety, strict behavioral norms, socio-political conservativism—practicing all these the CRC not surprisingly declared Fundamentalists their "cousins."[27] But *erring* cousins. Theological precision cut to the Right too, faulting such items in the Fundamentalist complex as dispensationalism, perfectionism, second blessings, and overt or implied Arminian conceptions of salvation. More broadly, the CRC still stood sufficiently in the Kuyperian tradition to question Fundamentalism's tendencies toward spiritual–material dualism, individualism (in church and society), truncated theology, millenarian fantasies, and association with the more noxious facets of the political Right.[28] Stylistic differences were probably sharpest of all. The Dutch Reformed, of course, required human confrontation with God but mediated that through classic theological and artistic forms (the Confessions and the Psalms) to check human volatility and to respect God's dignity and transcendence. Against this, Fundamentalism's obsession with personal experience, especially as channeled through heightened emotion and American cultural vulgarities, seemed to insult God, exaggerate man, and cheapen true religion. Partly to deepen the contrast, the CRC in these years so stressed the covenant—over against revivalism as a method of recruitment, over against dispensationalism as a sense of history. The virtues they saw in the doctrine implied their own critique. The covenant incorporated believers into the Kingdom of God, heirs to the rich development of Christian history, members of the present body of the faithful, rooted beyond the self and mere emotion against the storms of the times and the soul.[29]

These arguments reflect the character of the Americanized CRC: a Confessionalist regime with Neo-Calvinist variations, the latter finely balanced between antithetical and positive tendencies. But as the First World War catalyzed this settlement, the Second broke it. The early 1950s saw a startlingly close reprise of the battles of the early 1920s. The same four mentalities reappeared, Calvin Seminary was again nearly torn apart, and new journals were founded to carry on each party's cause. The profile of each camp tells something of the forces that led to the eruption. The new breed of positive Calvinists, speaking through the *Reformed Journal*, were largely young academics whom the war had pulled outside the ethnic network; they returned excited by the possibilities of bringing Calvinism to the larger American world. The Confessionalists comprised the denominational Old Guard, understandably content with the old settlement and creating *Torch and Trumpet* to enforce the same. This journal also gave space to resurgent Antitheticalism, buoyed by the influx of postwar Dutch immigrants to Canada. These groups' attention to Netherlandic traditions was not nearly as surprising as the fourth party's—a band of RCA Western leaders who in the *Reformed Review* sought to apply Dutch National Church models to their own situation.[30]

Only the outcome of the struggle was different. Rather than purging one or more directions, the CRC took an eclectic path, replacing its entire seminary faculty with moderates and increasing ever after its stress on the programmatic and administrative. Social forces made such a solution more likely, perhaps even inevitable. The affluence of the postwar decades brought regionalization to the CRC (the denomination now supports five colleges, not one) and at the same time drew the Dutch Reformed into the web of suburbia, mass media, and the consumer lifestyle, all of which held the possibility of overriding the ethnic social network, not to mention its value system. That value system, moreover, had been marked ever since the 1930s with features of

American culture religion (especially belief in free enterprise and national exceptionality), which trend the 1950s' anti-communist crusading brought to a peak. If the events from Bay of Pigs to Watergate broke that development, they left the community more with questions than with certitudes as to its character and the nation's, its future, its very goals and desires.

Present and Future

What is truly historic in the last twenty years will not be clear for some time, but we can begin to sort out the puzzle by comparing present patterns to those of the past. Certainly the sense of the community as an option rather than a limit is new; so is the sense of diminished momentum. The most important novelty, however, might well be the attraction of types of piety separate from Reformed orthodoxy. Devotion and confession have gone together ever since the conventicle era, but now the American revival syndrome on the one hand and the piety of success on the other beam into the community's living rooms with negative implications for Reformed doctrinal insistencies. That the second of these comes from the RCA's own Crystal Cathedral says enough in this light about assimilation.[31] But in a more traditional vein, the question of Dutch-Reformed acculturation has come to where it pointed from the start: not about relation to America in general but to the Evangelical sector of America, particularly the part of that sector descended from Calvinistic (as distinct from Wesleyan and Pentecostal) sources. And the Evangelicals with whom the Reformed have recently shown some signs of converging are precisely those who have pruned themselves of the Fundamentalist traits the Reformed so long resisted. Put more positively, they are those who have adopted signal features of the Reformed world view.[32] In this regard Americanization is proving to be, as Dutch immigrant pastors proposed, a two-way, not a one-way street.

Such is the view of the terrain from this vantage within intellectual history. What other directions or questions offer themselves for future research? First of all, correlation of the cultural and the social structural. I have made some speculations about the social positions associated with various mentalities: the outgoing pietism of the pre–World War I era with the established and more prosperous; positive Calvinism with CRC academics; the moderation of the CRC under the affluence of the 1950s. These and other conjectures should be more accurately measured. Second, the present case offers many possibilities for comparative analysis. This can be done with groups that immigrated more or less simultaneously with the Dutch: other Confessionalists (e.g., German Lutherans), other pietists (British and Scandinavian free-churchers), and ethnics searching out a place in American Catholicism. It can be pursued across religious lines, with that larger "people of the covenant," American Jews. It should also be done across time; for instance, with immigrants of the colonial era—not just the Dutch but the Scots-Irish, Germans, and (once again, but carefully) the Puritans. Most instructive of all might be a comparison across space. How did the Reformed in the Netherlands respond to the postwar Americanization of Western Europe? How do the Dutch Reformed in Europe now compare to the Dutch Reformed in North America?

Finally, the American community could most profitably be re-scanned with an anthropologist's eye. This is a growing trend in the historical profession anyway, but would be suitable in any case since its techniques can capture better than more formal intellectual history the flavors, nuances, and silent patterns at the heart of ethnic life.[33] Not only common grace and the covenant but also ham-bun wedding receptions in the church basement and the mystique of strawberry Jello at Sunday supper must be explored if we are to understand the soul of the wooden shoe.

Notes

1. See Rudolph Vecoli's bibliographical essays, "European Americans: From Immigrants to Ethnics," in William H. Cartwright and Richard L. Watson, Jr. (eds.), *The Reinterpretation of American History and Culture* (Washington: National Council for the Social Studies, 1973); and "The Resurgence of American Immigration History," *American Studies International* 17 (Winter 1979): 46–66.

2. The definitive review of this development is Milton Gordon, *As-*

similation in American Life (New York: Oxford University Press, 1964): 84–159.

3.   Carl Wittke, *We Who Built America* (New York: Prentice-Hall, 1939); Oscar Handlin, *The Uprooted* (New York: Grosset and Dunlap Publishers, 1951). Exemplary of the third school are Michael Novak, *The Rise of the Unmeltable Ethnics* (New York: Macmillan, 1973); Andrew Greeley, *Ethnicity in American Life* (New York: John Wiley and Sons, 1974); and Harold J. Abramson, *Ethnic Diversity in Catholic America* (New York: John Wiley and Sons, 1973).

4.   Robert Wiebe, *The Segmented Society* (New York: Oxford University Press, 1975); Arthur Mann, *The One and the Many: Reflections on the American Identity* (Chicago: University of Chicago Press, 1979); Richard Polenberg, *One Nation Divisible: Class, Race and Ethnicity in the United States since 1938* (New York: Viking Press, 1980); Catherine Albanese, *America: Religions and Religion* (Belmont, Calif.: Wadsworth Publishing Co., 1981).

5.   John Higham, "Hanging Together: Divergent Unities in American History," *Journal of American History* 41 (June 1974): 5–28.

6.   Samuel P. Hays, "Modernizing Values in the History of the United States," especially pp. 264–276, in *American Political History as Social Analysis* (Knoxville: University of Tennessee Press, 1979).

7.   Samuel P. Hays, "A Systematic Social History" and "The New Organizational Society," ibid., 133–186, 244–263 respectively.

8.   Novak, *Rise of the Unmeltable Ethnics*, 7–20, 33–45, 61–84, 103–136, demonstrates these points in detail. A few specific case studies are Frederick A. Luebke, *Bonds of Loyalty: German-Americans and World War I* (DeKalb, Ill.: Northern Illinois University Press, 1974); Richard Gambino, *Blood of My Blood: The Dilemma of the Italian Americans* (Garden City, NY: Doubleday, 1974); Philip Gleason, *The Conservative Reformers* (Notre Dame: University of Notre Dame Press, 1968).

9.   Timothy L. Smith, "Religion and Ethnicity in America," *American Historical Review* 83 (Dec. 1978): 1185.

10.   B. K. Kuiper, *Ons Opmaken en Bouwen* [Our Planning and Building] (Grand Rapids: Eerdmans-Sevensma, 1918), 128. This volume was a Dutch translation of an earlier (1911–1914) series on Americanization in the CRC's weekly, *The Banner*. The other major treatment of the subject was F. M. Ten Hoor's in *De Gereformeerde Amerikaan*; see especially the issues of Feb. 1897, 6–13; Aug. 1898, 289–296; Mar. 1909, 153–161.

11.   H. Algra, *Het Wonder van de 19e Eeuw* [The Marvel of the Nineteenth Century] (Franeker: T. Wever, 1966) (on the conventicle connection, see 99–100); D. H. Kromminga, *The Christian Reformed Tradition* (Grand Rapids: Wm. B. Eerdmans Publishing

Co., 1943); and Henry S. Lucas, *Netherlanders in America* (Ann Arbor: University of Michigan Press, 1955), 50–53.

12. The best surveys of Neo-Calvinism are found in studies of its leader, Abraham Kuyper. In Dutch, a fine short overview is Jan Romein, "Abraham Kuyper: Klokkenist van der Kleine Luyden" [Abraham Kuyper: Catalyst of the Common People], in *Erflaters van onze Beschaving* [Legators of Our Civilization] (Amsterdam: Em. Queridos, 1971); in English, Dirk Jellema, "Abraham Kuyper's Attack on Liberalism," *Review of Politics* 19 (Oct. 1957): 472–485. Two representative works of Kuyper in English translation are *Lectures on Calvinism* (Grand Rapids: Wm. B. Eerdmans Publishing Co., 1961), and *Christianity and the Class Struggle* (Grand Rapids: Piet Hein Publishers, 1950).

13. Herbert J. Brinks, "The CRC and RCA: A Study of Comparative Cultural Adaptation in America" (paper presented at the Great Lakes History Conference, Grand Rapids, May 1979), profiles the RCA West educational leadership in the nineteenth century, 18–19. Immigration trends are evident in Robert P. Swierenga, "Local-Cosmopolitan Theory and Immigrant Religion: The Social Bases of the Antebellum Dutch Reformed Schism," *Journal of Social History* 14 (Fall 1980): 123.

14. James D. Bratt, *Dutch Calvinism in Modern America* (Grand Rapids: Wm. B. Eerdmans Publishing Co., 1984), 38–40, 43–46, 67–74.

15. Ibid., 46–50, 72–73. Henry Zwaanstra, *Reformed Thought and Experience in a New World* (Kampen: J. H. Kok, 1973), 70–95.

16. The antithesis is concisely expressed in Kuyper's *Tweeërlei Vaderland* [A Twofold Fatherland] (Amsterdam: J. A. Wormser, 1887), and constituted the theoretical foundation for *Souvereiniteit in Eigen Kring* [Sovereignty in Each Circle] (Amsterdam: J. H. Kruyt, 1880) and *De Verflauwing der Grenzen* [The Fading of the Boundaries] (Amsterdam: J. A. Wormser, 1892). Kuyper elaborated common grace in *De Gemeene Gratie* [Common Grace], 3 vols. (Amsterdam: Hoeveker & Wormser, 1902–1904). For a statement in English of the first, see *Lectures on Calvinism*, 189–191, 198–199; of the second, 121–126. S. J. Ridderbos provides commentary on these ideas in *De Theologische-Cultuurbeschouwing van Abraham Kuyper* [The Theological-Culture Conception of Abraham Kuyper] (Kampen: J. H. Kok, 1947), 233–257, 30–131, respectively.

17. Bratt, *Dutch Calvinism*, 50–52; Zwaanstra, *Reformed Thought and Experience*, 95–118.

18. Bratt, *Dutch Calvinism*, 52–54; Zwaanstra, *Reformed Thought and Experience*, 118–131.

19. Bratt, *Dutch Calvinism*, 73–79; Zwaanstra, *Reformed Thought and Experience*, 210–294.

20. Harry Bultema, *Maranatha! Een Studie over de Onvervulde Pro-*

fetie [Maranatha: A Study of Unfulfilled Prophecy] (Grand Rapids: Eerdmans-Sevensma, 1917).

21. Ernest Sandeen develops this in detail in *The Roots of Fundamentalism: British and American Millenarianism, 1800–1930* (Chicago: University of Chicago Press, 1970).

22. A sample of Neo-Calvinistic hostility was John Van Lonkhuyzen, "Chiliastische Droomerijen" [Millenarian Fantasizing], *Wachter*, Sept. 19, Oct. 1, 1917. Showing congruences were the synodical president's closing address, heavy with millenarian tones (*Acta Synodi der Chr. Geref. Kerk, 1918* [Acts of Synod, CRC, 1918], 95, and two books by positive Calvinists on the "signs of the times": B. K. Kuiper, *De Vier Paarden uit Openbaring* [The Four Horses of Revelation] (Grand Rapids: Eerdmans-Sevensma, 1918), and R. B. Kuiper, *While the Bridegroom Tarries: Ten After-the-War Sermons* (Grand Rapids: Van Noord Publishing Co., 1919).

23. Bratt, *Dutch Calvinism*, 105–110. Harry R. Boer, "The Janssen Case Fifty Years Later," *Reformed Journal* 22 (Dec. 1972): 17–22; 23 (Jan. 1973): 22–28; 23 (Nov. 1973): 21–24.

24. *Acta Synodi, 1924* [Acts of Synod, 1924], 147–149. See also the principal commentators on this decision: Louis Berkhof, *De Drie Punten in Alle Deelen Gereformeerd* [The Three Points in All Parts Reformed] (Grand Rapids: Wm. B. Eerdmans Publishing Co., 1925), and Henry J. Kuiper, *The Three Points of Common Grace* (Grand Rapids: Wm. B. Eerdmans Publishing Co., 1925).

25. *Agenda: Synod of the CRC, 1928*, 4–41.

26. On orthodoxy, see Winfield Burggraaff, *The Rise and Development of Liberal Theology in America* (Goes: Oosterbaan & Le Cointre, 1928), and John Kuizenga, *The Relevancy of the Pivot Points of the Reformed Faith* (Grand Rapids: Society for Reformed Publications, 1951). On ecumenism, Herman Harmelink III, *Ecumenism and the Reformed Church* (Grand Rapids: Wm. B. Eerdmans Publishing Co., 1968).

27. Nicholas Monsma, *The Trial of Denominationalism* (Grand Rapids: Wm. B. Eerdmans Publishing Co., 1932), 72; Clarence Bouma, "Ecumenicity: Spurious and Genuine," *Calvin Forum* 15 (Nov. 1949): 61–62.

28. Bratt, *Dutch Calvinism*, 131–134.

29. James D. Bratt, "The Covenant Traditions of Dutch-Americans," in Daniel J. Elazar (ed.), *The Covenant Connection: Federal Theology and the Origins of Modern Politics* (in press).

30. The *Reformed Journal* and *Torch and Trumpet* (after 1970, the *Outlook*) were founded within a month of each other in 1951. Examples of RCA historical searching are the articles by W. L. Ietswaart (Mar. 1948: 7–11), Isaac Rottenberg (Mar. 1953: 4–7), and Lester Kuyper (May 1960: 18–31), all in *Reformed Review* (*Western Seminary Bulletin* before 1955).

31. Robert Schuller, who built the cathedral and its huge programmatic complex, including television's "Hour of Power," is an ordained RCA minister, raised in and educated through its network. His message of positive thinking and "success" is evident in any number of his published books. On the other side of the denominational divide, the CRC-rooted Amway Corporation promotes a similar ideology through its direct-sales empire.
32. See Richard Quebedeaux, *The Worldly Evangelicals* (San Francisco: Harper & Row, 1978), 145–161.
33. See John Higham and Paul Conkin (eds.), *New Directions in American Intellectual History* (Baltimore: Johns Hopkins University Press, 1979), xvi–xvii. A recent example is Henry Glassie, *Passing the Time in Ballymenone: Culture and History of an Ulster Community* (Philadelphia: University of Pennsylvania Press, 1982).

10. Religious Continuities in Europe and the New World

Herbert J. Brinks

Perceived from the tolerant ecclesiastical mode of the last few decades, many Dutch-American church constituents have concluded that their religious history in America is both confusing and embarrassing, for it appears that the founders of their churches were intolerant proponents of esoteric religious distinctions; and indeed the specific issues, which motivated the early immigrants to draw ecclesiastical boundaries, command but slight loyalty today. Few would argue any longer that rhymed Psalms are the only legitimate sources for congregational singing or that the pure church is marked by loyalty to the Netherlandic ecclesiastical secession *(afscheiding)* of 1834.[1] Since these and the other issues which segmented the immigrant churches in 1857 seem increasingly irrelevant, they have been largely ignored, and the vast majority of Dutch-Americans know little or nothing of their ecclesiastical origins.

Some blame for that condition must be attributed to the loss of the native language among the immigrants' descendants, for both their history and its sources are in Dutch. Still, it is also true that the history of the 1857 schism has been cast in an unattractively ascerbic polemic, and church historians have not been inclined to revive the topic because it could easily undermine fifty years of peaceful inter-church relations between the Christian Reformed and Reformed denominations.[2] Nonetheless, there is space for a careful re-examination of the 1857 secession's origins, and this essay will trace that ecclesiastical separation to its foundation in the three identifiable factions which grew out of the *afscheiding* in the Netherlands. It is particularly significant that these three partisan fragments flourished between 1840 and 1854, because that period also encompassed the initial phase of Dutch immigration to the American midwestern states. It is no surprise to discover, therefore, that the immigrants transported their ecclesiastical infighting to the New World.

Reduced to their essential characteristics, the contesting segments within the *afschieding* are distinguishable from their differing views of church polity and their contrasting interpretations of the *afscheiding* itself. In the center of this spectrum the Antony Brummelkamp and Albertus C. Van Raalte faction perceived the 1834 *afscheiding* as an ecclesiastically purifying event, but they also regarded segments of the national church as their legitimate religious cohorts. Similarly flexible in its views in church polity, the Brummelkamp and Van Raalte faction considered the church order of Dordrecht (1618–1619) as a helpful guide in maintaining the purity of the church, but they altered these rules to reflect changing circumstances.

Though on opposite sides of the centrist position, Hendrik De Cock and Hendrik P. Scholte shared common ground in defending the absolute necessity of the 1834 secession. For Scholte, however, the split was a prelude to organizing relatively independent congregations with local authority in formulating rules of conduct. By contrast, De Cock considered the seceded group as the only legitimate heir to the Dordracian succession, and he favored a rigid adherence to the rules which that synod formulated in 1619. Scholte, then, drifted toward non-denominationalism, while De Cock sought to organize the seceders as the continuing and pure remnant of the folk church.[3]

The divisive potential of these contrasting views was enhanced and perpetuated by the theological training which each of the leading clergy provided. Scholte conducted his school in Utrecht while Van Raalte and Brummelkamp taught respectively in Ommen and Hattem until 1844, when they joined forces in Arnhem. De Cock trained pastors in his Groningen parsonage and, following his death in 1842, the similarly minded T. F. De

Haan and W. A. Kok continued De Cock's work. These separate and frequently competing educational efforts were largely amalgamated in the Kampen theological school which was organized in 1854. For twenty years prior to that event, however, the seceded clergymen were trained to reflect their mentors' partisan views. Thus, long after the Kampen school superceded the parsonage schools, the pastorate educated before 1854 continued to reflect the partisan spirit which had divided them during the pre-Kampen era.[4]

Between 1846 and 1879 the Dutch-American immigrants acquired twenty-eight of these parsonage-trained pastors, and their behavior in America clearly reflected the partisan spirit that characterized the seceded church in the Netherlands before 1854 (see Table 10.1 for the specifics). H. P. Scholte's students joined several denominations, but they were inclined to disaffiliation and independence. Van Raalte's students followed him into the Dutch Reformed Church of America, while most of De Cock's disciples spurned the union that Van Raalte encouraged in 1850. Instead, the De Cock party in America attempted to establish intimate connections with the seceded church of the Netherlands, and they organized the Christian Reformed Church in 1857 to accomplish that goal. Thus, the patterns that had developed in Europe continued to mold ecclesiastical contours within the immigrant community.

More specifically, none of Scholte's six students invested their careers in the Christian Reformed Church, but, following their mentor, three of them pursued irratic courses with marked inclinations to independence. Three others joined forces with Van Raalte, but, since two of these died shortly after immigrating, only the Zeelander Cornelius Vander Meulen steadily represented the Scholte faction in the Reformed Church of America.

The nine immigrant pastors who adhered to Van Raalte's policies came from the whole spectrum of seceders. Two were Van Raalte's own students, while another trio had been Scholte's disciples. The remainder consisted of a pair of self-trained clerics and two others from the De Cock group. The breadth of Van Raalte's coalition, then, reflected his own more inclusive definition of the church. He had, in fact, never declared the national

Table 10.1. Parsonage-trained Pastors, 1846–1879

Name	Education	Date of ordination	Province served	Immig. date	Death	Susp.[a]	Affiliation in Am.[b]
I. de Cocksians (13)							
Ypma	de Haan	1845	Fr.	1847	1863	N	R
Smit	W. Kok	1847	Dr.	1851	1878	N	R, P, C.
v.d. Schuur	F. Kok	1840	Dr.	1848	1876	Y-1	R
Baron	de Haan	1844	Fr.	1869	1882	N	C
Coelingh	W. Kok	1852	Dr.-Fr.-Gr.-Ov.	1871	1895	N	C
Frieling	de Cock/W.Kok	1847	Ov.-Gr.	1866	1895	N	C
F. Hulst	de Haan	1855	Gr.	1868	1873	N	C
Kuiper	W. Kok	1850	Ov.-Gr.	1879	1894	N	C
v.d. Bosch	W. Kok	1848	Geld.-SH.	1857	1897	N	R, C.
v.d. Werp	de Cock/Haan	1844	Gr.-F.-NH-SH.	1864	1875	N	C
Koopman	W. Kok	1851	SH.	1865	1884	N	R, C, R.
Schepers	W. Kok	1852	Dr.	1852	1878	N	P, C.
Sum: C = 10	70.6%	7 prov. served					
R = 3	20.4%	3 prov. served					
II. Self-educated (6)							
Wust	Self (KK)[c]	1840	NH.	1847	1888	Y-2	R, I, C, Ret.
de Beij	Self/Postma	1848	Gr.	1868	1894	N	R
Duiker	Self/?	1850	Gr.	1867	1917	N	C, R, C, R.
v. Leeuwen	Self (KK)	1846	SH.-NH.-NB	1863	1882	Y-2	C

Duunewold	Self	1851	SH.	1851	1895	N	P, R
de Rooy	Self (KK)	1851	SH.	1851	1884	N	B, I, Ret., P, I, C.
Sum:	C = 2	40%	4 prov. served				
	R = 3	50%	2 prov. served				
	Ret. = 1	10%	1 prov. served				

III. Scholte Educated (6)

Baaji	Scholte	1840	Geld.	1848	1850	Y-1	R
Zonne	Scholte	1842	SH.	1847	?	Y-1	P
Betten	Scholte	1842	SH.	1847	1900	N	I
v.d. Meulen	Scholte	1839	SH.-Zee.	1847	1879	N	R
Gardenier	Scholte	1842	Zee.	1853	1855	N	R
Kiljn	Scholte	1839	Zee.-Ut.	1851	1883	N	R, C, R.
Sum:	R =	60.6%	4 prov. served				
	P & I =	30.4%	1 prov. served				

IV. Van Raalte Educated (3)

Bolks	v. Raalte	1841	Ov.	1851	1894	N	R
P. Oggel	v. Raalte	1849	Ut.-Zee.	1856	1869	N	R
Sum:	R	100%	3 prov. served				

Sources: Peter Vanden Berge, *Historical Directory of the Reformed Church in America* (New Brunswick, N.J.: Reformed Church of America, 1966); Algemeen Bureau van de Gereformeerde Kerken in Nederland, *Hondered Veerstig Jaar Gemeensten en Predikaten van de Gereformeerde Kerken in Nederland* [One Hundred and Forty Years of Congregations and Clergymen of the Reformed Churches in the Nederlands], (Goes: Oosterbaan & Le Cointre, 1974); Christian Reformed Church of North America *Yearbooks*; J. Wesseling, *De Afscheiding van 1834 in Groningerland* [The Secession of 1834 in Groningerland], (3 vols, Groningen: De Vuurbaak, 1972–1878); J. Wesseling, *De Afscheiding van 1834 in Friesland* [The Secession of 1834 in Friesland] (Groningen: De Vuurbaak, 1980); J. Smits, *De Afscheiding van 1834* (4 vols., Dordrecht: J. P. van den Tol, 1971–1982). Both Wessling and Smits have additional volumes in publication.

a Susp. = disciplinary suspension in the Netherlands or U.S.A., Y-1 = Yes in the Netherlands, Y-2 = Yes in America, and N = No.
b Reformed Church in America, C = Christian Reformed Church, P = Presbyterian, I = Independent, B = Baptist, and Ret. = returned to the Netherlands.
c KK = Kruiskerken or lay ordination.

church of the Netherlands to be utterly corrupt, but instead, both he and Brummelkamp supported the creation of educational ventures which joined members of the national and seceded churches.[5]

By contrast, the faction which organized the Christian Reformed Church in 1857, drew its whole clergy from the De Cocksian party in the Netherlands (Table 10.1). De Cock's group provided thirteen pastors to the larger immigrant community, and, as noted above, two of these linked with Van Raalte. Another pair affiliated with a conservative Scotch Presbyterian denomination, while the remaining nine served the Christian Reformed Church. Protesting Van Raalte's ecclesiastical policies in 1857, this new group highlighted its unreserved loyalty to the 1834 secession. But the Christian Reformed Church also espoused a rigid embrace of the Dordracian church rules. Thus, as nearly as possible, the dissenting group reincarnated the specific characteristics of De Cock's party.[6]

The founding pastor among the dissenters was Koene Vanden Bosch, and in addition to his suitably partisan educational credentials, his career in the Netherlands and America demonstrated the consistency of his factional loyalties. That process began auspiciously during his clerical examinations, which were scheduled during a synodical gathering in Zwolle. This 1848 synod was organized to unify the factions within the seceded denomination, for during the 1840s conflicting views of church polity divided Brummelkamp's adherents from those of De Cock. However, the two parties could not resolve their differences in 1848, and the De Cocksians withdrew. Vanden Bosch was caught in the middle because the synod which was to examine him had been captured by Brummelkamp. The De Cock faction attempted to solve the dilemma by gathering in a local church, but its pastor would not consent to that plan. Undeterred, the rump session marched seven miles down the road to Rouveen, where they received a welcome and where Vanden Bosch passed his exams.

Thereafter he served churches in Gelderland and Zuid-Holland, but in each case these congregations carried the wounds of disunity spawned by internal conflicts between the partisans of Scholte, Brummelkamp, and De Cock. Apeldoorn, where Vanden Bosch preached from 1848 to 1854, had once been split three ways, but after H. P. Scholte immigrated to Iowa in 1847, his partisans, together with their pastor, Gerrit Baay, followed Scholte to America. Despite initial controversies with the Brummelkamp faction in Apeldoorn, Vanden Bosch served the church for seven years, and then he moved to the Noordeloos, Zuid-Holland congregation in 1854. There he encountered a second church that had been fractured during the Scholte era. But again the Noordeloos group acquired greater unity after Scholte's adherents immigrated, and Vanden Bosch inherited the peace of their departure. Still, after a scant two-year ministry there, Vanden Bosch accepted the call of an immigrant church in Michigan, and several of his parishioners joined him in the trek to what became Noordeloos, Michigan.[7]

Although separated by an ocean and nearly half of the North American continent, Vanden Bosch encountered the same divisions among the immigrants in Michigan that had previously fractured the seceders in the Netherlands. To the last man of them, his denominational colleagues in the colony were students of Van Raalte or Scholte, and the prominent regional leader, Van Raalte, was a known theological cohort of Brummelkamp. Of all this, Vanden Bosch was probably forewarned, because both his father and brothers had preceded him to that region nine years earlier. Still, Vanden Bosch was no doubt shocked to discover that Scholte, who had been deposed from the seceded church of the Netherlands in 1840, could, nonetheless, gain access to the Zeeland, Michigan pulpit in 1856. Since Scholte had been the departed nemesis, whose divisive activity had troubled every church in Vanden Bosch's path,[8] it is hardly surprising that he listened attentively to those who favored secession from the Van Raalte coalition and reaffiliation with the seceders in the Netherlands. In so doing Vanden Bosch only reasserted an identity that had structured his whole career.

The Vanden Bosch career (though but one example) embodied the general contours of all the parsonage-trained pastors who joined him in the Christian Reformed Church.[9] But, no less than their pastors, the new denomination's parishioners were determined to preserve their peculiar De Cocksian identity in America. Consequently, their shifting denominational affiliations were directly related to the factional loyalties of the pastors they

Table 10.2. Thirty Lay Leaders and Officeholders
in the 1857 Secession, 1857–1861

Name	Source[a]	Office	Location in Michigan	Dutch origin	Affiliation in Netherlands[b]
B. de Graaf	B	Deacon	G.R.	Zee.	S
J. de Jonge	B	Deacon	G.R.	Zee.	?
H. Moerman	S	Deacon	G.R.	Zee.	S
A. Pleune	B	Elder	G.R.	Zee.	?
G. Haan	B	Elder	G.R.	Utrecht	S
J. Gelck	B	Elder	G.R.	Zee.	S
J. Gezon	S	Elder	G.R.	SH.	S
J. Van Tongeren	S	Elder	Noord.	Geld.	S
E. Everts	S	Elder	Noord.	Dr.	S
P. Vanden Bosch	S	Elder	Noord.	Dr.	S
J. S. R. Roos	S	Deacon	Noord.	SH.	H
A. Nijssen	S	Elder	G. Haven	Geld.	H
H. Bartels	S	Elder	G. Haven	Dr.	S
D. Groenveld	B	layleader	G. Haven	?	?
Lucas Elbers	B	Elder	Polkton	?	?
J. A. Vander Werp	S	Elder	Polkton	Gron.	S
H. Vinkmulder	S	Deacon	Polkton	Gron.	S
M. De Naaje	S	Deacon	Graf.	Zee.	S
J. F. Van Aanroy	S	Elder	Graf.	Dr.	S

acquired, and the history of two Chicago area churches clearly illustrates that phenomenon. Originally, in 1847, the Roseland and South Holland communities organized a single congregation which remained in Van Raalte's coalition until 1862. Their pastors during this period, W. C. Wust and Martin Ypma, were De Cocksian; but in 1862, with the arrival of Van Raalte's protege, Siene Bolks, the De Cocksians in South Holland left the Reformed Church. They remained apart until 1866 when H. R. Koopman replaced Bolks. A student of W. A. Kok, Koopman's career in the Netherlands bore clear evidence of his De Cocksian sympathies, and thus the dissidents in South Holland rejoined the Reformed Church in 1866. They remained in that denomination during Koopman's tenure, but his successor, Adrian Zwemer, was an outspoken proponent of the Van Raalte party

Table 10.2 (continued)

Name	Source[a]	Office	Location in Michigan	Dutch origin	Affiliation in Netherlands[b]
J. Rutgers	B	Elder	Graf.	Germany	S
H. K. Strabbing	S	Elder	Graf.	Dr.	S
S. Lucas	B	Elder	Graf.	Germany	S
H. Lucas	B	Deacon	Graf.	Germany	S
P. Boven	S	Elder	Graf.	Gron.	H
J. Rabbers	S	Elder	Zee.	Dr.	S
G. Kuipers	B	Deacon	?	?	?
H. W. Dam	S	Elder	Fries.	Fr.	S
C. Vorst	S	layleader	Holland	NH.	S
G. E. J. Ham	S	Elder	Holland	?	?
A. Krabshuis	S	Elder	Holland	Ov.	S

Sources: H. Beets, *De Chr. Geref. Kerk in N.A.* (Grand Rapids: Grand Rapids Printing Company, 1918), 79–87; Robert P. Swierenga, *Dutch Emigrants to the United States, South Africa, South America, and Southeast Asia, 1835–1880: An Alphabetical Listing by Household Heads and Independent Persons* (Wilmington, Del.: Scholarly Resources, 1983); Minutes of Noordeloos (Mich.) CRC; Centennial History 1857–1957: First Christian Reformed Church (Grand Rapids, Mich.).

[a] S = Swierenga's listing; B = Beets, *Chr. Geref. Kerk*, and others.

[b]Affiliation in the Netherlands: S = seceder; H = Hervormd Church; ? = Unknown.

and thus, when Zwemer occupied the South Holland pulpit, the De Cocksians reasserted their independence.

The Roseland community, which organized its own congregation in 1865, remained in the Reformed Church until 1877. But again, the departure of H. R. Koopman triggered secession, for when he left, the Roseland church fragmented, and the De Cocksian party organized the first Christian Reformed Church of that community. Koopman served the Roseland Reformed Church from 1870 to 1877, but his replacement, Cornelius Kriekard, who was a graduate of Hope College and New Brunswick seminary, did not carry proper De Cocksian credentials.[10] Describing the Roseland secession, one local pastor wrote, "It happened this way. Rev. Koopman, a minister from Pernis in the Netherlandic province of Zuid-Holland could not satisfy a portion of the

Roseland congregation. Dissatisfaction grew and developed from the time of his arrival. Then the Classis advised him to take another church, and when Koopman left, those who wanted him to stay resigned."[11]

Koopman, it would appear, spent much of his career leaving the scenes of his accidents. Yet he was more the occasion than the cause of the conflicts. He began his ministerial activity as a lay leader in the Netherlands, and while serving a fragment of the Noordeloos congregation there, he studied under W. A. Kok. Though not yet ordained, he led the anti-Scholte faction of the Noordeloos congregation; thus his credentials as a De Cocksian and an opponent of Scholte were well known. Furthermore, some of the immigrants in South Holland and Roseland originated from the churches that Koopman served in the Netherlands, which also accounts for his compatibility with the Chicago-area dissidents.[12] Though he never spearheaded secession from the Reformed Church in America, Koopman did desert the ranks for two years when he became the first pastor of the Pella (Iowa) Christian Reformed Church. Doubtless his anti-Scholte credentials encouraged the Pella dissidents to call him to Scholte's Iowa stronghold. Between 1868 and 1870 Koopman briefly left the Van Raalte coalition, but thereafter he returned to Reformed churches in Roseland and in Paterson, New Jersey, where he died in 1884.[13] Significantly, each of those congregations contained vigorous proponents of the De Cocksian faction who had no quarrel with Koopman, but when his successors failed to satisfy them, they formed new congregations.

In Michigan, where the chartering congregations of the Christian Reformed Church were concentrated, ideological cohesion also prevailed. For, like their pastors, the elected officials of the specific churches immigrated from eight different provinces in the Netherlands and Germany as well, with the widely separated regions of Drenthe and Zeeland providing the highest concentrations of provincial representation. No congregation's elders and deacons originated from a single Dutch province (see Table 10.2).[14] Thus, the evidence points to ideological rather than provincial cohesion, and since the dissenters systematically called their pastors from the De Cocksian party, logic suggests that they were well aware of their loyalty to that segment of the Dutch *afscheiding.*[15]

Whatever its convolutions, this recitation of ecclesiastical conjunction and disjunction discloses a consistent pattern of behavior, which modifies some widely regarded explanations for the 1857 secession. Certainly the founders of the Christian Reformed Church did not congeal along provincial lines,[16] for though their pastors were trained in the northern provinces of the Netherlands, they served churches throughout the land and the denominational constituency also originated from widely scattered points in the Dutch landscape. Then too, the assertion that the assertion that the behavior of one or twenty disgruntled malcontents adequately discloses the foundations of the 1857 secession cannot stand,[17] for though such folk were clearly agents of secession, their achievements depended upon the continuing vitality of established ideological distinctions. It appears that the primary and determining causes of ecclesiastical separation were intellectual, because partisan loyalties taken from Europe were vigorously reasserted in Michigan, Illinois, and Iowa, where the guiding reigns of intellect stretched back to the parsonage schools of Groningen, Arnhem, and Utrecht.

Notes

1. As is indicated in the April 8, 1857 notations in *Classis Holland Minutes, 1848–1858* (Grand Rapids: Wm. B. Eerdmans, 1950), 236–251, the dissatisfaction that pervaded the protests of the 1857 seceders focused on the Van Raalte group's failure to elevate the necessity of the 1834 secession and loosening the bonds of fellowship with the Netherlandic seceded church. The Graafschap consistory expressed this matter most directly, declaring, "what grieves our hearts most in all of this is that there are members among you who regard our secession in the Netherlands as not strictly necessary, or [think that] it was untimely" (242). The Polkton, Michigan consistory declared that they desired "no longer to belong to your denomination, and have betaken ourselves to the standpoint we had when we left the Netherlands, in order thus again to be in connection with the church of the Netherlands" (243). Rev. H. G. Klijn made a similar appeal as he reminded his colleagues, "we are together, ministers of the secession, in so far as your overseers in the midst of you walked that same path with us

in the Netherlands. Yea, we were separated from all Protestant denominations. Brethren, I exhort you in love not to lose this your character" (241). Less diplomatic, Koene Vanden Bosch simply announced, "I can not hold all of you who have joined the Dutch Reformed Church to be the true church of Jesus Christ, and consequently I renounce all fellowship with you and declare myself no longer to belong to you" (240). Apparently, for Vanden Bosch, the only legitimate belonging was with the seceded church of the Netherlands.

Other issues raised in the 1857 declarations of secession included the use by the Dutch Reformed churches of 800 hymns in worship services, together with its alleged practice of inviting members of other protestant groups to participate in the sacrament of the Last Supper. Complaints were also lodged over the Reformed denomination's fraternization with other churches whose doctrines conflicted with traditional Reformed confessions. These specific allegations of misconduct, including the denomination's inconsistent teaching and preaching from the Heidelberg Catechism, reflected the seceding group's attachment to the Dordrachian church rules of 1618–1619. In emphasizing these rules, together with the foundational character of the 1834 secession, the American seceders mirrored the views of De Cock's partisans in the Netherlands.

2.   Until the 1920s, inter-church relations between the Reformed and Christian Reformed churches were strained by a persisting barrage of pamphlets containing indiscreet and frequently brutal accusations. In 1918, Henry Beets, *De Chr. Geref. Kerk in N.A.: Zestig Jaren van Struijd en Zegen* [The Christian Reformed Church: Sixty Years of Strife and Blessing] (Grand Rapids: Grand Rapids Printing Company, 1918), 101–120, was the first effort to evaluate the 1857 secession from an historical perspective, but he concluded that the schism was both *"wettige en plichtmatige"* [legitimate and necessary], 120. Later church historians, D. H. Kromminga in 1943 and John Kromminga in 1949, refused to reassert the traditional justification for the 1857 separation. D. H. Kromminga, in *The Christian Reformed Tradition: From the Reformation till the Present* (Grand Rapids: Wm. B. Eerdmans, 1943), 106–111, provided a factual account generally free from judgmental conclusions. Still, he called it "regretable" that Van Raalte did not use "better methods to prepare the colonists for the 1850 union" with the Reformed Church. Although John Kromminga, in *The Christian Reformed Church: A Study in Orthodoxy* (Grand Rapids: Baker Book House, 1949), wrote: "We do not consider it within our province to determine whether this secession was justified or not." He nonetheless concluded that the seceders "may have over-emphasized the importance of the flaws they observed in the Reformed Church." Then to

balance the record, Kromminga added, "Van Raalte and his followers consistently minimized the dangers and errors of their own ecclesiastical community" (35). These relatively mild negations
stand in vivid contrast to the polemical literature of the early period before 1920.

3.   Both Netherlandic and U.S. church historians have described the
      fragmentation of the 1834 secession *(afscheiding)* with categories
      and definitions which are similar to those employed in this essay.
      Lubbertus Oostendorp, in *H. P. Scholte: Leader of the Secession of
      1834 and the Founder of Pella* (Franeker: T. Wever, 1964), 86–128,
      discussed the divisions of the seceders as crystalizing gradually
      "around the questions of baptism, church order, and the nature of
      the church in general" (103). De Cock's view that baptism should
      be available to children of both confessing and baptized members
      reflected his belief that the seceded church was equal to the na-
      tional or folk church in its obligation to serve the whole commu-
      nity. It was also a concession (akin to New England's halfway cove-
      nant) to the large number of pious doubters among the seceders
      who were faithful church folk but uncertain of their salvation.

      Beets, *Chr. Geref. Kerk*, 37–48; 79–84, discussed the distinc-
      tions between the Brummelkamp and De Cock factions in detail,
      and though Beets considered these intellectual postures to be
      significant forces leading to the 1857 secession, he concluded:
      "The deepest root and primary cause of the secession" was "dissat-
      isfaction with the teaching, worship and discipline of the church
      group with which the Colonists had united." On the contrary, this
      essay attempts to demonstrate that the partisan groupings which
      developed among the 1834 seceders did, indeed, become the foun-
      dation for the 1857 secession.

      H. Algra's "Broeder twisten," in H. Algra, *Het Wonder van de
      19ᵉ Eeuw* [The Wonder of the 19th Century] (Franeker: T. Wever,
      1976), 144–148, utilizes most of the traditional literature to re-
      count the chaos of fragmentation which characterized the Chris-
      tian seceded denomination between 1840 and 1854. But the most
      detailed analysis of that period is H. Bouwman's *De Crisis Der
      Jeugd* [The Crisis of Youth] (Kampen: J. H. Kok, 1914). More re-
      cently P. R. D. Stokvis in *De Nederlandse Trek Naar Amerika,
      1846–1847* [The Dutch Migration to America, 1846–1847]
      (Leiden: Universitaire Pers, 1977), 36–37 argued convincingly that
      the factious divisions within the seceded group provided motiva-
      tion for emigration, particularly among the adherents of Scholte
      and Van Raalte, i.e., the anti-synodical groups.

4.   The pre-Kampen parsonage schools and the founding of the Kam-
      pen Theological Seminary are described in W. De Graaf, *Een Monu-
      ment Der Afscheiding* [A Monument of the Secession] (Kampen:
      J. H. Kok, 1955), 20–26; and J. C. Rullmann, *De Afscheiding in de*

Nederlandsch Hervormde Kerk de XIXe Eeuw [The Secession in the Dutch Reformed Church in the 19th Century] (Kampen: J. H. Kok, 1930), 293–326.

5.   For Van Raalte's view of the 1834 secession, see Gerrit Ten Zythoff, "The Netherlands Reformed Church, Stepmother of Michigan Pioneer Albertus C. Van Raalte" (Ph.D. dissertation, University of Chicago Divinity School, 1967), who argues that Van Raalte was a reluctant seceder who "had done all that he could to avoid an open break, for he hated it" (255). Rullmann, *De Afscheiding*, 285–286, discussed the Brummelkamp faction's connection with members and groups within the national church.

6.   See note 1.

7.   H. Beets, "Ds. Koene Vanden Bosch," *Gereformeerde Amerikaan* [Reformed American], 6 (Mar., Apr., May 1902); Cornelius Smits, *De Afscheiding Van 1834: Tweede Deel, Classis Dordrecht* [The Secession of 1834: Second Part, Classis Dordrecht] (Dordrecht: P. J. van den Tol, 1974), 359–363.

8.   *Classis Holland Minutes, 1848–1858* includes the Oct. 9, 1856 notation, pp. 223–224, which reads: "Art. 18. The [question] whether Rev. Scholte should be allowed to preach in several churches was taken up. Rev. Van Den Bosch judges this not to be allowable. Brother Van Hees believes that it is unnecessary to discuss this at length, since we ought to leave one another free in this, and he, for himself, sees no objection to it, inasmuch as Rev. Scholte has never yet been suspended by any general assembly. Other brethren, however, wish to discuss it. After a long discussion about the person of Rev. Scholte, about his ecclesiastical standpoint, and the mutual alienation in church affairs, the following resolution is moved by Rev. Oggel: The assembly judging that those who have allowed Rev. Scholte to preach have not all done that to indicate thereby any fellowship with the ecclesiastical position of Rev. Scholte, but have merely lent to him their church building, judges that it can not prescribe to the consistories to what they may or may not lend their churches, and that this matter thus lies outside its competence: which motion was adopted."

9.   See particularly the list of parsonage-trained pastors (Table 10.1) in the De Cock party.

10.   *History of the First Christian Reformed Church of South Holland, Illinois* [1936], not paginated, and "Kroniek De Gemeente Roseland" [Chronicle of the Roseland Community], manuscript written by C. L. Clousing, 1902, located in the Christian Reformed Church Denominational Records of the Colonial Origins Collections, Calvin College and Seminary Library. Peter Vanden Berg, *Historical Directory of the Reformed Church in America* (New Brunswick, N.J.: Reformed Church of America, 1966) contains thumbnail sketches of the denomination's pastors and congregations.

11.   Letter of Bernardus De Beij to A. P. Lanting, Jan. 3, 1878, in the
      Dutch American Immigrant Collection of the Colonial Origins
      Collections, Calvin College and Seminary Library.
12.   For Koopman's career and other immigrant pastors who served in
      the Netherlands, see Algemeen Bureau van de Gereformeerde
      Kerken in Nederland, *Honderd Veertig Jaar Gemeenten en
      Predikanten Van De Gereformeerde Kerken in Nederland* [One
      Hundred and Forty Years of Congregations and Clergymen of the
      Reformed Churches in the Netherlands] (Goes: Oosterbaan & Le
      Cointre, 1974). More details about Koopman are available in Smits,
      Afscheiding Van 1834, 362, and the booklet, *Diamond Jubilee of
      the First Christian Reformed Church of Pella, Iowa* (n.p., n.d.),
      9–10.
13.   Dissident members of the Reformed Church in South Holland and
      Roseland certainly had prior acquaintance with H. R. Koopman
      since several of them had been founders of the Noordeloos church
      in 1836 or they were natives in regions which Koopman served
      (Gameren and Pernis) prior to his immigration. Some examples are
      Leenderd Vander Aa, G. Vogel, Baltus Van Baren, John De Mik, and
      Adrian Van Kleij.
14.   The officeholders originated from eight Dutch provinces and Graf-
      schaft Bentheim, a German region bordering the Netherlands.
15.   Since 70 percent of the officeholders can be identified with the se-
      ceders in the Netherlands (see Table 10.2), it seems reasonable to
      conclude that their pre-immigrant church affiliation probably did
      predispose them to join the 1857 secession. These findings conflict
      somewhat with Robert P. Swierenga's assertion in "A Denomina-
      tional Schism from a Behavioral Perspective: The 1857 Dutch
      Reformed Separation" *Reformed Review* 34 (Spring 1981): 180,
      which declares, "Thus, contrary to popular impressions, CRC laity
      were not notably more Afscheiding in background than were
      RCA members."
16.   See note 3.
17.   Arie Brouwer, *Reformed Church Roots* (Grand Rapids: Reformed
      Church Press, 1977), 124–126.

11. The Dutch in Canada: The Disappearing Ethnic

Herman Ganzevoort

A number of years ago the Dutch government expressed an interest in forming closer ties with the Dutch immigrant community in Canada for the purpose of cultural enrichment and exchange. To explore such possibilities it sponsored the visit to Canada of Dr. A. S. Tuinman, a former agricultural attaché, who had played a prominent part in the post–World War II immigration to Canada. After a series of stops and numerous meetings with Dutch-Canadians, Tuinman began to doubt the feasibility of any serious interchange between the Dutch in Canada and their compatriots at home.

He found to his disappointment that no national Dutch-Canadian organization spoke for or responded to the needs of all the immigrants. Furthermore, the three organizations which did serve the community, the churches, the credit unions and the clubs, represented only small parts of the larger ethnic community and had few connecting ties. Of the three, only the clubs evinced any interest at all in a cultural exchange, but they seemed unsure as to what contribution they could make. Tuinman unwillingly came to conclude not only that the Dutch-Canadian community was divided into many groups but that it seemed to be merging and disappearing into the Canadian multicultural mosaic.[1]

Dr. Tuinman was not the first nor will he be the last to reach these conclusions. The evidence suggests that the Dutch-

Canadian is an ethnic who should be put on the "vanishing species" list. It may seem strange, that in a country which is legally
bilingual and which publicly prides itself on its multicultural
composition, the sixth-largest ethnic group (426,000) should be in
the process of evaporation. But that is the case. An examination
of certain aspects of the immigrant community clearly delineates
and highlights this ongoing process.

One of the most important vehicles for retaining cultural
identity among immigrant groups in Canada and elsewhere has
been the retention of the native language. Such retention has
helped to solidify and maintain ethnic boundaries, community
solidarity, and differentiation from the dominant culture. *The
Non-Official Languages Study* (N.O.L.) of 1975 indicated that the
Dutch along with the Scandinavians expressed the lowest interest in language retention of the ten ethnic groups studied.[2] While
actual retention of the native language remains high among the
first generation (68 percent), it declines rapidly by the third generation to an almost negligible 0.8 percent.[3] Clearly, as death begins to take its toll among the first generation, the use of the
Dutch language in Canada will cease to have any function as a
cultural retainer.

The viability of the ethnic press obviously depends upon
language retention, and it can serve an important function in
keeping the language alive. Yet 52 percent of the respondents in
the N.O.L. study (some 38,000 people) never read the ethnic
press.[4] This disinterest clearly affects the only two exclusively
Dutch newspapers being published in Canada: *The Nederlandse
Courant* and the *Hollandse Krant*, which have a combined and
steadily declining circulation of 10,000. The two bilingual newspapers, *The Windmill Herald* and *Hollandia News*, with a combined circulation of some 12,000, are making a concerted effort to
increase the amount of English language material. Declining interest in ethnic newspapers and a diminishing language competency increasingly threatens the survivability of the ethnic press.[5]

The most successful Dutch-Canadian publication is the
English-language weekly *Calvinist Contact*, which has a circulation of 11,000. It owes its success to the fact that it serves as the
official organ of the Christian Reformed Church in Canada. It

functions less as a newspaper and more as a forum for church news and the interpretation of events from a "Reformed Christian" perspective.[6]

Also available to Dutch-Canadians are a number of church magazines such as *The Pioneer*, *The Banner*, and *The Clarion*, and church newsletters. Club and society bulletins and even credit union publications such as the *DUCA Post*, with a 5,000 circulation, are also distributed to the community.[7] The majority of these publications are printed in English and, without apology, recognize the changing language competency of their subscribers. It is doubtful, given the increasing use of English, that exclusively Dutch newspapers or other publications can survive in Canada without a dramatic increase in immigration from the Netherlands.

The teaching of Dutch as a second language also seems to have a very low priority among Dutch-Canadians. While some private tutors give instruction in the language and the Dutch Credit Union of Toronto (DUCA) has offered Dutch-language courses, the demand has been small when compared to that expressed by such groups as the Italians, Portuguese, or even Germans. The Christian parental schools, which are closely connected to the various Dutch-Canadian Calvinist churches, have shown little desire to institute Dutch-language programs. The N.O.L. study clearly reflected the Dutch community's disinterest in language training when it noted that Dutch-Canadians scored the highest of all ethnic groups in their lack of concern toward their children taking Dutch courses if they were available in local public and secondary schools.[8]

Although some attempt has been made to support Dutch-language retention in radio and television programming and in other media, the result has not been notably successful. Radio CHIN in Toronto broadcasts 90 minutes a day, with news, songs and music of the Netherlands, but its audience seems to be largely limited to first-generation immigrants. The rebroadcast of Dutch-language programs from Radio Nederland also reaches a limited public.[9] Dutch-Canadian theater groups presenting Dutch plays are hampered and increasingly discouraged by the declining language competency of their patrons. It is little wonder that Book IV of the *Report on Bilingualism and Biculturalism* suggested that "it seems most unlikely that the Dutch language will survive in Canada except as a language of immigrants."[10]

If language, then, cannot be regarded as a bulwark against cultural disappearance or evaporation, what about the three most important Dutch-Canadian institutions: the church, the credit union, and the club? An examination of these three, in the context of agents of cultural survival, does not hold out much hope for the preservation of the Dutch culture in Canada or for its bearer, the Dutch-Canadian.

The Canadian national census of 1971 indicated that 98,000 Dutch-Canadians were Roman Catholic, 83,000 Christian Reformed, 80,000 United Church of Canada, 127,000 adherents of other churches, and 38,000 of no professed religion.[11] With the largest number of Dutch-Canadians, the Roman Catholic church would seem to be an important body in the preservation of the Dutch-Canadian and his culture. This, however, has not been the case. While early in the immigration history the Roman Catholic church did favor Dutch settlements in the prairie west served by Dutch priests such as Plumas, Manitoba and Strathmore, Alberta, its general policy has been to avoid the creation of a Dutch "national" church. Integration into existing Catholic parishes and absorption into Canadian society was preferable to the creation of religious ethnic enclaves. Because the Dutch were culturally and socially acceptable to the Canadians, this appeared to be eminently possible.[12]

This policy was continued in the post–World War II era as the church sought to rebuild rural parishes which had been depopulated due to wartime and post-war urbanization. Again, integration and assimilation were the order of the day. Although Catholic laymen and priests of Dutch and English origin worked among the Dutch immigrants they were encouraged to help the new arrival fit into the English-speaking church. The Latin mass, the acceptance of ethnic intermarriage, and the welcome offered by fellow parishioners helped to bridge the language and cultural gaps. By the second generation, itself a product of the separate or parochial school, the process had been virtually completed.[13]

With nothing to distinguish themselves religiously from other Canadians and finding full acceptance in the Canadian

Catholic community, the Dutch immigrant saw little need to retain his Dutch culture or identity. Certain traditions in regard to family, food, or ideas could be maintained, but they naturally began to breakdown under the influence of the dominant society and the passage of time. The integration and assimilation urged by the church appeared to be beneficial, and therefore the loss of native culture and identity seemed to be an indifferent thing.[14]

The Christian Reformed Church found itself in a unique but, perhaps ultimately, not different position. Those immigrants who favored a Calvinist religious orientation were encouraged, both in the Netherlands and Canada, to think of themselves as secular missionaries bringing a new dispensation to Canada.[15] Church leaders encouraged them to integrate to the extent of learning the language and becoming an active part of the Canadian society so that they might share their reformed heritage and give service to the community. Assimilation; which meant the abandonment of religious principles, was to be eschewed, however. The immigrants were to be in the world but not of the world.[16]

The Christian Reformed Church, true to its calling as a source of Calvinistic enlightenment and responsive to the needs of its members, began the transition from Dutch to English in its services, organizations, and publications. It also sought to reach out to the larger Canadian community around it. In the process, religious ideas and traditions increasingly came into conflict with the values of Canadian society. The battlefield for this conflict was the hearts and minds of first- and second-generation Dutch-Canadian youth. Problems relating to out-group dating, dancing, movie attendance, and makeup created church and familial disruption. It soon became obvious that the retention of religious orthodoxy in the face of the "insidious liberal" influences of Canadian society was a constant and never-ending challenge.[17]

Out of this Christian Reformed collision with Canadian society have come two streams of response. The majority of immigrants were prepared to compromise and accommodate themselves and some of their principles. Largely regarding the church simply as a kind of Dutch Presbyterian religious organization, similar to its Canadian counterpart, they have sought to fit into their surroundings with the minimal amount of disturbance.

They have taken on most of the attitudes and ideas of the host society and, like the Catholics, retain some very basic Dutch customs, ideas, and folkways.[18]

The minority, perhaps a third, have made what appears to be
the most lasting and certainly most noticeable "Dutch" contribution to Canadian society. These "reformed" activists have helped
to establish Christian parental schools, a number of Christian
colleges within the Canadian university system, and some determined, if not highly successful, ventures in the fields of labor, agriculture, and human rights. Neither group, however, nor the
church, sees any real value in retaining the Dutch language or
culture which bred their unique variety of religion. In fact, the
church as a whole is quite vehement in its opposition to fellow
Canadians who persist in labelling it as the "Dutch Church."[19]

Other "reformed" churches find themselves in a similar situation. Although some are more orthodox than the Christian Reformed and see a greater danger in assimilating into the
"worldly" Canadian society, none see their survivial tied to the
retention of the Dutch language or culture. Indeed, many reject
what they regard to be the "liberal" sins of their churches in the
Netherlands and regard themselves as the chosen remnant. The
Reformed Church of America in Canada, while the most liberal
of the reformed, regards, with some disquiet, the more advanced
ideas of the *Hervormde Kerk* in the Netherlands and certain of
their own church leaders on the east and west coasts of the
United States.[20]

It is clear, then, that even in the "Dutch" churches in Canada little value has been placed upon the maintenance of the native language, culture, or identity. No great expectations, then,
have to be held for those who joined the United Church or other
Canadian Protestant churches. They and their children have
fitted themselves with the cloak of religious and ethnic invisibil-
ity. To them, their origins may be interesting, some customs and
traditions may be preserved, but their home and allegiance is to
Canada.

The second institution which should be briefly looked at is
the Dutch-Canadian credit union. Spread across Canada wherever there are heavy enough concentrations of immigrants, the
credit unions are a post-1950 development. Building upon Dutch

experience with cooperative lending and savings institutions, Dutch immigrants, in some cases with the help of the Dutch government, sought to provide easier access to credit than was available from the Canadian chartered banks. Some were organized by co-religionists such as the Catholic St. Willibrord's of London, Ontario or a number of Christian Reformed credit unions or on a purely secular basis such as the DUCA of Toronto. Most have been very successful and have expanded their financial services over the years.[21]

With the possible exception of DUCA and a few others, they have functioned largely as financial institutions and have had little cultural impact upon the Dutch community. They have undergone the same language transition as the churches and their meetings and financial services are carried out primarily in the English language. All the credit unions seek to serve clients beyond the narrow confines of the ethnic group and, while they might sponsor an occasional Dutch film or speaker or even conferences, fiscal responsibility and profit are more important than functioning as cultural repositories. Money has no ethnic connotation except that the credit unions have aided in the achievement of economic affluence for their members and have helped them to take part in the material growth of the Canadian society as a whole and to break down many economic barriers between the immigrant and his Canadian hosts. In other words, the credit unions have themselves been a vehicle of acculturation.[22]

The last part of the institutional trinity is the Dutch-Canadian club. Like the credit unions and the churches, clubs are to be found in the center of immigrant population concentrations. They are locally organized and run and have no national umbrella organization. Clubs were already in evidence in the early years of settlement but have had a notorious tendency to be short-lived due to their dependence on a few first-generation organizers and members.[23]

Organized in the main by non-Calvinist Dutch, they have had limited appeal to the orthodox religious groups who have made up at least a third of the immigrant group. Dances, card games, the consumption of alcohol, and theatrical or film entertainment have made such clubs unacceptable to a significant number of immigrants. While some did join to take advantage of organized charter flights to the homeland or annual celebrations of St. Nicholas Day, they did not become involved in other club activities.[24]

In recent years, with stimulation from the federal government's multicultural program and building grants, the clubs have been able, at least in larger urban centers, to become permanently housed and more firmly established. They have become involved in local ethnic festivals and in "Thank you Canada" programs to finance tulip plantings, organs, and carillons in rememberance of the Canadian role in the liberation of the Netherlands; they support choirs and dance groups and have a variety of dinners and social occasions. They do not, however, attract or represent a broad spectrum of support within the Dutch community.[25]

Faced with a general disinterest in their activities by the majority of the Dutch community, which either does not identify itself as ethnic or sees no relevance in folk dances and costumes which are already archaic in the Netherlands, the clubs have opened their membership to the community. As the non-Dutch element is further increased by intermarriage, they become Canadian social clubs with a veneer of Dutch culture and *gezelligheid* (conviviality). As protectors or preservers of the Dutch culture, they are quaint and interesting but largely irrelevant.[26]

If the three most prominent institutions of the Dutch-Canadian community have done little to preserve its culture or ethnicity and have in some cases even sought to erase it, perhaps it would be appropriate to look at the Dutch-Canadians and to draw some conclusions as to why they were and are so willing to give up their birthright.

Between 1890 and 1980 some 200,000 Dutch immigrants came to Canada from the Netherlands and the United States.[27] The nature of the immigration has been dictated by Canada's economic and developmental needs. The homestead era (1890–1914) required agricultural pioneer settlers. The inter-war period (1918–1930) saw a need for agricultural laborers, and the early post–World War II period called for agricultural laborers who could make the transition to independent farmers. The post-war urban and industrial boom required industrial and skilled labor, service workers, and some professionals.[28] This recruitment resulted in an immigration which was overwhelmingly lower middle class (66 percent), with the remainder largely lower class.[29]

Post–World War II immigrants, observers have pointed out, tended to have loose social and cultural ties at home, and many had backgrounds of cultural alienation.[30] These are characteristics, I believe, which were also shared by the majority of earlier immigrants—as, indeed, was a lack of formal education and the use of dialect or Frisian rather than formal Dutch among rural immigrants. None of these factors encourages the belief that the majority of immigrants had more than a passing interest in or knowledge of anything other than their own working-class or bourgeois culture. The conclusion that must be drawn is that the immigrants were hardly the most ideal carriers or transmitters of high native culture. Any examination of the Dutch literature which the immigrants brought with them or imported to Canada or even produced there, with the exception of religious publications, will corroborate such a view. It would seem that their lifestyle and culture meshed easily with that of the Canadians.[31]

When they arrived in Canada seeking economic security and advancement, they found themselves to be relatively acceptable immigrants. The Canadians regarded them, often above others, as culturally adaptable and assimilable, as they generally seemed to fit the norms of Canadian society. In terms of labor, they were immediately exploitable and a benefit to the developing nation. Very little about the Dutch was objectionable, strange, or could not be modified.

Similarly, from the immigrants' point of view, Canadian society, although different, seemed to offer plenty of opportunity and was open to change. An apparently classless society—at least, one based on wealth rather than birth—with European origins and founded on the work ethic, it opened up new avenues of personal struggle and achievement. Ideas and techniques from their own experience were appreciated and valued in Canada, and conditions there promised personal acceptance after a necessary period of economic and social apprenticeship. The immigrants were prepared to accept the promise until circumstance proved otherwise.

Such tempered acceptance from both sides permitted an easier integration or even assimilation than was possible for other immigrants, particularly those from eastern or southern Europe or Asia. It also prevented the development of an antagonistic or protective or even aggressively nostalgic ethnicity which is so often the compensation for non-acceptance by the dominant society.

The dispersal of the immigrants across the country, first to areas of highest labor need or settlement potential, and then to areas close to developing Dutch settlement, if they were economically viable, effectively prevented ghettoization. This was a policy encouraged by the Canadians and generally accepted by the individuals and organizations involved in immigrant settlement. Perhaps responding to their past experience of over-crowding in the Netherlands, the immigrants seemed to prefer it that way.

Encouraged by government, church, and their own pragmatic evaluation of what was necessary to achieve economic welfare, the immigrants began to discard many of the recognizable ethic identifiers. The positive economic and social returns of such a policy seemed to justify their actions. While a few might question the wisdom of abandoning the keys to their past, the majority believed that if the cost of success and achievement was the loss of their "Dutchness," it was well worth paying. Little wonder, then, that almost 60 percent identify themselves as Canadians rather than some kind of "ethnic"[32] and that perhaps less than 2 percent have ever gone back to the Old Country.[33]

The Dutch-Canadian is a "vanishing species." He is in the process of disappearing, and willingly so. But before his is gone, how may he yet be identified? Are there characteristics, tribal marks, ideas, and differences which distinguish him from his fellow Canadians? There are, indeed, cultural remnants and social memories which can be guideposts to the discovery of the elusive ethnic.

For example, family names remain an important means of identification. Since they were generally not as unpronounceable to the Canadian tongue as some other foreign ones, the Dutch have generally chosen to keep them. English Canadians quickly recognized that a "van," as in Vander Berg, or a "de," as in De Groot, indicates a Dutch name. There are, of course, many more names which are not so recognizably Dutch, but Canadians have never been loath to ask about ethnic origin, and an accent only encourages such an inquiry. Some immigrants did change their last names if such names were either unpronounceable or had sexual or derogatory connotations in English.

First names such as Sjoerd and Wietzke were also often Canadianized, and many immigrant children simply took on Canadian equivalents. Children of immigrants have usually received Canadian names if they were born in Canada. Although the general rule which dictated naming children after their grandparents was followed at first, this custom has begun to disappear. In recent years, the naming of children has been determined by popular Canadian fashion, while in some religious circles Biblical names have made a resurgence.

In rural areas, Dutch farmsteads are sometimes marked by the names of the districts from which the immigrants came or by names of Old Country farms themselves. Family names are prominently displayed on barns throughout the country and on many city dwellings. The fad to mark automobiles with the country of origin of the driver has also led to the appearance of NL bumper stickers on Canadian roads. Frisian pride has even produced an occasional sticker or flag from that province. The Dutch do not seem at all reluctant to display their origins in this fashion.

Another obvious sign of Dutch residency, visible to outsiders, is the continued use of the picture window valance or curtain. This curtain, the predominant fashion in the Netherlands, hangs across the top quarter of many Dutch-Canadian front windows. Made of figured lace, it has been retained by many first-generation immigrants, along with a profusion of houseplants, and is noticeable both in rural and urban areas.

Dutch businesses are often identifiable by the names of the proprietors (Voortman's Cookies) or the inclusion of the windmill logo or the use of "Dutch" in the name of the business itself. In Canada today, anything "Dutch" connotes cleanliness, hard work, and acceptability, and Dutch-Canadian businessmen take advantage of that association in their financial dealings with the general public. Most "Dutch" businesses could not exist without the patronage of Canadians outside the ethnic group. The only exception to this rule might be Dutch credit unions, whose membership remains predominantly Dutch.

Certain enterprises do, however, continue to cater to the ethnic community's needs. Dutch bakeries, delicatessens, butchers, fish markets, and specialty stores carry products which whet the appetites of the immigrants and their children. Bakeries make *bokkepotjes* (goats' feet); delicatessens carry croquettes, meat, and cheese; butchers produce Dutch cuts and *blinde vinken* (veal birds); fishmongers have smoked eel and mackerel; and the "Dutch Store" carries the familiar textiles, spices, and assorted other goods. Most of them also serve an increasing non-Dutch-Canadian clientele which have adopted many of the Dutch specialties and products and made them part of their daily necessities.

Dutch foods and products are available to the general public, and many supermarkets have "Dutch" or "ethnic" sections. Here one can find such foods as chicory, endive, kale, and broad beans, some imported from Holland, as well as Dutch pastries and other sweets. Since the Dutch cuisine is made up basically of meat, potatoes, and vegetables, it has little to distinguish it from the Canadian. Only Dutch restauranteurs serving Indonesian or French dishes have had any impact upon the Canadian restaurant scene.

As far as alcoholic beverages are concerned, Dutch-Canadians have in the past limited themselves in their selection. Canadian beer, although judged not as good as Dutch beer, has always been regarded as satisfactory and less costly than the imported variety. Canadian whiskey quickly displaced *Genever* (gin), although some might be returning to youthful tastes, as it is now abundantly available. Since many of the Dutch were not wine drinkers at the time of their emigration, their consumption in this area has perhaps lagged behind. Specialty drinks of Dutch manufacture such as Advocaat or Curaçao are more readily available than in the past, but there is little evidence to suggest that Dutch-Canadians consume more than anyone else. Moderate consumption of alcohol seems to be the general rule in the Dutch community, particularly in the orthodox circles. Restraint, not prohibition, is the determining factor; it is not uncommon to see alcoholic beverages served in homes after the Sunday morning church service. Alcoholism seems, however, to be no more common in the Dutch community than in the general public.

While the Dutch-Canadians may be adapting themselves

more and more to Canadian business practices and foods, they do preserve the family solidarity which was so important in the Netherlands and in their settlement in Canada. Birthdays, baptisms, marriages, funerals, and ordinary Sunday get-togethers remain important in preserving family contacts. Christmas, Thanksgiving, Mother's and Father's Day bring extended families, often from great distances, to the homes of family elders. Birthdays are seldom forgotten or uncelebrated, and the visit of, or to, an Old Country relative is generally a joyous occasion. Letter writing, whether overseas or to other places in Canada, although diminished by time, has been kept up. Telephone calls, even to the Netherlands, have helped to retain a certain family closeness, in spite of the great distances which sometimes separate members. Many still preserve the time-honored custom of keeping birthday and events calendar in a convenient and prominent place, often the back of the bathroom door.

The close family ties have, in some ways, been a support in the increasingly unstable social conditions of the changing Canadian society. While the authoritarian and patriarchal nature of the family unit has mellowed over time, respect for parents and elders is still prominent. Many second- and third-generation children still go to parents and grandparents for help and advice and look to their personal relationships as models for their own. Even as democratic marriage relationships begin to predominate in the community, replacing authoritarian structures, many reformed Dutch-Canadians see value in the traditional value system which places the man at the head of the family. This, and their religious orientation, no doubt accounts for their low divorce rate.

The strong sense of family has also encouraged the Dutch to extend themselves in the community at large. Orthodox Calvinists have regarded social outreach as true Christian service to the Canadian society and have encouraged it at all levels. Given their religious orientation, they have attempted to set up social service organizations which deal with the clients' problems from a "Christian" perspective. Christian counselling services and organizations to treat the mentally ill and the handicapped have developed from this interest.

As opportunities expanded in Canada in the 1960s and

1970s, the Dutch immigrants, particularly in urban areas, began to take advantage of them both for themselves and for their children. Dutch-Canadian professionals made their appearance in the fields of education, engineering, medicine, law, architecture, business, and even the fine arts. There were few occupations which they did not enter in or succeed at. As in the rest of Canadian society, women began to expand their role and leave behind the rigid patriarchal constraints which had inhibited them or their mothers in the Netherlands.

The scale of success measured against that of other Canadians exhibited no difference; in fact, except for their names, few could be identified as being peculiarly Dutch-Canadian. A few of the more prominent Dutch-Canadians recently have been: Senator George Van Roggen of British Columbia, William (Bill Woodenshoe) Vander Zalm of the British Columbia Legislature; Debbie Van Kiekebelt, the athlete; Aretha Van Herk, the author; John De Visser, the nationally famous photographer; Petra Burka, the skater; and the Voortman cookie kings. All have been recognized for their individual accomplishments, not their ethnic backgrounds.

The record of Dutch-Canadian achievements is evident for those who know where to search, but where is the "Dutch cultural" imprint on Canadian society? What is peculiarly Dutch-Canadian about what the first or second generation have achieved? What has distinguished the efforts of this group from any other ethnic group which immigrated to Canada? With the exception of the Christian Reformed activists, who have sought to make Calvinism relevant to Canadian society, a few dance groups, choirs, and theater groups, Dutch culture seems to have had no serious impact on the Canadian scene. It is true that a small body of literature dealing with the immigrant experience is beginning to develop, but only recently have writers begun to use English as a medium of expression. None have yet achieved any national prominence or notice, nor has a serious immigrant novel been written. Sociologists, historians, and other academics have merely scraped the surface in their examination of Dutch-Canadians.

The question remains: What has grown out of the Dutch

experience in Canada that is worthwhile preserving, developing, and sharing with fellow Canadians and others? Perhaps it is too soon to give an answer—perhaps too late!

Notes

1. Interview Dr. A. S. Tuinman, 1978, Calgary, Alberta.
2. K. G. O'Bryan, J. G. Reitz, O. Kuplowska, *Non-Official Languages: A Study in Canadian Multiculturalism* (Ottawa: Ministers Responsible for Multiculturalism, 1975), 389.
3. Ibid., 109.
4. Ibid., 329, 331.
5. Interview A. vander Heide, 1980, Burnaby, British Columbia.
6. Ibid.
7. Ibid.
8. K. G. O'Bryan, et al., 299.
9. For Dutch immigrant attitudes towards Dutch-language TV and radio programming, see K. G. O'Bryan, et al., 330–339.
10. Canada, *Royal Commission on Bilingualism and Biculturalism,* Book IV (Ottawa: Queen's Printer, 1969), 135.
11. *Census of Canada,* 1971, Volume I, Table 18.
12. For more on Catholic settlement prior to 1940, see Herman Ganzevoort, "Dutch Immigration to Canada 1892–1940" (Ph.D. dissertation, University of Toronto, 1975).
13. Interview Fr. F. Ver Hagen, 1979, High River, Alberta; interview Mrs. A. Felix, 1980, Toronto, Ontario.
14. Ver Hagen interview; Felix interview.
15. William Petersen, *Planned Migration: The Social Determinants of the Dutch Canadian Movement* (Berkeley: The University of California Press, 1955), 188; T. C. Van Kooten, *Living in a New Country* (Hamilton: Guardian Publishing Co. Ltd., 1959), 146; Ganzevoort, Chapter I.
16. Van Kooten, Chapters III, IV.
17. Ibid.; interviews Dr. J. Hielema, 1978–1979, Calgary, Alberta.
18. Hielema interview.
19. Ibid.
20. Interviews Rev. D. DeJong, 1979–1980, Calgary, Alberta; interviews Rev. P. Nulton, 1979, Calgary, Alberta.
21. Interviews, 1972–1975, St. Catharines, Ontario; 1980, Toronto, Ontario; 1977–1980, Calgary, Alberta.
22. Ibid.
23. Interview Cathy Cosgrove, 1980, Toronto, Ontario; Ganzevoort, Chapter V.
24. Interviews, 1972–1975, St. Catharines; 1977–1980, Calgary.

25. Cosgrove interview; for an examination of one Ontario club see Cathy Cosgrove, "Profile on the Dutch Canadian Club of North Bay." Unpublished manuscript in author's collection, 1978.

26. Ibid.

27. This final figure has been arrived at by an examination of the Canada Census 1871–1971, Dutch and American government statistics, and emigration society figures, and M. C. Urquhart and K. A. H. Buckley, *Historical Statistics of Canada* (Cambridge: Cambridge University Press, 1965). It is the author's own figure.

28. Gordon Oosterman, et al., *To Find a Better Life: Aspects of Dutch Immigration to Canada and the United States* (Grand Rapids: The National Union of Christian Schools, 1975), 95.

29. G. Beijer, et al., *Characteristics of Overseas Immigrants* (The Hague: Government Printing and Publishing Office, 1961), 132.

30. Ibid.

31. This and the following material is a personal evaluation based on hundreds of interviews with ministers, fieldmen, government officials, and most important, immigrants.

32. K. G. O'Bryan, et al., 427.

33. My studies have indicated that the returns to the Netherlands were few and largely took place in the first year, with homesickness being the primary motive. The percentage has been arrived at only after numerous interviews and discussions with government officials, fieldmen, and immigrants.

PART FOUR

Literary Culture and the Popular Press

12. Dutch Literary Culture in America, 1850–1950

Walter Lagerwey

One of the first scholarly comments on immigrant literature in the Dutch language was made by Henry S. Lucas. His observation is still worth noting:

> The Dutch immigrant deeply enjoyed reading. He was fond of theological works, even though these required concentrated thought and some familiarity with Scripture. . . . Next to writings on theology and the life of the spirit, the Dutch immigrant loved poetry. Most of the Dutch newspapers in this country carried poetry fairly regularly. It was usually didactic or patriotic, or else devoted to topics of local interest. An anthology of the Dutch poetry written here would accurately reflect the life and problems of the Dutch immigrant.[1]

This characterization, however apt in many respects, needs correction. The commentary of Lucas applies only to the Dutch orthodox Protestant community and ignores the Catholic Dutch and Flemish immigrant communities. In actuality, there is much greater variety in Dutch literary culture, especially if it includes the entire body of prose: memoirs, sketches, essays, editorials, folk tales, and even sermons. In my judgment, a significant and meaningful panorama of immigrant life is only possible if we include both poetry and prose.[2]

There is a very clear line of demarcation between Dutch Protestant communities and Dutch-Flemish Catholic communities in regard to the quantity and character of their literature. The Dutch language has had continuing significance in the life of the orthodox Reformed community for at least a century, and Dutch language publications united scattered settlements from the first Dutch-language newspaper, *De Sheboygan Nieuwsbode* (1846–1861) to the last newspaper, *De Volksvriend* of Orange City, Iowa (1874–1951). The church paper, *De Wachter,* has appeared continuously from 1868 to the present. Catholic communities were much more quickly Americanized and assimilated into the mainstream of American life; thus there is far less literature in the Dutch language produced in this community. This accounts for the preponderance of Protestant literature in almost every category.

I focus first on literature written during the founding of the Dutch and Flemish settlements, and second on writings during the period of their florescence as foreign-language ethnic groups. For the Protestant Dutch the tale of the immigrant experience begins with the sorrows of leave-taking and, after resettlement in the new homeland, continues in the nostalgic remembrance of things past. It is a tale of the struggles and sufferings of the new settlers, the Pilgrim Fathers of the West they have been called, but one that eventually climaxed in commemorative celebrations of gratitude in communities that not only survived but prospered.

It is also the story of Americanization, of Dutch Reformed Americans living in their church-centered communities, especially in Michigan and Iowa, struggling to remain Dutch as they became American, citizens who had to take sides in the Civil War, the Boer War, World War I, and World War II. As citizens they learned to celebrate American holidays, to become proud burgers of their newly adopted land even when they were not so politically involved. Here the Holland-American communities grew, narrow in their petty bourgeois ways and theological disputes and schisms, but broad in their religiously rooted way of life, their theologically defined and oriented life-style, and their commitment to Christian educational institutions, a Christian press, Christian institutions of mercy, and even a Christian labor organization. The hopes and aspirations, the joys and sorrows of these people, are poignantly expressed in their literature.

Several poems were written even as the departing ships were beginning the long journey to America. Two stanzas from an

1853 poem by J. C. v. d. B. of Rochester, New York reflect the turmoil and tension in the heart of one who left the homeland in
search of a better living and never would return:

> Vaarwel! Vaar eeuwig wel! O, dierbaar Nederland,
> 't Was op uw grond, dat ik voor het eerst het licht
>   aanschouwde,
> Daar leerde ik d'eerste tred aan moeders lieve hand,
> Daar was het dat 'k voor 't eerst tot God mijn handjes
>   vouwde...
>
> O, harde ballingschap—alleen om een bestaan
> Naar evenredigheid van zijn bestaan te vinden,
> Verlaat' hij Vaderland! Maar stort zoo menig traan
> Bij 't scheiden van zijn land, van magen en van vrienden.[3]

("Farewell! Fare forever well, Oh dearest Netherland, / It was upon
thy soil that first I beheld the light; / There I learned my first step at
mother's dear hand, / There it was I first folded my little hands to
God. / . . . Oh, hard exile—only to make a living, / Comparable to
his present living / He leaves the Fatherland! But tears pour from his
eyes / As he parts from his land, relatives and friends.")

The commemorative celebrations of 1887 at Zeeland and of
1907 at Holland, Michigan were the occasion for poems by Henry
E. Dosker and J. A. De Spelder. Dosker's rhetorical poem ex-
presses the marvel and mystery of the ancient primeval forest
with its vapor-filled swamps, majestic and forbidding to those
who settled there. Two stanzas from the long poem follow:

> O somber oord, waar dof de echos galmen
> En smoren in het woud of stillen waterplas.
> Hier zweven nog de doodelijke dwalmen
> Op 't groene slijm van 't slibberig moeras. . . .
>
> O, somber oord, wie zal uw grootschheid teek'nen?
> Wie schetst naar waarde, uw trotsche majesteit?
> Wie maalt den reuzenkamp, waarop de mensch moet
>   reek'nen,
> O woud, die naar uw kroon de stoute handen breidt.[4]

("O somber region where dull the echoes resound / And are smoth-
ered in the forest or quiet water pond, / Here the deadly fumes still

drift / On the greenish slime of the slippery swamp. . . . O somber region, who can portray your grandeur? / What portrayal can do justice to your proud majesty? / Who depict the gigantic struggle with which men must reckon / Oh forest, who would with bold hand reach for your crown")

Indeed, it was a dark and somber forest to the Dutchman who came from a civilized world of cultivated woods and who scarcely knew how to fell a tree!

Already in 1886 Dingman Versteeg published a history of the Michigan colony, including several anecdotal tales, which he entitled *Pelgrim-Vaders van het Westen* (Pilgrim Fathers of the West). The title suggests myth forming. To be sure, Dominie Albertus C. Van Raalte and his people are presented as a noble, valiant band who, like the Pilgrims before them, fled to America for freedom of religion. It is a moving account, soberly told, of the departure from the Netherlands to the arrival at the Black Lake, and then to the settlement at Holland. It is perhaps more story than history, but passages like "Ziekte en Dood" (Sickness and Death) and "De Plaag van 1851" (The Plague of 1851) are unforgettable tales of sickness and suffering.[5] Versteeg also tells anecdotal tales, like that of the inexperienced Dutchman who negotiated with an Indian by sign language to have a tree felled so that it would not crash on his log cabin. There is also the story of the Dutchman who came to work only to find that no one else had arrived on the job. When the boss arrived later in the day to check the shop, he found the worker, who did not know that it was Independence Day.[6]

Many memoirs of the early settlement survive. One of the most delightful reminiscences by an old settler appeared in *De Grondwet* (The Constitution) in July of 1927. It is Albert Kampferbeek's "De Oude Koloniale Dagen Vergeleken Bij De Dagen Die Wij Thans Beleven" ("The Old Colonial Days Compared with the Days We Presently Experience"). Kampferbeek's delightful style is evident from the following passage in which he talks about candle illumination:

Vetkaarsen, die men zelf kon gieten, waren veel goedkooper, en kwamen derhalve meer overeen met het finantie-wezen,

Waarover men beschikken kon. Want, men vergete niet, dat die eerste baanbrekers muskietus, vlooien, krekels en slangen in overvloed hadden, maar klinkende munt, ziedaar, die was zoo schaarsch als gevederde varkens.[7]

("Grease candles, which one could pour himself, were much cheaper, and therefore accorded more with the finances that one had at his disposal. For, let the reader not forget, that those first pioneers had an abundance of mosquitoes, fleas, crickets, and snakes, but hard cash, lo, that was as scarce as feathered pigs.")

The original cottages were not very bug-proof:

Hoe goed ook dichtgesmeerd, er kwamen hier en daar gaatjes in voor, waardoor muskieters, vlooien, krekels en soms zelfs slangen en ander klein kruipend onttuig naar binnen konden dringen. Men had in die dagen weinig gezelschap, en geen wonder, men kon in die kleine cabins er ook niet veel bergen. Maar dit kruipend, tergend en stekend gezelschap die, als zooveel ongenoode gasten, met al de brutaliteit van den middernachtelijken roover binnendrongen, had men in overvloed, en men was niet zelden ten einde raad hoe er mede huis te houden.[8]

("However tightly sealed, there were still little openings through which mosquitoes, fleas, crickets, and sometimes even snakes and other crawling riff-raff could enter. One had little company in those days, and no wonder, one could not lodge many people in those small cabins. But this crawling, tormenting, biting company which, like so many uninvited guests entered with the boldness of a midnight robber, were present in abundance and not seldom one was at his wit's end in knowing how to live with them.")

Kampferbeek was a good observer as well as a good storyteller who chose the right metaphor to make a point. A lighted cabin in the dark forest draws curious deer who "peer through the windows like so many shameless peeping Toms to see what was going on in such a hut."[9]

Despite all these hardships, the energetic Dutch colonists succeeded. I conclude this brief review of the literature of the early settlement at Holland with a statement by Versteeg that highlights the growing respect of the Americans for the persistence and diligence of the Dutch colonists:

> Hoewel de Amerikanen in het begin dikwijls lachten om het onhandig hanteeren der bijl door ons volk en soms zeiden: 'Die menschen houden het hier niet uit', hadden zij zooveel achting voor hunnen standvastigen ijver dat zij hen gaarne onderrichtten en bijstonden. Spoedig echter, toen zij de vorderingen zagen die gemaaakt werden, veranderde hunne meening, en kregen de Amerikanen zooveel verwachting voor de toekomst der nederzetters, dat zij thans zeiden: 'Het duurt maar weinige jaren, dan zijn die menschen welvarend.' En hunne voorspelling werd bewaarheid.[10]

> ("Although in the beginning the Americans often laughed at the clumsy way in which our people handled the axe and sometimes said: 'Those people will never stick it out here', still they had so much respect for their steadfast diligence that they gladly taught and assisted them. Soon however, when they saw the progress which they had made their opinion changed, and the Americans had so much expectation for the future of the settlers, that they now said: 'It will take only a few years and then these people will be prosperous.' And their prediction came true.")

One of the best accounts of early Flemish settlements is Charles Louis Desmedt's letter dated "Milwaukie 24 Februari 1845." A few passages demonstrate the writer's skill and the troubles of the immigrant. Desmedt described a storm that broke out at sea, a tempest lasting eighteen hours that forced the ship far off its course:

> Een doodelijke stilte heerschte op het schip. Een ieder was in het gebed. Men hoorde niets dan een treurige klok, die van tijd tot tijd, volgens de beweging van het schip huere tragzame kloppen liet hooren. De armen der masten die sloegen in 't water. De vogels kwaemen op ons schip om ruste te neemen. De zwaerste kisten verliepen van hunne plaetsen. Men moest zig in het bed vast houden. Ik alleen bleef langst op het dek de golven beschouwen, die van tijd tot tijd over het schip sprongen. Zoo wierden wij noordwaers gedreeven, tot wij begonnen den welvisch en

den vliegende visch te ontmoeten. Eenige zeijden dat wij de golven van Mexico(!) in dreeven. En dat men ons in het menschmoorden Virrapas zoud laeten. Hier op antwoorde mijn vrouw, dat God het stiert waer het hem beliefd, als hij ons naer het verdrukte Vlaenderen niet terug zend. 6 dagen moest men vaeren om weder op onze weg te geraeken, zo dat er den 23 Sept. uijt den mast geroepen wierd, om 1 uer van den nacht: Land, Land. Alle reijzigers sprongen uijt het bed, tot zelfs de kranke om de nieuwe wereld te beschouwen.[11]

("A deadly silence reigned on the ship. Everyone was praying. There was no sound but that of the sad clock, which from time to time, slowly tolled with the movement of the ship. The arms of the masts were beating in the water. Birds came to rest on the ship. The heaviest trunks were moving about. One had to hold tightly to stay in his bunk. I alone remained on deck the longest watching the waves which from time to time washed over the ship. We were driven northward until we began to see whales and flying fish. Some said that we were drifting in the gulf of Mexico! And that we would be left in the murderous 'Virrapass'. To this my wife replied that God sends us where it pleases him, if only he does not send us back to oppressed Flanders. Six days we had to sail to get back on course, so that on September 23rd, at one o'clock in the night, the call came from the mast: Land, Land. All travelers leaped out of bed, even the sick, to see the new world.")

Desmedt finally arrived at Milwaukee, a city with a bishop and four priests, that is surprisingly egalitarian:

Hier is nooit getwist aangaande de Religie. Doopen, trouwen, en begraven kost hier niets. Gendarmen, heeren, priesters, kan men zelfs aan geene kleedinge kennen en zijn al burgers. Niemand is hier heere, zoo rijcke hij wezen moge.[12]

("There never have been religious disputes here. Baptism, marriage, and burial cost nothing. Policemen, gentry, and priests are not distinguished by their clothing and are all [ordinary] citizens. No one is a lord here, as rich as he may be.")

Another interesting Flemish literary account is by the gifted writer Philemon Sabbe, whose reminiscences about childhood first appeared in *De Gazette van Detroit.* Henri, a young man from his village, experienced the lure of America:

> Dat zat al lang in zijn kop te gisten en te borrelen gelijk kokend water, die gedachten van naar Amerika te gaan.[13]

> ("Those thoughts of going to America had been fermenting in his head for a long time already and bubbling like boiling water.")

While waiting for the train to take him to work in the "French sweat fields," he saw the advertisements of:

> . . . machtige rookpluimende schepen zachtjes door de blauw-groene zee ploegen met zwenkende zeemeeuwen die er rond wieken als twee witte boogjes never mekaar in den blauwen hemel getrokken. . . . Ginder ver lag weelde en fortuin! . . . Dat wilde maar uit zijn kop niet.[14]

> ("mighty smoke-plumed ships gently plowing through the blue-green sea with wheeling seagulls circling beside each other like two small arches, drawn in the blue sky. . . . Yonder, faraway, lay wealth and fortune! . . . He could not get that picture out of his head.")

At that same time, Letten Aerens, who had "made it" in America, returned to the homeland for a visit.

> Hij sprak Vlaamsch met vreemde woorden er tusschen, zoodat men maar den helft verstond en zei altijd 'jis' in plaats van ja. Hij droeg schoenen die kraakten als eiken plankskens met appelronde blinkende toppen. Een gouden ketting bengelde aan zijn keurige ondervest zoo dik dat men er een hond had kunnen mee vastbinden, en in zijn mond glom meer goud dan tanden. Die had fortuin gemaakt in America, waarom zou hij dat niet kunnen.[15]

> ("He spoke Flemish interspersed with foreign words so that one understood only the half of it, and always said 'jis' instead of *ja.* He wore shoes with apple round shining tops that creaked like little oaken boards. On his neat vest there dangled a gold chain so thick that one could have tied up a dog with it, and in his mouth gleamed more gold than teeth. He had made a fortune in America, why couldn't he?")

Henri had spoken often to his mother about his intention to go to America, but she had never even bothered to listen. What would a whippersnapper like him do in America? The dialogue between them in Flemish dialect is delightful:

> Zoo een snotneuzege, wuk zoie gi doen in Amerika. 'n vrimd land, waadat er nog wilde loopen. . . . Bluuft gie maar zeere hier!
>
> Neen, moeder, ik ga naar Amerika; 't mag zien dat 't wilt.[16]

("You little snot nose, what would you do in America, a strange land where the wild [Indians] still walk around. . . . You had better stay right here. No, mother, I'm going to America, whatever it may be.")

The night before he left, everyone watched as Henri packed his bags. It was a sentimental scene, sad for those who stayed behind, but one of hope and joy for Henri:

> Hij zat over valiezen geknield, bloozend van fierheid en geluk. Wij slikten een paar tranen door. . . . Morgen vertrekt hij. Zouden we hem nog ooit terug zien? . . . Zoo'n geestige jongen; hij kende al de laatste liedjes en zong als een lijster. Waar hij was, was er leute![17]

("He sat kneeling over his suitcases, cheeks aflush with pride and happiness. We swallowed a few tears. . . . Tomorrow he leaves. Would we ever see him again? . . . Such a spirited lad; he knew all the latest tunes and sang like a lark. Wherever he was there was fun.")

But the final morning of departure was the saddest scene of all:

> "'t Was er dien morgen triestig in huis, persies alsof iemand over eerde lag. Onder den tafel stonden twee nieuwe valiezen, met roode etiketjes beplakt waarop een stoomschip vaarde. Moeder liep doelloos rond met gezwollen oogen en vader zat zwijgend neven de stoof door 't venster starend, zijn pijp te rooken. Broeders en zusters stonden elkaar verloren te bekijken en soms snoot iemand zijn neus met een gerucht dat tranen verried.[18]

("It was dreary in the house that morning, exactly as if there were a wake. Under the table stood two new valises, with red labels on which a steamship was sailing. Mother walked around in circles with red swollen eyes and father sat silent beside the stove staring through the window, smoking his pipe. Brothers and sisters stood about with a lost look and occasionally someone blew his nose with a sound that betrayed tears.")

This scene of leave-taking, repeated as every emigrant embarked for the distant shores of America, no writer has so movingly recorded in the Dutch language as Philemon Sabbe.

Americanization: Patriotic Literature

Immigrants characteristically displayed an almost idealistic admiration for the new fatherland. That admiration was often expressed in poetry. J. Quintus, editor of the *Sheboygan Nieuwsbode,* already in 1850 translated into Dutch a poem, "Greetings to America," which was a tribute to the land of the free. Quintus also wrote editorials about slavery and, like many Dutch immigrant writers, he saw America and its wars from the perspective of Dutch history. America, like Holland, always fought for freedom against tyranny. In an editorial "Slavernijuitbreiding of Slavernijbeperking" (Expanding or Limiting Slavery), Quintus reminded his Dutch compatriots that in the old country, the Dutch, unitedly, had shaken off the bonds of slavery, and he asked them whether they would then tolerate tyranny in their new fatherland?[19]

In a patriotic poem, H. Grootemaat called upon the Holland-Americans to enlist on the Union side in the Civil War to preserve the republic:

> Op nu Nederlandsch wakkre zonen!
> Burgers van Amerika,
> Wilt u uwer waardig tonnen,
> Volgt der vad'ren voorbeeld na,
> Hebt gij eens dit land verkoren
> Voor uw tweede Vaderland,
> Aan de Unie trouw gezworen,

U aan haar in nood verpand
Op Bataven! Dan te wapen,
Nu het vuur des oproers brandt![20]

("Arise now, vigilant sons of Netherlands! / Citizens of America, / Show yourselves to be worthy / Follow the example of your
Fathers, / Once you have chosen this land / As your second
Fatherland, / Have sworn loyalty to the Union, / Pledged yourself
to her in need, / Arise Batavians! Take up arms, / Now the fires of
insurrection are burning!")

One of Van Raalte's sons who enlisted expressed disgust for the
students who would rather study than fight:

Het zou vrij wat beeter lijken dat de helft van de studenten
hier in de ranks waren, dan daar als cowards te huis te
blijven, en te wachten tot dat ze gedraft worden, en als ze
gedraft worden dan gaan ze nog beedelen om geld om hun
zelven vrij te kopen. Ik zeg elke een van de studenten die
zijn eigen kost niet kan betalen om school te gaan die moet
maar voor zijn kost gaan werken of maar enlisten.[21]

("It would look a good deal better that half of the students were
here in the ranks, than to stay at home there as cowards, and to
wait until they are drafted, and if they are drafted they go begging
for money to buy themselves free. I say to all students who can't
pay their own way to go to school, that they should work for a living or enlist.")

Another amazing Dutchman, Bastiaan Broere, recalled as an
example of God's marvelous providence his daring escape from
Confederate troops who had seized the area where he lived.
Broere, an oyster fisherman, refused to take up arms with the
Confederates and sought to flee north in a rowboat. First he
fell into the hands of Confederates and then of the Yankees, both
of whom took him to be a spy. The life of the dauntless, god-
fearing Broere was miraculously spared, and eventually, after
hair-raising adventures, he was re-united in the north with his
wife and children.[22]

The Boer War elicited even deeper emotional involvement
than the Civil War. Henry Van der Werp's poem "Aan mijn Stam-

genooten in de Transvaal" captures the theme of the British Lion, the traditional enemy of the Dutch, who is on the loose:

> De Britsche Leeuw, als immer tuk op roof,
> Heeft weer zijn klauw in 't Hollandsch bloed geslagen;
> De trotsche Brit, voor recht en rede doof,
> Schroomt niet, om boos gewin, zijn eer te wagen![23]

("The British Lion, eager as ever for booty, / Again has struck its claw in Dutch blood; / The proud Brit to reason and justice deaf, / Does not hesitate to risk honor for ill-gotten gain.")

B. A. Hendriksen, in a poem about World War I entitled "de Oorlogsgruwel" (The Abomination of War), devoted a stanza to explaining that England was being punished by God for its evil ways, notably in the Boer War:

> Gij Groot-Britanniers—der wereld door berucht—
> Door wiens laaghartigheid thans 't Boerenvolk nog zucht,
> Wiens weerga niet bestaat op heel deez' zondig' aarde
> Ontvangt alree uw loon, voor 't geen g'uzelven baarde. . . .[24]

("You Englishmen—infamous throughout the world— / Through whose baseness the Boers still sigh, / Whose equal does not exist in all this sinful world, / Already you receive your reward, for what you engendered. . . .")

World War I also stimulated the writing of poetry among the Flemish. Their homeland, after all, was overrun by the Germans. Father Van Tighen, in a poem "Brabanconne," lamented the treacherous German betrayal:

> Ons Vaderland werd vreselijk neergeslagen,
> Door eenen snoodaard laflijk aangerand;
> Op, Belgen, in deze akelige dagen
> Waar kerk en school en huizen zijn verbrand.
> Vooruit, vooruit, wij moeten roem behalen,
> Zoo zingen en herzingen we allen nog;
> Vooruit, vooruit wij moeten zegepralen
> In onzen kamp met 't laffe Duitsch bedrog.[25]

("Our Fatherland was terribly struck down, / Cowardly ravished by a villain; / On Belgians, in these dismal days / Where church and school and homes were burned. / Forward, forward, we must gain fame, / So we all sing and sing again; / Forward forward, we must triumph / In our battle with cowardly German deceit.")

Another Fleming, G. A. De Keyser, mourned the loss of a son, who was apparently a member of the American expeditionary forces:

Mijn jongen is bezweken
Bezweken onder het brutaal
Geweld van 't stikgas, 't schroot en 't staal
Die de overweldiger onzer streken,
—Wreed, als een hun . . . vandaal,—
Op 't vreedzaam volk, dat hij verplicht
Was te beschermen, heeft gericht.[26]

("My son has succumbed / Succumbed to the bald power / Of poison gas, of shrapnel and of steel / Which the usurper of our lands, / —Cruelly, like a Hun . . . a vandal,— / Thrust upon the peaceful people / Whom he was pledged to protect.")

Jacob H. Hoekstra, who wrote under the pseudonym Hans Hansen, remembered the dead of World War I in a poem "Decoration Day 1934."[27] He expressed bitterness about the causes for the war and asserted that our boys were sacrificed to the God of Mammon. In an article 'Amerikaanisme' (Americanism), he asked whether it was Americanism to send our sons to the battlefields of Europe just to accommodate the "temple robbers" of Wall Street.[28] The capitalism of Wall Street is un-American, says Hoekstra:

. . . Dat razend woekeren om met eens anders vermogen het volk uit te persen (en dat is Wall Street kapitalisme) is de pest der wereld. Dat is de pest die oorlog wil om zich zelven vet te mesten met het bloed der jeugd en de tranen der moeders. Dat kapitalisme, die ziekte, die pest, die uitheemsche razernij in Europa gebakerd en in de hel uitgevonden is on-Amerikaansch.[29]

("That mad profiteering, bleeding the people with other people's capital [that is what Wall Street capitalism is] is the pest of the world. That is the plague that wants war in order to fatten itself on the blood of youth and the tears of mothers. That capitalism, that sickness, that pest, that foreign madness, nursed in Europe and invented in hell, is un-American.")

That is the stirring, militant, critical prose (and poetry) of Hoekstra! The patriotic Hoekstra praised the American flag as unique among all others:

> Waai, wapper zeer beminde vlag; uw glorie klapper dag aan dag op berg en dal en zeeën. U sterren stralen lang en kloek op 't blauw gekleurde zijdedoek aan alle wereld ree-en. Waai, wrapper prachtvol kleuren-schoon, gij pronkstuk en der natie's kroon, waai in des hemels geuren. Geen volk, hoe groot of sterk of klein, wane met u gelijk te zijn in sierlijkheid van kleuren.[30]

> ("Wave and flutter, dearly beloved flag; let your glory wave day by day on mountain and dale and seas. Let your stars shine long and bold on the blue colored silken cloth in all the roadsteads of the world. Wave and flutter, splendid array of colors, thou showpiece of the nation's crown, wave in the fragrant heavens. Let no people, great or small, think to equal you in the grace of colors.")

Many Dutch-American poems and editorials commemorated national holidays. In these the process of Americanization is evident. A. Zwemer translated Whittier's centennial hymn "God of our Fathers" and told the story of the first Independence Day in a poem "De Eerst Vierde-Juli Dag 1776." I cite a few lines:

> d'Oude Bel is nu gebroken
> En verstomd haar ijz'ren tong.
> Maar de Geest der Vrijheid leeft nog
> Is en blijft voor altijd jong.[31]

> ("The Old Bell now broken / And stilled its iron tongue. / But the Spirit of Freedom lives on / Is and remains ever young.")

What is even more striking was the translation into Dutch of American national songs. B. D. Dijkstra translated "America the Beautiful" and "America." One wonders what inspired this translation. Did the mother tongue still remain the best vehicle for expressing one's deepest feelings, even about the new fatherland?

> Schoon zijn uw heem'len uitgebreid
> Op velden golvend graan.
> Op bergen vol met majesteit,
> En 't dal met ooft belaan.

Amerika, Amerika
God gaf Zijn gunst u mee.
Gij staat gekroond
Waar eenheid troont
Van zee tot blauwe zee.

Amerika, mijn land,
Der vrijheid dierbaar strand
Zijt lof mijns zangs!
Der Vaad'ren graf was daar;
Gij roem der Pelgrim schaar;
Daar rolt een vrijheids maar
Uw bergen langs![32]

American holidays were also celebrated in the poems of Philemon Sabbe: "Memorial Day," "Sterrenvlag, Flag Day, June 14th," Sterrenvlag, July 4th," and "Thanksgiving." The first stanza of "Memorial Day" reads:

Ach! wie beschrijft 't onzeglijk wee
Door al die kruisjes hier gebaard!
Wat weduwleed, wat weezengrief,
Wat moedertranen hier vergaard! . . .[33]

("Ah, who can describe the unspoken woe / Engendered by all those crosses here! / What widow's grief, what orphan's sorrow, / Gathered here what mother's tears.")

The poet Sabbe also wrote "In Memoriam Franklin Delano Roosevelt" to commemorate the death of the president, who was Dutch on his fathers's side and Flemish on his mother's. Sabbe praised Roosevelt especially as a defender of the laboring man, of the oppressed and persecuted:

Verdediger van 's werkers lot,
Vervolgden en verdrukten,
Met 't geloof in 't hart en 't oog op God
Een wil die nimmer bukte! . . .

Gij dapp'ren telg uit Hollands stam
En Vlaand'rens bloed gesproten,
Geen puiker zoon heeft Nonkel Sam
In gansch zijn heem genoten.[34]

("Defender of the worker's lot, / Of persecuted and oppressed, / With faith in his heart and an eye on God / A will that
never bowed. . . . / Thou courageous scion sprung from / Holland
stock and Flander's blood, / No finer son has Uncle Sam / Among
all his countrymen.")

C. De Bode's rimed greeting to Roosevelt upon his inauguration completes the circle. How proud Bode is of the president,
who is of Dutch descent and took his oath of office on an old
Dutch family Bible:

Hooggeeerde President!
Al is mijn naam u onbekend
'k Ben geen geboren Amerikaan,
Toch ben ik uwe onderdaan.
Een burger van dit groote land,
Schoon geboren in klein Nederland.[35]

("Highly honored President! / Although my name to you is
unknown / I am not an American by birth / Still I am your
subject. / Citizen of this great land, / Though born in little Netherland.")

The rimed letter of C. De Bode is very long, but its Calvinist conclusion is worth noting. The humble writer does not hesitate to
tell the president of the United States that he and the nation
must bow the knee before God before the chastisement of the depression will be lifted. That is the prayer and wish of every
good Calvinist:

Buigt gij uw knie voor God uw Koning
In de binnenkamer van uw woning
En wij, als volk met u te saam
Wij buigen voor Gods grooten naam.
Dan zal de Heer de tijden wenden.
En ons opnieuw Zijn zegen zenden.
Dan komt het land weer uit zijn noode.
Dat is de wensch van C. de Bode.[36]

("If you bow your knee before God your King, / In the inner chamber of your dwelling / And we as people together with you / Bow
before the great name of God. / Then the Lord shall turn the
times. / Once again send us His blessing. / Then the land will
again come out of its distress, / That of C. de Bode is the wish.")

Dutch Immigrant Poetry

Dutch immigrants enjoyed and discussed the literature of
the Netherlands. D. Veltman wrote a column "Literarisch" that
appeared regularly in *De Calvinist*. He says that when he wanted
to relax he still always reached for Dutch literature.[37] The col-
umnist obviously knew and understood the literary movements
of Dutch poetry in the nineteenth century. He discussed especially Willem Bilderdijk and Izaac da Costa.

Bilderdijk (1756–1831), great Calvinist poet-philosopher
and source of inspiration to many of the Reformed immigrant
poets, was an acerbic critic of the Enlightenment. Bilderdijk and
his disciple Da Costa (1798–1860) were too militant, too impas-
sioned, too subjective, and too critical for their rationalistic con-
temporaries. Veltman cites with approval the Dutch critic Allard
Pearson's attack on early nineteenth century poets:

> Men was zoo genoeglijk bijeen in zijn knollentuin. Wat
> behoefde me deze of gene zich excentriek aan te stellen en
> over de muur te klimmen! Dat staat hem lelijk. . . . Het
> rustelooze der hongerigen naar beter en hooger, in elk geval
> naar iets anders, is blijkbaar overdrijving, te ver gegaan.[38]

> ("They were so comfortably together, pleased as Punch. Why
> would anyone, here or there, act like an eccentric and 'want to
> climb over the walls!' That makes him look ugly. . . . The restless
> search of those who hunger for higher and better things, in any case
> for something other, is apparently exaggeration, excess.")

In contrast to the Rip Van Winkle mentality of contemporary
poets, Bilderdijk and Da Costa were men of passion; their lyrics
expressed deeply felt and intensely experienced emotions. This
led Veltman to ask: "Have we, with our penchant for being
whole or half-Americans denied this characteristic that is so typically Dutch?"[39] The answer to that question may be found in
Dutch immigrant poetry that often focusses on *het alledaagse*
(the commonplace, the trite), as well as expressing *hartstocht en
gloed* (passion and fervor), "Climbing over the Wall," and the
"restless search of those who hunger for higher and better."

The *alledaagse,* or commonplace, includes first of all the

gelegenheidsgedichten (occasional poetry) written for every possible occasion. The number of such poems appearing in newspapers and periodicals is astounding. They deal with every aspect of immigrant life: a birthday poem for a beloved pastor or a memoriam to a deceased friend; the completion of a new parsonage or the paying off of the mortgage on the Christian school; the description of a Sunday school picnic or an ecclesiastical visit; the opening of a hospital for tuberculosis patients; the commemoration of the 350th anniversary of John Calvin's birth; the celebration of Thanksgiving Day or Christmas; a meditation on *Oudejaarsavond* (Old Years's Night) or a New Year's Day sermon in rhyme! Doubtless, the immigrants were carrying on a Dutch tradition of long standing. Every special occasion in the community called for the rhetorician's art to articulate its sentiment and spirit in words set to rhyme. An occasional one, like P. Jonker's "Oudejaarsavond," qualifies as a poem:

> Uren, dagen, maanden, jaren
> Vliegen als een schaduw heen,
> Met hun zorgen en gevaren
> Droefheid, treuren en geween.[40]

("Hours, days, months, years / Like a shadow fly past, / With their cares and dangers / Sorrow, mourning and tears.")

An occasional verse like "De Zondagschool Picnic" (The Sunday School Picnic) reminds us how the Dutch immigrant adapted to American church ways, socializing with fun and food. A church picnic is a day for recreation and edification in God's great outdoors.[41] The best and most delightful account of a Sunday school picnic is in the Yankee-Dutch prose of Dirk Nieland: "Sonnieschoel Pikkenik." Nieland is a keen observer, and he does not hesitate to expose the human side of the pious parishioners:

> Wel, efter 'n luddel wail staarte de bisnis. Dominee preede en gaf 'n nais spiets. 't Was over 'n tekst uit Prediker, geloof ik, of meebie de Psalms. Somting laik dat. Maar 't was nais, dat's rielie troe. Som piepel gelooven niet in zulke sieries spietsen op 'n benkwet of pikkenik, maar ik zeg 'tis arraid. Je voelt later dan beter om fon te maken. En je kunt toch ook

niet van dominee ekspekten dat hij aan die kreezie ekterij
mee zal doen. No, ik zeg, zoo belangt het, want de wais
koning Salomo zegt toch ook dat er 'n taim is om te leffen en
'n taim om te kraaien.[42]

("Well, after a little while the business started. Dominie prayed
and gave a nice speech. It was about a text from Ecclesiastes, I believe, or perhaps the Psalms. Something like that. But it was nice,
that's really true. Some people don't believe in such serious
speeches at a banquet or picnic, but I say it is all right. Then you
feel better about having fun later on. And you can't expect the minister to participate in all the crazy acting. No, I say, that is the way
it belongs, for after all the wise King Solomon says that there is a
time to laugh and a time to cry.")

A very special type of occasional poem, beloved in immigrant circles, was the recitation. At every festive occasion a selection was recited, generally in rhyme; it was often humorous,
sometimes serious, but always didactic! There were even recitation clubs. There was such a demand for these recitations that
two volumes were published, one by H. Van der Werp—*Lentebloemen voor de Huiskamer en het Reciteervertrek* (Spring Flowers for the Living Room and the Recitation Parlor)[43]—and another compiled by the publisher William B. Eerdmans Sr.—*Mijn
Recitatieboek: Ernst en Luim* (My Recitation Book: Serious and
Humorous Selections).[44] The Yankee-Dutch poems of John Lieuwen are primarily intended as recitations. In "Een Wedding
Speech" he gives the newly weds some practical advice:

> Now when you get een argument
> —En—dit moet je weten
> De Mrs. heeft het laatste woord
> So start niet met debaten.[45]

("Now when you get into an argument / —And—this you must
know / The Mrs. has the last word / So don't start debating.")

Another category of poetry is the religious hymn. The Reverend H. Van der Werp, one of the most gifted poets, wrote children's poems and original hymns and translated American gospel
hymns. From his children's poetry, I quote a stanza from an evening and a morning prayer:

O God, ik dank u dat de nacht
Een zoete rust mij heeft gebracht,
En dat dit nieuwe morgenlicht
Mij toont uw vriendlijk aangezicht.[46]

("Oh God, I thank thee that the night / Sweet rest to me has brought / And that this new morning light / Shows me they friendly face.")

Och, lieve Heer,
Ik bid u zeer,
Eer ik ga slapen,
Hou gij van nacht
Bij mij de wacht
En al uw schapen.[47]

("Oh, dear God / I do pray to you / Ere I go to sleep / Do thou keep watch / Over me this night / And all thy sheep.")

The good pastor sympathized with children who had to memorize the Ten Commandments and the ten plagues, so he put these to rhyme! Among the hymns he translated from the English is "Come Holy Spirit, Heavenly Dove":

Kom, Hemelduive, Heil'ge Geest,
Gij trooster aller smart,
Bereid een heilig liefdefeest
In dit ons koude hart.[48]

("Come Holy Spirit, Heavenly Dove, / Thou consoler of all sorrows, / Prepare a feast of love / In this our cold heart.")

An immigrant teacher, Dewey Westra, was especially fond of the Dutch Psalms, many of which he translated into English. He was unhappy with a new versification of the Dutch Psalter, *Liedboek voor de kerken,* which appeared in 1973. His own attempts at a new versification were not very successful in my judgment.[49]

Another interesting class of poetry is polemic verse which deals with a religious subject. Generally, it is a sharp attack on heterodoxy of various kinds. Several writers excel at this type of verse, notably Hans Hansen and B. H. Hendriksen. A good example of Hansen's polemic is "The Prayer Meeting" (Het biduur), the midweek worship so characteristic of many American churches. In this instance the ladies at a midweek prayer meeting are the object of the poet's ire and irony: The ladies, "deftig, vroom en fijn" (stately, pious and fine), have come from hither and yon for a morning of Bible study and prayer and are ready for lunch. Before they go to the tables, they get out their cosmetic cases:

> . . . moesten eerst die waarde vrouwen neusjes
> poetsen van belang, en kleuren de
> wenkbrauwen, verven kinnebak en wang.
> Nu is 't waar dat echte mannen haten
> het dat "paint" gefleur uit die potjes
> en die kannen met die vreemde valsche
> kleur. Zou dan God dat valsche verplaten
> van het hart en 't aangezicht dan niet
> duizendmaal meer haten? *Hij* is de *waarheid*
> en het *licht.*[50]

(" . . . those worthy ladies first had to really polish their noses, color eyebrows, and chin and cheek. Now it is true that real men hate that "paint" coloring from little pots and cans with those false foreign colors. Would not then God hate that false coating of heart and face a thousand times more? *He* is the *truth* and the *light.*")

B. H. Hendriksen, a layman, regularly published his poems in the newspapers. Many were collected in a volume, *Uit het Hart tot Het hart* (From Heart to Heart). His didactic religious verse is difficult to appreciate, but his polemic verse is strident and sharp, whether he is attacking people within the Reformed churches or Roman Catholic heretics outside of it:

> Die altijd preekt, en nimmer kerkt,
> Die altijd bidt, en nimmer werkt,
> Den naaste sticht, doch steeds van huis is, —
> 'k Vrees, dat hij voor zijn huis een 'kruis' is.[51]

("He who always preaches and never goes to church, / Who always prays, and never works, / Edifies his neighbor, but is always away from home, — / I fear, that he is a 'cross' to his own.")

> Catholicisme,
> Maakt niemand vrij;

Neen, Calvinisme
Dat minnen wij!

("Catholicism, / Makes no one free; / No, Calvinism, / That love
we!")

Geen trotsche kerken,
Van Rome's rot—
NOCH 'goede werken'
Volstaan bij God.[52]

("No proud churches, / Of Rome's gang- / NOR 'good works' /
Suffice for God.")

Most Dutch immigrant poetry is religious, it is intended to
instruct and to edify. The older poems of edification, like the occasional verse, are generally very long and very rhetorical. Only
rarely were the poems that first appeared in newspapers or periodicals published separately. Except for B. H. Hendriksen and Jacob
H. Hoekstra, the poets who published in book form were all clergymen: B. D. Dijkstra, H. Van der Werp, A. Zwemer, H. Van Hoo-
gen (a sermon in rhyme), H. Hoeksema (a drama in rhyme while
he was still a student), and G. Vos. The poems are often a kind of
meditation in rhyme. In the introduction to *Cardiphonia:
Geestelijke Liederen voor Christelijke Gezinnen en Vereenigingen* (Cardiphonia: Spiritual Hymns for Christian Families and Societies), H. Van der Werp explicitly stated that goal was edification, admonition, and consolation. Van Der Werp added that he
was writing and publishing hymns in order to maintain the beautiful Dutch language in the home and in young people's societies
as a variation to the English hymns. In a world that is becoming
ever more materialistic, Van Der Werp says, "It behooves the
Christian all the more to raise heart and voice to his God and
Saviour in Heaven, his future fatherland"[53] (my translation). The dominie's pietistic longing for heaven finds expression in an original hymn: "Verlangen naar den Hemel" (Longing
for Heaven):

Mijn hart verlangt naar Boven,
Mijn ziele dorst naar God
En 't storeloos genot

Waarmee Hem de Englen loven
Mijn hart verlangt naar boven.

O, mocht ik U aanschouwen,
Mijn lust, mijn licht, mijn lied.
Reeds zie ik in 't verschiet
De hemelkusten blauwen
O mocht ik U aanschouwen.[54]

("My heart longs for heaven, / My soul thirsts for God / And undis-
turbed delight / With which the Angels praise him / My heart
longs for heaven. / "O, that I might behold thee, / My joy, my light,
my song. / Already on the horizon I see / The coasts of heaven
turning blue / O, that I might behold thee.")

In the twentieth century, second-generation immigrants
had enjoyed higher education, and poetry definitely changed for
the better. Poems became less didactic, less rhetorically sentimental, and more reflective of deep inner emotional experiences.
There is greater concentration in the poem, the emotion is expressed in a metaphor, and on occasion the poem is highly structured, as in a sonnet. The poem is no longer "een uitboezeming"
(a passionate outburst), but a song in which the poet seeks to give
expression to his or her desire, his or her joy and sorrow. Thus
Geerhardus Vos introduces his poems, saying:

Schoon simpel hun gemoed, 't zijn toch mijn eigen zangen
Een lied is als een kind gezien door moederoog,
Getroeteld in een droom van dat het werd ontvangen,
En trots de smartgeboort, een voorwerp van verlangen.[55]

("Though their tone is simple, still they are my songs, / A lyric is
like a child seen through mother's eye, / Cuddled in a dream from
the moment of conception / And despite its painful birth, an object
of desire.")

It is worth noting that in the second decade of the twentieth
century, poems by women were being printed in conservative
church papers, but the identity of these poets was disguised by
pseudonyms like Donna and Lydia and Nellie. The latter poet,
who is identified sometimes as Nellie Van Kol, describes this poetry well:

In alle dingen ligt een lied;
Maar 't lied ligt in de ziel der dingen,
En diep moet gij daarinne dringen
Of 't liedeke en vindt gij niet.

In alle dingen ligt een lied;
Maar 't liedeke laat zich niet dwingen:
't Wil weten of gij 't ook kunt zingen,
Of 't liedeke en krijgt gij niet.[56]

("In all things there is a song; / But the song lies in the soul of
things, / And deeply must thou enter in / Or thou wilt not, not find
the song. / In all things there is a song; / But the song will not be
forced; / It wants to know if thou canst also sing it, / Or thou wilt
not, not get the song.")

Thus the poem must find an echo in the reader, and the enjoyment of a poem requires sensitivity to its form and content.
Nellie van Kol can be frank and honest with her deeply existen-
tial question:

Waartoe besta ik?
Leef en verga ik?
Het is mij raadsel,
Mysterie, Heer!
Maar op U bouw ik,
Op U vertrouw ik
En kniel aanbiddend
In 't stof ter neer.[57]

("Why do I exist? Live and die? / It is a puzzle, / A mystery to me,
O Lord! / But on thee I build, / In thee do I trust / And in adoration
kneel / Down in the dust.")

The poet Geerhardus Vos excels in expressing a variety of
deeply felt thoughts and emotions in poems that exist in their
own right, poems that do not have to edify or to entertain:

Haar lijf was lelieblank, en op haar leden
Lag als een godenkleed de schoonheid uitgespreid.
Haar stem klonk als muziek uit heilige gebeden,
En wien haar groeten gold die was gebenedijd.

Zij ging op verre reis; toch blijft ze mij omzweven;
Door ieder visioen dat ziel of zinnen streelt
In een hooger schoon haar lieflijkheid geweven;
Al mijn genieten is herinnring aan haar beeld.[58]

("Her body was lily white, and on her limbs / Beauty lay spread like
a garment of the gods. / Her voice sounded like the music of sacred
prayers, / And whom her greeting favored he was blessed. / She
went on a distant journey; still she hovers about me; / By every vision that gratifies the soul or senses, / In a nobler beauty woven
about her loveliness; / All my enjoyment is the remembrance of
her image.")

There is subtlety of expression, and much is left to the intui-
tive, imaginative response of the reader who ponders the poem
and its imagery. How different is the theme of love in the following poem:

De wonde duif wil rijzen
Zij weet niet Oost of West.
Wat baat den weg haar wijzen
Terug naar het leege nest?
Geen wind uit dorre hoven
Brengt gloed en geuren weer
Der passie-bloem verstoven;
De plaats kent haar niet meer.[59]

("The wounded dove desires to rise / She knows not East nor
West. / What good to show her the way / Back to the empty
nest? / No wind out of barren gardens / Brings fervor and fragrance
again / To the passion-flower blown away; / Its place knows her
no more.")

In the poems of Wybe J. Van der Meer, one finds a sensitive
portrayal of the beauty of nature, whether a wintry night on the
prairie or the beauty of a summer sunset. Yet the very stillness
and silence of the snow-covered prairie or the golden glow of the
setting sun is at the same time a metaphor of celestial order and a
transcendent life that does not end, and a prayer that consecrates
the day and night:

De zommerzon staat op den wereldrand.
In zee van goud ontvangt het land

Gods benedictie voor den nacht,
In wonderkleur van vrome avondpracht.
In stil gebed langzaam de dag verstomt;
Tot vrede na de benedictie komt.
Als in betoov'ring, diepe wijding, ligt
Het eenzaam land, als in een droomgedicht.
Een symphonie van zoete kleur-akkoorden,
Zingt, met onhoorbre stille woorden,
Bij stervend goud, van zonneschijn
Van hooger leven en van eeuwig zijn.
Tot alles in meditatie rust,
En bleeke nacht de slapende aarde kust.[60]

("The summer sun stands on the world's edge. / In a sea of gold
the land receives / God's benediction for the night, / In wondrous
color of pious evening splendor. / In silent prayer the day is slowly
hushed; / Till peace follows on benediction. / As in enchantment,
deep consecration, lies / The lonely land, as in a visionary
poem. / A symphony of sweet color chords, / Sings with inaudible,
silent words, / As gold is dying, of sunshine, / Of higher life and
eternal being. / Until all in meditation rests, / And pale night the
sleeping earth doth kiss.")

Perhaps the meditative rest of "Zomeravond" (Summer Evening)
best befits our mood as we reflect that the sun has set on the
poets of Dutch and Flemish America, poets whom we honor even
as we remember them.

Notes

1.   Henry S. Lucas, *Netherlanders in America: Dutch Immigration to
      the United States and Canada, 1789–1950* (Ann Arbor: University
      of Michigan Press, 1955), 606. See also Harry Boonstra, "Dutch-
      American Newspapers and Periodicals in Michigan, 1850–1925"
      (master's thesis, University of Chicago, 1967), 17–18.

2.   See, for example, Walter Lagerwey, *Neen Nederland, 'k Vergeet U
      Niet: Een Beeld Van Het Immigrantenleven in Amerika Tussen
      1846 en 1945 in Verhalen, Schetsen en Gedichten* [No Nether-
      lands, I Won't Forget You: A Picture of Immigrant Life in America
      between 1846 and 1945 in Narratives, Sketches, and Poems]
      (Baarn: Bosch & Keuning, 1982).

3.   J. C. v. c. B. "Vaarwel aan Nederland" [Farewell to the Netherlands]

Sheboygan Nieuwsbode [Sheboygan News Messenger] 6 (Sept. 1854).

4. Henry E. Dosker, "Het Veertigjarig Gedenkfeest te Zeeland, 31 Aug. 1887" [The Fortieth Memorial Commemoration at Zeeland, 31 Aug. 1887] in C. Van Loo, A. La Huis, H. C. Keppel, eds., *Historical Souvenir of the Celebration of the Sixtieth Anniversary of the Colonization of the Hollanders in Western Michigan, Held in Zeeland, Michigan, August 21, 1907* (Zeeland, Mich., 1908), 88–91.

5. Dingman Versteeg, "Ziekte en Dood" [Sickness and Death], in *De Pelgrim-Vaders van het Westen: Eene Geschiedenis van de Worstelingen der Hollandsche Nederzettingen en Benevens Eene Schets van de Stichting der Kolonie Pella in Iowa* [The Pilgrim Fathers of the West: A History of the Struggles of the Dutch Settlements together with a Sketch of the Founding of the Colony of Pella, Iowa] (Grand Rapids: C. M. Loomis, 1886), 73–78.

6. Versteeg, "Het Rooien der Bosschen" [Clearing the Woods], 94–95, and "Onder de Amerikanen" [Among the Americans], in *Pelgrim-Vaders van het Westen*, 106–107.

7. Albert Kampferbeek, "De Oude Koloniale Dagen Vergeleken bij de Dagen die Wij Thans Beleven" [The Old Colonial Days Compared with the Days that We Now Experience], *De Grondwet* 65 (22 July and 9 Aug. 1927).

8. Ibid.

9. Ibid.

10. Versteeg, *Pelgrim-Vaders van het Westen*, 95.

11. Arthur Verthé and Bernard Henry, *Vlaanderen in de Wereld* [Flanders in the World] (Brussels: D. A. P. Reinaert Uitgaven, 1971–1972), 431.

12. Ibid., 433.

13. Philemon Sabbe, *Beelden Uit Mijn Kinderjaren* [Images from My Childhood] (2 vols.) (Detroit: *Gazette van Detroit*, 1944), I, 68.

14. Ibid., I, 68.

15. Ibid.

16. Ibid.

17. Ibid., I, 69.

18. Ibid.

19. J. Quintus, "Slavernijuitbreiding of Slavernijbeperking" [Slavery Expansion or Slavery Reduction], *De Nieuwsbode* 7 (19 Aug. 1856).

20. H. Grootemaat, "Te Wapen voor de Unie" [To Arms for the Union], *De Nieuwsbode* 12 (13 Feb. 1861).

21. D. B. K. Van Raalte, Letter to A. C. Van Raalte, written during the Civil War, cited by Wynand Wichers in *A Century of Hope* (Grand Rapids: Wm. B. Eerdmans, 1968), 59.

22. Bastiaan Broere, *Korte Beschrijving van het Leven en de Wonderbare Leidingen Gods met Bastiaan Broere in Nederland en in Amerika* [A Brief Description of the Life and Wonderful Guidance

of God with Bastiaan Broere in the Netherlands and in America].
Met een Inleiding van J. J. A. Ploos Van Amstel, red. H. De Vries.
Amsterdam: J. A. Wormser, 1887).

23. H. Van Der Werp, "Aan Mijn Stamgenooten in de Transvaal" [To
My Fellow Countrymen in the Transvaal], *De Gereformeerde
Amerikaan* [The Reformed American] 3 (1889/1900): 526–527.

24. Bernard Antonius Hendriksen, "De Oorlogsgruwel" [The Horror of
War], *Uit Het Hart Tot Het Hart: Een Bundel Gedichten* [From
Heart to Heart: A Volume of Poetry] (Kalamazoo, Mich.: Gebr.
Hendriksen, 1916, 105–108.

25. Van Tighen, "Brabanconne" (Belgian national anthem), *Gazette
van Moline*, 2 Sept. 1915.

26. G. A. De Keyser, "Mijn Jongen" [My Boy], *Gazette van Moline*, 14
Oct. 1918.

27. Jacob H. Hoekstra [Hans Hansen] "Decoration Day," *Het Oosten*
30 (24 May 1934).

28. Hoekstra, "Amerikaanisme" [Americanism], *Het Oosten* 30 (29
Mar. 1934).

29. Ibid.

30. Jacob H. Hoekstra, "Onze Vlag" [Our Flag], *Hans Hansen* (Chicago:
n.p., 1920), 96–97.

31. A. C. Zwemer, "De Eerste Vierde-Juli-Dag, 1776" [The First Inde-
pendence Day, 1776], *Hartestemming en Leering* [freely trans.:
Emotional and Didactic Verse] (Grand Rapids: Van Dort &
Hugenholtz, 1887), 66–68.

32. B. D. Dijkstra, "Het Schoone Amerika. America, the Beautiful"
[The Beautiful America. America the Beautiful], and "Amerika.
America," *Stichtelijke Liederen* [Edifying Songs] (Orange City,
Iowa: B. D. Dijkstra & Zoons, n.d.), 26 and 8.

33. Philemon Sabbe, "Memorial Day," *Gazette van Detroit* (24 May
1946).

34. Philemon Sabbe, "In Memoriam Franklin Delano Roosevelt," *Gazette Van Detroit* (20 Apr. 1945).

35. C. De Bode, "Aan den President der Vereenigde Staten" [To the
President of the United States], *De Volksvriend* [The Peoples'
Friend] 59 (16 Mar. 1933).

36. Ibid.

37. D. Veltman, "Literarisch" [Literary], *De Calvinist* 7 (27 Jan. 1917).

38. Ibid.

39. Ibid.

40. P. Jonker, "Oudejaarsavond" [New Year's Eve], *De Gereformeerde
Amerikaan* [The Reformed American] 13 (1909): 614–615.

41. John T. Youngsma, "De Zondagschool Picnic" [The Sunday School
Picnic], *De Bereer* [The Berean] 11 (1929/1930): 223–224.

42. Dirk Nieland, *'n Fonnie Bisnis. With 14 Pen Drawings* [A Funny

Business. With 14 Pen Drawings] by D. Lam; Preface by Frederick Ten Hoor; Vocabulary by Anna Wieland De Boer (Grand Rapids: Wm. B. Eerdmans, 1929), 42.

43. H. Van Der Werp, *Lentebloemen voor de Huiskamer en het Reciteervertrek* [Spring Flowers for the Living Room and Recitation Parlor] (Kampen: G. Ph. Zalsman, 1896).

44. Wm. B. Erdmans, comp., *Mijn Recitatieboek: Ernst en Luim* [My Recitation Book: Serious and Humorous Selections], (Grand Rapids: Eerdmans-Sevensma, n.d.).

45. John Lieuwen, *Sweat en Tears* [Sweat and Tears] (Holland, Mich.: Schreur Printing Co., 1947), 55.

46. H. Van Der Werp, "Morgenbede en Dank" [Morning Prayer and Thanks], *De Kleine Samuel: Bede, Dank en Lof uit Kindermonden, Een Boekje voor het Christelijk Huisgezin* [The Little Samuel: Prayer, Thanks and Praise from the Mouths of Children: A Booklet for the Christian Family] (3rd ed. Grand Rapids: B. Sevensma, 1908), 24.

47. H. Van Der Werp, "Avondbede" [Evening Prayer], *De Kleine Samuel*, 12.

48. H. Van Der Werp, *Lentebloemen voor de Huiskamer*, 64.

49. Dewey Westra, manuscript in the Colonial Origins Collection, Calvin College and Seminary, Grand Rapids, Michigan.

50. Jacob H. Hoekstra, "The Prayer Meeting *(Het biduur),*" *Het Oosten* [The East] 30 (17 May, 1934).

51. B. A. Hendriksen, *Uit het Hart tot het Hart* [From Heart to Heart], 105–108.

52. Ibid.

53. H. Van Der Werp, *Cardiphonia: Geestelijke Liederen voor Christelijke Gezinnen en Vereenigingen* [Songs of the Heart: Spiritual Songs for Christian Families and Societies] (Holland, Mich.: De Grondwet Drukkerij, 1894), 6–7.

54. H. Van Der Werp, "Verlangen naar den Hemel" [Longing for Heaven], in Wm. F. Peters, ed., *De Kroon: Liederenbundel. Christelijke Liederen voor Zondagschool en Huisgezin verzameld door Ds. H. Van Der Werp* [The Crown: A Collection of Songs. Christian Songs for Sunday School and Family], compiled by Reverend H. Van Der Werp] (Chicago: Paul H. Wezeman, 1907).

55. Geerhardus Vos, "Praeludium" [Prelude], *Spiegel der Natuur* [Mirror of Nature] (Princeton, N.J.: n.p., 1927), 9.

56. Nellie Van Kol, "Het Lied" [The Song], *De Wachter* [The Watchman] 59 (1926): 374.

57. Nellie Van Kol, "Aan U de Glorie" [To Thee Be the Glory], *De Wachter* 59 (1926): 580.

58. Geerhardus Vos, "Absentis Imago" [Absent Image] *Spiegel der Natuur*, 83.

59. Geerhardus Vos, "Dulcia Non Redeunt," *Spiegel der Natuur*, 96.
60. Wybe J. Van Der Meer, "Zomeravond" [Summer Evening] *Yn 'E Frjemdte* [In a Strange Land] (Ljouwert [Leeuwarden]: W. A. Eisma, 1926), 56.

13. Dutch-American Newspapers: Their History and Role

Conrad Bult

This essay has three purposes. The first is that of describing the more important journal articles, chapters in books, and monographs concerning the Dutch-American periodical press. The second is that of listing a brief and very selective inventory of extant files of Dutch-American newspapers and magazines. The third function is that of suggesting further use of resources found in these publications.

Before the turn of the century, a few items appeared in print about Dutch journalism. In 1886, a book written by Dingman Versteeg, *De Pelgrim-Vaders van het Westen*, was printed in Grand Rapids, Michigan, and here the author included a few comments written by an H. Van Eijk, who, during the 1860s, served as editor of Holland, Michigan's first newspaper, *De Hollander* (1850–1895).[1] Van Eijk, as quoted by Versteeg, mistakenly believed that *De Hollander* was the oldest Dutch newspaper in America, an honor belonging to *De Sheboygan Nieuwsbode* (1849–1861), which came out in Sheboygan, Wisconsin, in 1849, one year before *De Hollander* made its debut. Also, Van Eijk contended that *De Grondwet*, which appeared in Holland during the years 1860–1938, did much to promote the ideals of the Republican party among the early immigrants.[2]

Also in 1886, A. S. Kedzie contributed a piece "Newspapers

273

in Ottawa County" for the ninth volume of the *Report of the Pioneer Society of the State of Michigan*.[3] Between a few paragraphs in which he generalized about the value of newspapers, the author listed the papers in sequence by date of appearance and gave a few details about those titles he knew to exist. One, for example, is that *De Grondwet* was the first paper in Ottawa County to be printed on a steam press.[4] He noted that eleven out of seventeen English-language papers had perished, while, on the other hand, only three of the six Dutch-language papers no longer existed, and, in one of his final paragraphs, he says this about the Dutch and their newspapers:

> The Dutch papers seem to have a more vigorous vitality. The Dutch are marked for their intelligence, as well as for their probity and industry; yet they are not a more reading people than the Americans, though having of reading matter fewer sources of supply.
>
> Many of them are content with the Bible, Psalm-book and one newspaper, the latter thus becoming quite essential in the family.[5]

Although not specifically interested in Dutch journalism, Albert Baxter, editor of the Grand Rapids *Eagle* and author of *History of the City of Grand Rapids*, devoted a few words to Dutch journalism in the chapter "The Press of Grand Rapids."[6] Here he mentioned at least nine titles with Dutch-language names, of which four were still alive in 1891, the book's publication date. Baxter commented briefly on each title, and his more extensive remarks concern two Dutch newspapers, *De Vrijheid's Banier* (1868–1904?) and *De Standaard* (1875–1918). For Baxter, these were the two earliest newspapers other than the dailies which flourished in Grand Rapids.[7]

A few statements having to do with early Pella, Iowa, journalism can be found in *Geschiedenis van Pella, Iowa en Omgeving* by Kommer Van Stigt. First published in 1897, this work has recently been translated by Elisabeth Kempkes under the title, *History of Pella, Iowa and Vicinity*. Throughout the book are scattered statements about Pella's first paper, *The Pella Gazette* (1855–1860) and other early titles such as the Democratic *Pella's Weekblad* (1860–1942), the Republican *Pella Blade* now the

Chronicle,[8] and the specifically religious *Pella's Maandblad*
(1862–1863).[9] The Pella pioneer, Rev. Hendrik P. Scholte
founded both the English-language *Pella Gazette* and *De
Toekomst* (1866–1868), which he published toward the end of his
life. Van Stigt's high regard for both Scholte and *De Toekomst* can
be seen in the following quotation:

> As we have stated before, Scholte, particularly during the
> last two years of his life went back to the same normal atti-
> tude that had characterized him in The Netherlands. During
> those years he gave us those glorious exhortations in "De
> Toekomst" (The Future) a monthly magazine.[10]

Van Stigt presented the reader with several pages of articles taken
directly from *De Toekomst* which have such headings as "Cor-
rupting God's Word," "Regeneration," "Philosophy," and "Sanc-
tified in Christ."[11] Here and there in the volume are a few biographical statements about such individuals as the Reformed
Church minister Pieter J. Oggel, founder of *Pella's Weekblad* and
Pella's Maandblad, and H. Neyenesch, who purchased the *Pella
Blade* in 1865 and *Pella's Weekblad* in 1870 from its owner and
co-founder, Henry Hospers, who later began the first Dutch paper
in Orange City, Iowa, *De Volksvriend* (1874–1951).[12] What Van
Stigt said nearly a century ago about the Dutch-American press
no doubt came from what he had gleaned from his reading of past
files of *Pella's Weekblad* and conversations with those who
shared his interest in the history of Pella.[13]

Just a few random comments are inadequate for describing
what is available on the subject in the *Gedenkboek van het
Vijftigjarig Jubileum der Christelijke Gereformeerde Kerk* A.D.
1857–1907. As a contributor to this volume, Andrew Keizer, a
Christian Reformed minister, wrote a fourteen-page chapter,
"Onze Pers," devoted to journals related to the Christian Reformed Church both officially and unofficially. Keizer was the
logical choice for an author of this section since in 1894 he had
begun his twenty-five year tenure as editor of *De Wachter*
(1868–), the Dutch-language voice of the denomination he
served. When Keizer penned his words in the *Gedenkboek, De
Wachter* (started in 1868) had had an almost forty-year history of
continuous publication. For Keizer, significant elements in the

history of *De Wachter* were how what was said in this paper aided the growth of the Christian Reformed Church and the mode of expression of those who wrote in it. Keizer neatly combined these two strands of thought in his following words about *De Wachter*:

> It was born in stormy times amid the sometimes heated struggle of those days. The first volumes give evidence of very turbulent times in our ecclesiastical life, so that *De Wachter* was constantly involved in heated strife, especially with those who contested the right of existence of our churches.[14]

Also, the author is not overly impressed with the argumentative tone found in early volumes of *De Wachter*, and he stated at one point that "recently *De Wachter* could occupy its position more calmly and only now and then it considered the calling to become polemic, . . ."[15] Other Christian Reformed journals such as *The Banner*, which began as the *Banner of Truth* in 1866; the German language *Reformierte Bote Berichte aus der Christlichen Reformierten Kirche* (1899–1920?), started in Freeport, Illinois, in 1899 to answer the needs of a few German-speaking congregations in the Midwest; and *De Gereformeerde Amerikaan*, though not an official church publication, edited during the years of its life, 1897–1916, by the Christian Reformed minister, Foppe Ten Hoor are given a few paragraphs, where the author in a separate brief chronological narrative about many titles, offered some of the earliest commentary on the character, contents, and circulation of all periodicals related to the Christian Reformed Church.

Researchers will find Theo De Veer's "Hollandsche Journalistiek in America" in the March 1909 issue of *Elsevier's Geïllustreerd Maandschrift* essential for early and somewhat objective criticism. Written by a Dutch journalist who visited America in 1907, it is a description for those in the Netherlands of the efforts of Dutch-American newspapermen.[16] This article, according to Linda Pegman Doezema, author of *Dutch Americans: A Guide to Information Sources*, contains what can be considered ". . . the earliest record concerning the Dutch press in the United States."[17] De Veer's statements of facts concerning when and where newspapers first appeared are in a few instances either incorrect or vague and must be checked against other studies.

(This criticism is not meant to detract from the value of this piece as a source for circulation figures, history, and evaluation of each title, biographical details about certain editors, quality of the Dutch language used, and for an understanding of the attitude of a journalist who came to America in 1907 to observe first hand the success and failures of the Dutch-American press.) Although he rates *De Grondwet* from Holland, Michigan; *De Volksvriend* from Orange City, Iowa; and *De Volksstem* (1890–1919) from De Pere, Wisconsin, very highly, De Veer still believed that a good paper could compete with those he mentioned. Needed for such a paper, he contended, are journalists with more skills and education than those writing and publishing papers at the present time.[18]

Not a journalist, but a Rhodes Scholar and historian, Jacob Van der Zee is the author of *The Hollanders of Iowa*, published by the State Historical Society of Iowa in 1912, which includes a chapter titled "The Dutch Press in Iowa." About the author's qualifications, the editor of Van der Zee's book stated: "Born of Dutch parents in The Netherlands and reared among kinsfolk in Iowa, he has been a part of the life which is portrayed in these pages."[19] Van der Zee's eleven pages on the topic are filled with footnoted details about the journalists H. P. Scholte, Henry Hospers, and H. Neyenesch and the papers they founded and owned. Also, Van der Zee noted those Holland-Americans who published English-language newspapers in Iowa towns other than Pella, Orange City, and Sioux Center, where the *Sioux Center Nieuwsblad* (1892–1930) was the first Dutch-language newspaper.[20] Written expression in English, according to Van der Zee, was a difficult chore for such individuals as Scholte, and for this reason and general disinterest, his early attempt to edit and produce an English-language paper, *The Pella Gazette*, failed. Also, the author closes his brief history of this paper and its financial woes with a remark that it is very hard to comprehend why a settlement of more than 2,000 could not, before 1860, support a Dutch-language paper. Also here are the fears and hopes of a few of the early newspaper editors, at times in their own words. Van der Zee noted too, that immigrants, who had formed clubs to buy high-priced papers in the Netherlands were amazed at the number of low-cost papers available in America. The Dutch-language newspapers, Van der

Zee concluded, will continue to exist as long as new immigrants find homes in established Dutch communities. His hopes for the welfare of the Dutch press reveal the high regard he had for the Dutch language and those who wrote in it. Furthermore, he relied heavily on newspaper editors whom he knew personally and past files of papers extant at the time of his research, for background not only for this chapter, but also for much of what appears throughout his book.[21]

While editor of the official Christian Reformed periodical, *The Banner*, and associate editor of *De Gereformeerde Amerikaan*, Rev. Henry Beets penned no fewer than three articles on the topic of Dutch journalism. One of Beets's pieces is in the December 1916 issue of *De Gereformeerde Amerikaan*. Here Beets presented a list of Dutch-language papers which includes a few printed in locations where neither the Reformed or Christian Reformed Church flourished. Among these are *Gazette van Moline* (1907–1940), a Flemish paper from Moline, Illinois, and the Catholic *De Volksstem* from De Pere, Wisconsin. Beets claimed that the Wisconsin *Sheboygan Nieuwsblad* was the first Dutch newspaper in America. He is right about it being first but in error about the title, which is actually *De Sheboygan Nieuwsbode*.[22]

With information about papers known to him, Beets interspersed such tantalizing items as, for example, the fact that the editors of the Paterson, New Jersey, *Het Oosten* (1904–1940) and the Kalamazoo, Michigan, *De Hollandsche Amerikaan* (1890–1945) were not fond of the ideas of Abraham Kuyper, the Dutch theologian-politician who served as prime minister of the Netherlands during the years 1901–1905 and who believed that God must be served in all areas of human endeavor. Kuyper's ideas can be found in his two newspapers *De Heraut* (1872–1945) and *De Standaard* (1872–1944). Beets did not see a bright future for the Dutch-language press, for reasons such as competition among the ethnic papers themselves, little desire among the people to read, and especially to read good literature. Also, an English-language paper was always present as an alternative choice for many of the immigrants. Beets ended his article with words which combined both nostalgia and warning: "Considering what a power the press is—for good or for bad—it is a very sad fact that our Holland folk do not demand more sound reading matter. The coming generations will reap bitter fruit as a result—that is equally unavoidable."[23]

On the same melancholy note, in his "Dutch Journalism in Michigan," in the 1922 volume of *Michigan History Magazine*, Beets offered little hope for the future of Dutch papers in Michigan. For him, they had a few more decades of life with survival being most possible in areas where rural readers were served. Even though soon to be dead, Dutch newspapers had, according to Beets,

> . . . tried to make true American patriots of the Dutch immigrants, and their descendants, instilling love for only one flag, the Stars and Stripes, and inspiring supreme devotion to only one country, that of the land of the free and the home of the brave.[24]

Beets noted that both the Reformed and Christian Reformed denominations now published official English-language journals in Michigan. For the Reformed it was first *The Leader* (1906–1934), later *The Intelligencer Leader* (1934–1943), and still later *The Church Herald* (1944–). *The Banner* (1866–) became the denominational organ of the Christian Reformed Church in 1915. Other remarks given by Beets in this article are very similar to what he had said in the *Gereformeerde Amerikaan*, which, as we have seen, revealed his fears about the impending demise of the Dutch language as a mode of conversation and a means of communication in newspapers.

A Chicago newspaper, *The American Daily Standard* (Dec. 22, 1920–Mar. 12, 1921?), which first came off the press on December 22, 1920, was an attempt to fill the need of those who desired a Christian paper. The Christian Reformed minister John Clover Monsma founded the paper, and for this reason no history of Dutch journalism is complete without a few remarks about this unique and short-lived publication modeled after Abraham Kuyper's famous *De Standaard*, which for many years was a force to be reckoned with in the Netherlands. After less than three months, *The American Daily Standard* perished, a victim of unwise management, too small a circulation, and lack of managerial skills among those who ran the enterprise.[25]

Monsma did not take the defeat of his project lightly, and as a result he wrote a self-justifying polemic pamphlet of over a hundred pages, *Why The American Daily Standard Failed and How It Is Going to Win*. For Monsma, one of the most difficult matters to understand was the lack of support among other religious papers for his early fund-raising ventures. Specifically, as the following quotation demonstrates, he was bothered by the lukewarm encouragment, or lack of it, exhibited in those periodicals read by members of the Reformed and Christian Reformed Church.

> The editor-in-chief of *The Banner* said absolutely nothing. *Onze Toekomst*, a Dutch weekly published in Chicago, was as silent as a tomb at this time. A couple of Dutch-language sheets, the one distributed in Kalamazoo, Mich., and the other in Paterson, N. J., and both carrying a distant odor of foreignism, barked and bit at us with all the clamor of a couple of mad poodles, afraid that they would lose their patronage as soon as our paper was put on the market. The Reformed "Leader," published in Holland, Mich., copied the biting editorial of the Chicago "Continent," and with evident satisfaction.[26]

The demise of *The American Daily Standard* did not end Monsma's forays into the field of journalism. With a group of ministers from various denominations, he formed the non-profit World Publishing Company in 1937. This organization produced four issues of *The World: An International News Weekly* (May 12–July 28, 1937), an imitation in both format and news coverage of *Time*, the popular American news magazine. *The World*, under Monsma as editor, was not to be concerned about profit, would be free from the demands of commercial interests, political leaders, and particular religious denominations.[27] The fourth, and assumed to be the last, issue of *The World*, dated July 28, 1937, brought to an end what Monsma and his fellow ministers had hoped would be a truthful Christian weekly. Other than the usual pleas for support and subscribers, the final number of *The World* nowhere indicates why *The World* was forced to cease. Both *The World* and *The American Daily Standard* were victims of Monsma's Old World concept that a national magazine or newspaper based on Christian ideas could survive and, indeed, thrive

in America. Writing about *The American Daily Standard*, Jacob
Van Hinte, author of *Nederlanders in Amerika* (1928) declared:

> Its Dutch background betrayed it, in spite of the American
> appearance (catchy headlines and many pictures) by the
> names of co-workers and advertisers, its religious character
> and by the nature of the articles and especially the news
> which was not placed in it.[28]

The World, as the front cover of each issue proclaimed, was
"Founded on Christian Principles." Featured in its first number
was a prominent article on the religion of President Franklin
Roosevelt. Van Hinte's analysis of the failure of *The American
Daily Standard* also explains the short life span of *The World*.

"Spiritual Growth—The Dutch Press" is the translated title
of chapter 15 in Van Hinte's *Nederlanders in Amerika*.[29] In the
newspapers serving the Dutch immigrant, religious material was
essential, Van Hinte noted. Also, both politics and local and de-
nomination-wide church news were covered in almost every issue of the various Dutch-American publications. In other words,
without this religious news, a paper's prospects of survival were
very poor. Van Hinte even maintained that many newspapers
continued to exist only because their editors saw fit to print what
he described as religious "gossip," that is, the religious difficulties
and controversies in the various Dutch settlements.[30]

Van Hinte wrote about both English- and Dutch-language papers and explained that their circulation was not limited to the
location where each was printed. For this reason, the Dutch-
American press tended to increase the cohesiveness among all
immigrants and made them aware of the Dutch background.
Also, in his view, the strident doctrinal and theological writing in
the official denominational papers, and others as well, somewhat
counterbalanced the good effects that these publications had in
the life of the Dutch-American.[31] Van Hinte described *De Hope*
(1865–1933), a paper related to the Reformed Church and Hope
College, as being free from polemics, especially while under the
editorship of Dr. Nicholas M. Steffens, a Reformed minister and
professor at Western Theological Seminary, who often tilted with
the liberal Rev. F. W. N. Hugenholtz, editor and publisher of *De
Stemmen uit de Vrije Hollandsche Gemeente* (1886–1890) and a

man who was not a member of either the Reformed or Christian Reformed Church.

The quality of the Dutch language used, Van Hinte believed, was gradually declining. Also, as he saw it, love for the Dutch language was never a primary reason for the establishment of the early Dutch-American papers, while financing from political interests often did play a crucial role. About the general decay in the quality of the contents and editorials and Dutch language in Reformed and Christian Reformed papers he stated:

> Those newspapers that had as editors ministers or teachers recently immigrated from the Netherlands, constituted favorable exceptions. This was especially the case among the Christian Reformed, and is still occasionally true. Thus we see the apparently conflicting phenomenon that the most ordinary people had the best newspapers in Dutch, complete with some really noteworthy editorials, while, from a Dutch point of view, the newspapers that served the wealthier and more educated members of the Reformed Church made a decidedly poor impression.[32]

In addition, Van Hinte discussed Dutch-American journalism in "Het Geestelijk Leven in de Nederzettingen,"[33] the fifteenth chapter of the second volume of his study. In a part of this chapter titled "De Pers,"[34] he claimed that what is contained in newspapers will give a good idea of just how the immigrant became a part of American life. Here, as before, the author has emphasized that to continue, a paper must be theologically conservative. How the Dutch language is used, and the inevitable decline in circulation are matters, though discussed before, again given additional space here. *De Hope* and *Onze Toekomst*, he stated, are still very healthy and have increased in size. Newspapers, denominational publications, other religious journals, college yearbooks, and even such college student papers as the *Central Ray* (1876–) and the *Calvin College Chimes* (1907–) have been described in detail. Included are the author's characterizations of newspapers and journals alive and dead. About editors, contents, and advertisements, Van Hinte has both generalized and made specific comments. What he has stated about the politi-

cal and religious views of those who published and edited the various papers, will give the reader a good survey of what the immigrant read, and the ideas which competed for his political and
religious allegiance. For the author, papers such as *De Grondwet*,
De Hollandsche Amerikaan, and *De Volksvriend*, by their news
from other settlements and their countrywide circulation, contributed to a sort of familylike awareness among the immigrants.

Also valuable in Van Hinte is his state-by-state listing of
publications which were alive when he visited America. He has
given the date of origin, politics, type of contents, editor's name,
and, for most, circulation figures. Moreover, Van Hinte has
brought to the student of the Dutch press items not necessarily
found in other sources. Among these are, first, that the Paterson,
New Jersey, *Het Oosten* and *De Hollandsche Amerikaan* contained more than the average number of articles which criticized
ministers; second, that the best Dutch is found in the most orthodox papers; and third, that American Calvinism, as seen in college newspapers, is of a different brand than that found among
students in the Netherlands.[35]

As previously stated, Van Hinte did make use of the work of
Beets and De Veer. Also, the point must be made that most of his
footnotes which concern newspapers indicate that he perused for
the most part issues dated in the 1920s and did little work with
extant earlier files.[36]

Americans from Holland, by the author, journalist, and English professor Arnold Mulder, a man described as "gifted" by Van
Hinte, appeared in 1947.[37] This volume, the first book-length
study in English of the Dutch in America, contains a chapter
"Dutch Nose for the News." Here, Mulder did not add much that
is new with his thought that the immigrants realized the value of
a newspaper since they had often consulted them in the Netherlands and his remarks that newspapers contributed to the Americanization process. About *De Grondwet* he said:

> *De Grondwet*, like other journals in its class had served the
> Dutch people well for three quarters of a century. It made
> the path to a difficult Americanism a little smoother for
> thousands of immigrants as they kept arriving from Holland
> through the decades; in its own undramatic way it had

occupied a place of some importance in the American scene.[38]

He, as did those before him, discussed the stormy relationship between *De Hollander* and Van Raalte, and the ventures to establish Calvinistic papers. He devoted several paragraphs to the failure of *The American Daily Standard.* In summary, this chapter, not accompanied by footnotes, or a great many source references in the text, reflects Mulder's fascination with somewhat trivial matters, his condescension, and his high regard for the benefits of Americanization. In short, he did not bemoan the passing of the Dutch-language papers, nor did he think Dutch journalism to be unique in any way. For the author, Dutch-language newspapers arose, made a contribution, and died as did journals in other languages.

Neither Mulder nor Van Hinte reflected the sympathetic attitude toward the immigrant found in the very impressive *Netherlanders in America,* written by the historian Henry S. Lucas and published in 1955, almost a generation ago. In his chapter "Press and Politics," the section "The Dutch American Press" is an excellent sketch of Dutch-American journalism by someone very familiar with both past critical comment and extant newspaper and journal files. In his search for the earliest Dutch-language newspaper in America, he relied on the 1849 and 1850 issues of *De Sheboygan Nieuwsbode* for articles about two short-lived titles, *De Volksvriend,* supposedly published in Grand Rapids in 1849, and *De Nederlander in Noord-Amerika,* founded in New York in 1849 by a group of individuals who wished to swindle the immigrant as soon as he came off the boat. Both enterprises failed, and not a single copy of either paper exists. For Lucas and other students of the Dutch-American press, *De Sheboygan Nieuwsbode,* founded by Jacob Quintus, is the first successful Dutch-language newspaper in America.[39] In his view, *De Grondwet* wielded the most influence; *De Volksvriend* carried the best news about the Dutch settlements, usually written by the immigrants in letters to the editor; and Chicago's *Onze Toekomst* (1894–1953), especially under the editorship of the Christian Reformed minister Johannes Van Lonkhuizen, reflected what was written in Abraham Kuyper's two papers *De Standaard* and *De Heraut*.[40]

Not slighted by the author are such Wisconsin Catholic titles as the *De Pere Standaard* (1878–1896) and *De Volksstem*. About such Flemish papers as the Illinois *Gazette van Moline* (1907–1940) and the *Gazette van Detroit* (1914–?), the author has these words: "It would be a mistake to think that many Hollanders ever read either the *Gazette van Moline* or the *Gazette van Detroit*. These papers devoted themselves almost entirely to news about Flanders and about Flemings settled in the United States."[41]

De Hope and *De Wachter* were, in Lucas's view, the Dutch language religious papers most popular with the immigrants. Based in New York City, the official paper for the entire Reformed Church, *The Christian Intelligencer* (1830–1934), written in English, did not, Lucas asserted, find its way into the homes of many immigrants who came to America in the last half of the nineteenth century.[42] Less critical of the Dutch press than Van Hinte, Lucas concluded with the remarks that financial instability made it impossible for Dutch-American journalists to provide their readers with day-to-day news about America, and in particular, about the American political scene. Lucas believed that the attention these papers gave to church affairs, religious news, and theological questions provided the immigrant with something he could find nowhere else. Also, Lucas has written: "The conclusion is clear: it was fondness for the mother tongue and love for the faith brought from the homeland that kept the Dutch-language press alive."[43]

In 1967 Harry Boonstra, a faculty member at Hope College, Holland, Michigan, submitted a masters thesis, *Dutch American Newspapers and Periodicals in Michigan 1850–1925*, to the University of Chicago. This thesis contains more information than found anywhere else about the Dutch press in Michigan. Early in this work, Boonstra evaluated the work of Van Hinte and Lucas and his following words are illuminating: "Both Van Hinte and Lucas borrowed from Beets and De Veer, although Van Hinte provides more independent analysis."[44]

In chapter I, "Setting," Boonstra concerned himself with a few general remarks about the American immigrant press which is followed by a brief history of Dutch settlements in America and in particular of the colonies in Michigan. In the second chapter, the author described the general contents of both newspapers and church-related journals. Local news, national and international coverage borrowed from English-language papers, an ever present section of news from the Netherlands, editorials, much poetry written by laymen and ministers, and serialized fiction based on significant events in Dutch history, all had a place in almost every issue of many of the papers. Also, Boonstra noted that the religious papers carried doctrinal discussions, inspirational articles, and denominational news. He closed the second chapter with a few words about advertising and "journalistic feuds," to use his phrase.[45] In the third chapter, "Main Issues," we read how these papers reported and editorialized about national politics and elections, the Boer War, World War I, prohibition, the Dutch-English language problem, and Americanization. The secession of the Christian Reformed from the Reformed Church in 1857, Freemasonry, Common Grace, and Christian Schools are mentioned as items receiving more than average attention in the religious papers.

In his brief concluding chapter, Boonstra noted that editors believed their responsibility embraced informing the immigrant about America and urging him to live a morally upright life. Also, the author implied that the advertising in the Dutch press often revealed aspects of immigrant life not found in the written articles. Typical for most papers, he found, was a conservative attitude bolstered by the notion that change was not necessarily a good thing. For the author, the spiritual, intellectual, and emotional life of the immigrants and the problems that beset them, can best be studied by use of the papers provided for them by journalists who were often immigrants themselves. Lastly, Boonstra stated this about his concern for the religious character of Dutch-American journalism: "The analysis of the religious issues as found in the press is a major part of this study, because one cannot do justice to a study of the Dutch-American people and their writing without a careful scrutiny of their religious life."[46]

At the end of the volume, Boonstra has added two appendices. The first, "Individual Papers," contains a separate section on each of the newspapers the author deemed most significant.[47] In the second appendix, "Masterlist," all Michigan Dutch papers known to exist have been indicated. Extant back files, the location of each, dates of publication, and a note or two about any changes in the titles or mergers of different journals have been given here. It is unfortunate that this rich and essential source for any person who intends to do research on Dutch journalism in Michigan, remains unpublished. A model of research, Boonstra's work might have been slightly enhanced if he had made use of a few rather lengthy quotations from the newspapers he studied.

Though not primarily concerned with Dutch journalism, Henry Zwaanstra's doctoral dissertation, *Reformed Thought and Experience in the New World: A Study of the Christian Reformed Church and Its American Environment 1890–1918*, published in 1973, is for the most part based on the contents of *De Wachter, The Banner, De Gereformeerde Amerikaan, De Gids* (1885–1911), and its successor *De Calvinist* (1911–1918). Both *De Gids* and *De Calvinist* ardently espoused the the ideas of Abraham Kuyper. Zwaanstra judged *De Wachter* the best source for *Christian Reformed Church* history, *The Banner* to be very well written and meant to serve those who read English, and the *Gereformeerde Amerikaan* second only to *De Wachter* in popularity among Christian Reformed readers.[48] This history of trends of thought in the Christian Reformed Church during the years of Americanization is basic for an understanding of the multitude of issues written about by Dutch-American journalists who fought their battles about doctrine, theology, and the relation of the church to the world, in the papers they edited.

Still another historian, Gerald De Jong, in his book *The Dutch in America 1609–1974*, sketched in a general way how the contents of Dutch-American newspapers formed the attitudes of the people who read them.[49] Information about the Paterson, New Jersey, newspapers *De Telegraaf* (1882–1921) and *Het Oosten* can be located in his article "Dutch Immigrants in New Jersey before World War I," in the Summer-Autumn 1976 issue of *New Jersey History*. Here, he pointed out, *De Telegraaf* focused more on national and international news, while *Het Oosten* had greater coverage of the Dutch settlements in the United States. Also *Het Oosten* contained more religious news than *De Telegraaf*. Both papers are quoted by De Jong to prove that Dutch-

language papers aided the immigrants in retaining their ethnic identity.[50]

In his doctoral dissertation, *Dutch Calvinism in Modern
America: The History of a Conservative Subculture,* James Bratt
made heavy use of the journals which served readers in the Reformed and Christian Reformed Churches.[51] He perused the contents of these titles to determine both what editors and contributors had to say about the doctrinal and theological problems
peculiar to the two denominations and how these writers viewed
the social, political, and religious problems of the day. Primarily,
Bratt is fascinated by these publications for the reason that what
they contained can be used to better comprehend how the intellectual leaders in the Reformed and Christian Reformed denominations reacted to the American scene during the years
1900–1950 and also to examine what elements of denominational consciousness and ethnic identity can still be found among
the members of these two denominations.

In *Neen Nederland, 'k Vergeet U Niet* which appeared in
1982, Walter Lagerwey included a section "De Nederlandse Pers
in Amerika."[52] Here the author has listed geographically the
more important titles and has quoted items from many papers in
which the founder or editor of each revealed his hopes for the paper and the reasons for his journalistic venture. Also, Lagerwey
has provided pertinent remarks from both Van Hinte and Lucas
on Dutch-American newspapers. In other sections of his book,
"Hollandse Amerikanen" and "Immigrantenpoëzie," the author
collected many selections of prose and poetry, taken, in most
cases, from the newspapers.

Future research concerning Dutch-American journalism depends on extant back files of the papers. For Holland, Michigan,
the file of *De Grondwet* (1860–1938) begins in 1871. Extant years
of *De Hollander* are 1850–1860 and 1872–1880. The Zeeland
Michigan, *Zeeland Expositor* (1892–), now the *Zeeland Record,*
lacks only one year, and the back files are in the hands of the publisher. The Kalamazoo *De Hollandsche Amerikaan* (1890–1945)
back holding lacks only the years 1900–1903. Files of Grand Rapids papers are meager. Of *De Gids,* only about six years have survived.[53] For *De Standaard* (1875–1918) and its successor, the
Standard Bulletin (1918–1943), only a total of three years are ex-

tant.[54] Sparse holdings are known of the two Paterson, New Jersey, papers *De Telegraaf* (1882–1921) and *Het Oosten*, (1904–1940).[55] Extant files of the Chicago *Onze Toekomst* (1894–1953) begin in 1920 and after that date are fragmentary. Most issues of *The American Daily Standard* (Dec. 22, 1920–Mar. 12, 1921) exist.

Files of Rev. Scholte's two Pella, Iowa, papers, *The Pella Gazette* (1855–1860) and *De Toekomst* (1866–1868) are complete. The back run of the *Pella Blade,* now the *Chronicle* (1865–), lacks many issues for the period 1865–1900. Missing from the file of *Pella's Weekblad* (1860–1942) are the years 1860–1886 with the exception of 1870. A complete file of the Orange City, Iowa, *De Volksvriend* (1874–1951) can be found. Of the *Sioux Center Nieuwsblad* (1892–1930) file, the years 1892–1895 and the decade of the 1920s cannot be located. This title continues to exist as the *Sioux Center News.*

The Wisconsin *Sheboygan Nieuwsbode* (1849–1861) holding is complete. The back file of the Catholic *De Volksstem* (1890–1919) from De Pere, Wisconsin, lacks two years in the 1890s. This paper merged with the Illinois *Gazette van Moline* (1907–1940), a Flemish paper for which a complete back file is extant. Of the Catholic *De Pere Standaard* (1878–1896), only the first two years are known.

Complete runs of the official papers of the Reformed and Christian Reformed denominations exist with the exception of *Der Reformierte Bote Berichte aus der Christlichen Reformierten Kirche* (1899–1920?), for which only the years 1915–1919 can be located. Files of papers not having official status but read by members of the two denominations are with one or two exceptions complete. Holdings of the theologically liberal Grand Rapids journal *Stemmen Uit de Vrije Hollandsche Gemeente* (1886–1890) are known for the years 1886–1889. *De Wachter* and the *Holland News* (1979–) from Bellflower, California, are the only papers in the Dutch language currently being published in the United States. A complete listing of both retrospective and current Dutch-American publications is given in the annotated bibliography *Dutch Americans: A Guide to Information Sources* by Linda Pegman Doezema.[56]

Dutch-American journalism offers many opportunities for

the researcher, particularly for the one who can read Dutch. Anthologies of editorials, letters to the editor, and news articles on the various Dutch settlements in America, would contribute much to our understanding of the journalists themselves and those who read their papers. Those who desire to know more about the economic life of the immigrant can make use of advertisements and prices given for farms and agricultural commodities. Book advertisements, serialized fiction and poetry can be scrutinized to determine the intellectual tastes of the Dutch-Americans. Essential for any study of the immigrant's religious life, his preoccupation with fine points of doctrine and theology, or of his attempts to relate what he believed to the world he lived in, are past files of newspapers and journals, all of which, to one degree or another, contained religious material. Lastly, the Dutch-American journalists themselves deserve more attention. Their motives for publishing; what they thought of other papers; their use of the Dutch language and, for that matter, the English; their political and religious ideas; and how they viewed America are topics which, if better comprehended, will contribute greatly to what we already know about those editors and publishers who originated and wrote in these papers which, today, embody the Dutch-American heritage in a way unrivaled by any other sources.

Notes

1. Dates in parenthesis indicate known or assumed years of publication.
2. Dingman Versteeg, *De Pelgrim-Vaders van het Westen* [The Pilgrim Fathers of the West] (Grand Rapids: C. M. Loomis, 1886), 162–163.
3. S. Kedzie, "Newspapers in Ottawa County," *Report of the Pioneer Society of the State of Michigan* 9 (1886): 295–300.
4. Ibid., 297.
5. Ibid., 300.
6. Albert Baxter, *History of the City of Grand Rapids, Michigan* (New York and Grand Rapids: Munsell & Company, 1891), 260–277.
7. Ibid., 268.
8. Kommer Van Stigt, *History of Pella, Iowa and Vicinity*, trans. Elisabeth Kempkes (n.p.: n.p., n.d.), 87, 112–113, 127. The *Pella Blade* began in 1865.

9. Ibid., 113.
10. Ibid., 18.
11. Ibid., 18–26.
12. Ibid., 112–113, 126–127.
13. Ibid., 2.
14. *Gedenkboek van het Vijftigjarig Jubileum der Christelijke Gereformeerde Kerk A.D. 1857–1907* [Memorial Volume of the Fiftieth Jubilee of the Christian Reformed Church, A.D. 1857–1907] (Grand Rapids: n.p., n.d.), 170.
15. Ibid., 171.
16. Theo De Veer, "Hollandsche Journalistiek in Amerika" [Dutch Journalism in America] *Geïllustreerd Maandschrift* (Mar. 1909), 114.
17. Linda Pegman Doezema, *Dutch Americans: A Guide to Information Sources* (Detroit: Gale Research Company, 1979), 195.
18. De Veer, "Hollandsche Journalistiek in Amerika," 114.
19. Jacob Van Der Zee, *The Hollanders of Iowa* (Iowa City: State Historical Society of Iowa, 1912), 5.
20. Ibid., 254–255.
21. Ibid., 242–255.
22. Henry Beets, "Hollandsche Tijdschriften en Couranten in de Vereenigde Staten," [Dutch Journals and Newspapers in the United States], *De Gereformeerde Amerikaan* 20 (Dec. 1916): 515. Much of the material in this article first appeared in "Amerikaansche Brieven," *Neerlandia,* 19 (1915): 182–183, written by Beets under his pen name, Melis Stoke Jr.
23. Ibid., 521.
24. Henry Beets, "Dutch Journalism in Michigan," *Michigan History Magazine* 6 (Sept. 1922): 441.
25. Henry S. Lucas, *Netherlanders in America: Dutch Immigration to the United States and Canada, 1789–1950* (Ann Arbor: University of Michigan Press, 1955), 572.
26. John Clover Monsma, *Why the American Daily Standard Failed and How It Is Going to Win* (Grand Rapids: Seymour & Muir, 1921).
27. "By Way of Introduction," *The World an International News Weekly*, May 12, 1937, first unpaginated page after front cover.
28. Jacob Van Hinte, *Nederlanders in Amerika: Een Studie over Landverhuizers en Volkplanters en in de 19e en 20ste Eeuw in de Vereenigde Staten van Amerika* [Netherlanders in America: A Study of Emigration and Colonization in the 19th and 20th Century in the United States of America] (2 vols.) (Groningen: P. Nordhoff, 1928), II, 494.
29. For comments on Van Hinte by American scholars, see Doezema, *Dutch Americans: A Guide to Information Sources*, 238; Lucas, *Netherlanders in America*, xi.

30. Van Hinte, *Nederlanders in Amerika*, I, 478–479.

31. Ibid., I, 489.

32. Ibid., I, 488.

33. Ibid., II, 405–521.

34. Ibid., II, 472–496.

35. Ibid., II, 484–485, 489–490.

36. Henry Beets's perceptive review of *Nederlanders in Amerika* is in *The Banner*, (Dec. 14, 1928), 946.

37. Van Hinte, *Nederlanders in Amerika*, II, 492.

38. Arnold Mulder, *Americans From Holland* (Philadelphia: J. B. Lippincott, 1947), 218.

39. Lucas, *Netherlanders in America*, 529–530, 710.

40. Ibid., 537.

41. Ibid., 539–540.

42. Ibid., 540. During the years 1826–1830 the *Magazine of the Reformed Dutch Church* appeared. It was published in New Brunswick, New Jersey, and merged with the *Christian Intelligencer* in 1830.

43. Ibid., 541.

44. Harry Boonstra, "Dutch-American Newspapers and Periodicals in Michigan, 1850–1925" (M.A. thesis, University of Chicago, 1967), 2.

45. Ibid., 23.

46. Ibid., 78.

47. Those papers considered in this appendix are: *De Hope* (1865–1933), *The Banner* (1866–), *De Wachter* (1868–), *De Gids* (1885–1911), *De Calvinist* (1911–1918), *De Hollander* (1850–1895), *De Grondwet* (1860–1938), *De Hollandsche Amerikaan* (1890–1945), and *De Standard* (1875–1943?).

48. Henry Zwaanstra, *Reformed Thought and Experience in a New World: A Study of the Christian Reformed Church and Its American Environment 1890–1918* (Kampen: J. H. Kok, 1973), 3–4.

49. Gerald F. De Jong, *The Dutch in America, 1609–1974* (Boston: Twayne, 1975), 207–209.

50. Gerald F. De Jong, "Dutch Immigration in New Jersey Before World War I," *New Jersey History* 94 (Summer-Autumn 1976): 88.

51. James Donald Bratt, *Dutch Calvinism in Modern America: The History of a Conservative Subculture* (Grand Rapids, Mich.: Wm. B. Eerdmans, 1984). In the "Selected Bibliography," Bratt listed the following periodicals: *The Banner, The Leader, The Christian Intelligencer-Leader, The Church Herald, De Gereformeerde Amerikaan, De Gids, De Calvinist, The Christian Journal, Religion and Culture, The Witness, The Reformed Herald*, and *The Calvin Forum*.

52. Walter Lagerwey, *Neen Nederland, 'k Vergeet U Niet: Een Beeld van het Immigrantenleven in Amerika Tussen 1846 en 1945 in*

Verhalen, Schetsen en Gedichten [No Netherlands, I Won't Forget You: A Picture of Emigrant Life in American between 1846 and 1945 in Narratives, Sketches, and Poems] (Baarn: Bosch & Keuning, 1982), 70–83.

53. The years extant are Feb. 20, 1905–Feb. 4, 1911.
54. For *De Standaard*, Sept. 26, 1916–Sept. 7, 1917. For *Standard Bulletin*, July 1, 1938–Dec. 27, 1940.
55. For *De Telegraaf*, Dec. 3, 1917–Dec. 28, 1921. For *Het Oosten*, Dec. 7, 1917–Jan. 2, 1920, and the years 1934–1936.
56. Doezema, *Dutch Americans*, 238.

Contributors

JAMES D. BRATT, Professor of Religious Studies, University of Pittsburgh. Author of *Dutch Calvinism in Modern America: The History of a Conservative Subculture* (1984) and of articles related to religion and ethnicity in American life.

HERBERT J. BRINKS, Professor of History and Director of Heritage Hall Archives, Calvin College. A Fulbright Research Fellow in the Netherlands in 1976 and author of *Schrijf Spoedig Terug: Brieven van Immigranten in Amerika, 1847–1920* (1978).

ELTON J. BRUINS, Evert J. and Hattie E. Blekkink Professor of Religion, Hope College and Director of the Archives, Netherlands Museum, Holland, Michigan. Author of *The Americanization of a Congregation* (1970) and numerous articles and bibliographical guides.

CONRAD BULT, Reference Librarian and Assistant Library Director for College-Related Matters, Calvin College and Seminary Library. Specialist in Dutch-language press and periodical literature in the United States and Canada.

HILLE DE VRIES, Professor of Economic History, University of Leiden. Author of *Landbouw en Bevolking Tijdens de Agrarische Depressien in Friesland (1878–1895)* (1971) and many articles.

RICHARD L. DOYLE, Professor of History, Mount Union College. Author of *The Socio-Economic Mobility of the Dutch Immigrants to Pella, Iowa, 1847–1925* (1982).

HERMAN GANZEVOORT, Professor of History, University of Calgary. Author of *Dutch Immigration to Canada, 1892–1940* (1975) and other books and articles; co-editor of *Dutch Immigration to North America* (1983).

295

WALTER LAGERWEY, Queen Juliana Professor Emeritus of Dutch Language, Literature, and Culture, Calvin College. Author of *Neen Nederland, 'k vergeet u niet* (1982); *Speak Dutch: An Audio-lingual Course* (1968); and other books and articles on Dutch language and culture.

YDA SAUERESSIG-SCHREUDER, Professor of Geography, University of Delaware. Author of *Emigration, Settlement, and Assimilation of Dutch Roman Catholic Immigrants in Wisconsin, 1850–1905* (1982).

PIETER R. D. STOKVIS, City Historian, The Hague. Author of *De Nederlandse Trek Naar Amerika, 1846–1847* (1977) and other articles.

ROBERT P. SWIERENGA, Professor of History, Kent State University. Recipient of Fulbright-Hays Silver Opportunity Research Fellowship to the Netherlands (1976) and Fellow of the American Council of Learned Societies (1981); co-editor (with J. W. Schulte Nordholt) of *A Bilateral Bicentennial: A History of Dutch-American Relations, 1782–1982* (1982). Author of *Pioneers and Profits* (1968); *Quantification in American History* (1970); *Acres for Cents* (1976); *History and Ecology* (1984); *Dutch Emigrants to the United States, South Africa, South America, and Southeast Asia, 1835–1880* (1983); *Dutch Immigrants in U.S. Ship Passenger Manifests, 1820–1880* (1983).

DAVID G. VANDERSTEL, Senior Historian, Conner Prairie Pioneer Settlement, Noblesville, Indiana. Author of *The Dutch of Grand Rapids, Michigan: 1848–1900. Immigrant Neighborhood and Community Development in a Nineteenth Century City* (1983).

HENRY A. V. M. VAN STEKELENBURG, Instructor in History, Vught, The Netherlands. Author of "Rooms-Katholieke Landverhuizers naar de Verenigde Staten," *Speigel Historiael* (1977); and "Tracing the Dutch Roman Catholic Emigrants to North America in the Nineteenth and Twentieth Centuries," in Herman Ganzevoort and Mark Boekelman, eds., *Dutch Immigration to North America* (1983).

Index